# 60HIKES
## WITHIN 60MILES

### 3rd Edition

# BALTIMORE

## Including Anne Arundel, Baltimore, Carroll, Harford, and Howard Counties

# 60 HIKES WITHIN 60 MILES: BALTIMORE

**Library of Congress Cataloging-in-Publication Data**
Names: Sturm, Allison, 1987– author. | Balkan, Evan, 1972– author.
Title: 60 hikes within 60 miles : Baltimore : including Anne Arundel, Baltimore, Carroll, Harford, and
    Howard Counties / Allison Sturm and Evan Balkan.
Other titles: Sixty hikes within sixty miles Baltimore | 60 hikes within 60 miles.
Description: Third Edition. | Birmingham, Alabama : Menasha Ridge Press, [2019] |
    Evan Balkan is the sole author of the previous editions. | "Distributed by Publishers
    Group West"—T.p. verso. | Includes index.
Identifiers: LCCN 2019001222 | ISBN 9781634041522 (paperback) | ISBN 9781634041539 (ebook)
Classification: LCC GV199.42.M32 B342 2019 | DDC 796.5109752—dc23
LC record available at https://lccn.loc.gov/2019001222

Cover and text design: Jonathan Norberg
Cover photo: Kilgore Falls at Rocks State Park: Falling Branch Area © Allison Sturm
Interior photos: Allison Sturm unless otherwise noted
Cartography and elevation profiles: Scott McGrew, Tim Kissell, and Allison Sturm
Index: Rich Carlson

**MENASHA RIDGE PRESS**
An imprint of AdventureKEEN
2204 First Ave. S., Ste. 102
Birmingham, AL 35233
menasharidge.com

DISCLAIMER This book is meant only as a guide to select trails in the Baltimore area and does not guarantee hiker safety in any way—you hike at your own risk. Menasha Ridge Press, Allison Sturm, and Evan Balkan are not liable for property loss or damage, personal injury, or death that result in any way from accessing or hiking the trails described in the following pages. Please be aware that hikers have been injured in the Baltimore area. Be especially cautious when walking on or near boulders, steep inclines, and drop-offs, and do not attempt to explore terrain that may be beyond your abilities. To help ensure an uneventful hike, please read carefully the introduction to this book, and perhaps get further safety information and guidance from other sources. Familiarize yourself thoroughly with the areas you intend to visit before venturing out. Ask questions, and prepare for the unforeseen. Familiarize yourself with current weather reports, maps of the area you intend to visit, and any relevant park regulations.

# DEDICATION

To Steven—life's best partner, both on and off the trail.

# 60 HIKES WITHIN 60 MILES

3rd Edition

## BALTIMORE

Including Anne Arundel, Baltimore, Carroll, Harford, and Howard Counties

**Allison Sturm**
**Prior edition by Evan Balkan**

**MENASHA RIDGE PRESS**
Your Guide to the Outdoors Since 1982

# 60 Hikes Within 60 Miles: Baltimore

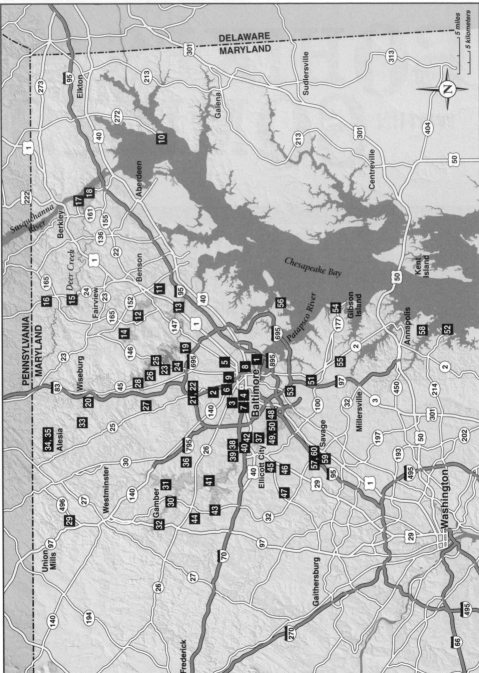

# TABLE OF CONTENTS

## NORTHERN SUBURBS 100

## NORTHWESTERN SUBURBS 144

## WESTERN SUBURBS 180

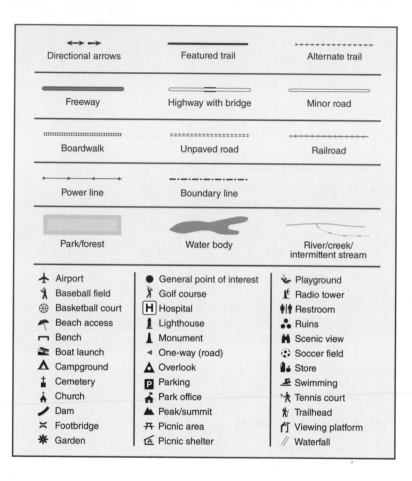

| | | |
|---|---|---|
| ⟵ ⟶ Directional arrows | Featured trail | Alternate trail |
| Freeway | Highway with bridge | Minor road |
| Boardwalk | Unpaved road | Railroad |
| Power line | Boundary line | |
| Park/forest | Water body | River/creek/ intermittent stream |

| | | |
|---|---|---|
| ✈ Airport | ● General point of interest | Playground |
| Baseball field | Golf course | Radio tower |
| Basketball court | H Hospital | Restroom |
| Beach access | Lighthouse | Ruins |
| ⌐ Bench | Monument | Scenic view |
| Boat launch | ◄ One-way (road) | Soccer field |
| Δ Campground | Δ Overlook | Store |
| Cemetery | P Parking | Swimming |
| Church | Park office | Tennis court |
| Dam | ▲ Peak/summit | Trailhead |
| ✕ Footbridge | Picnic area | Viewing platform |
| ✳ Garden | Picnic shelter | // Waterfall |

# ACKNOWLEDGMENTS

**My biggest debt of gratitude** goes to my wonderful husband, Steven Sturm, who has been my constant source of encouragement. His faith in me has been unyielding, and I'm forever thankful to have him by my side. Not only did Steven forgo countless game days to keep me company on the trail, but he also readily accepted the task of mapping the trails toward the end, when we happily learned we were expecting a baby due the same month as my book.

Writing this book wouldn't have been nearly as enjoyable without my wonderful family and friends who accompanied me along the way: my sister, Catherine Aldrich, who braved some blistery cold and rainy-day hikes with her characteristic enthusiasm; my cousin Lauren Brown, who didn't miss a single detail along the trail; as well as Angie Mangum, Kelly Brown, Julie Markowitz, Tina Ruppert, Heather Consla, and Holly Lefcourt, all of whom made these trails a joy to hike. I'd also like to acknowledge my wonderful parents, Gary and Nina Aldrich, who instilled in me a love of the outdoors, a strong sense of independence, and the knowledge and tools needed to feel safe on my own, even when miles away from a cell signal.

Special thanks goes to everyone I encountered along the trails and in the parks who were so helpful in offering their guidance and sharing their abundant knowledge, especially Ken Grimm, who knows Patapsco like the back of his hand and helped provide updates regarding flood damage on some of the trails, as well as inspiration for the Daniels Area hike. I'd also like to thank Evan Balkan, *60 Hikes Within 60 Miles: Baltimore*'s original author, who responded to my list of reader-suggested updates quite charitably. Thanks to him and the team at Menasha Ridge Press for this opportunity.

—*Allison Sturm*

# FOREWORD

Welcome to Menasha Ridge Press's 60 Hikes Within 60 Miles, a series designed to provide hikers with information needed to find and hike the very best trails surrounding metropolitan areas.

Our strategy was simple: First, find a hiker who knows the area and loves to hike. Second, ask that person to spend a year researching the most popular and very best trails around. And third, have that person describe each trail in terms of difficulty, scenery, condition, elevation change, and all other categories of information that are important to hikers. "Pretend you've just completed a hike and met up with other hikers at the trailhead," we told each author. "Imagine their questions; be clear in your answers."

An experienced hiker and writer, author Allison Sturm has selected 60 of the best hikes in and around the Baltimore metropolitan area. This third edition includes new hikes, as well as additional sections and new routes for some of the existing hikes. Allison provides hikers (and walkers) with a great variety of hikes—all within roughly 60 miles of Baltimore—from urban strolls on city sidewalks to aerobic outings along beaches, rivers, and piedmont foothills.

You'll get more out of this book if you take a moment to read the Introduction explaining how to read the trail listings. The "Topographic Maps" section will help you understand how useful topos are on a hike and will also tell you where to get them. And though this is a where-to, not a how-to, guide, readers who have not hiked extensively will find the Introduction of particular value.

As much for the opportunity to free the spirit as to free the body, let these hikes elevate you above the urban hurry.

*All the best,*
*The Editors at Menasha Ridge Press*

**A good walk is therapy.** The fresh air, sights, sounds, and smells of the natural world: these things can fill a person's senses better than any artificial stimulant. Maryland has long been a leader in programs combating urban sprawl and preserving open spaces. Indeed, what makes Maryland, and specifically the Chesapeake watershed, the Land of Pleasant Living is the wonderful mix of suburban and rural. There is nothing, whether a cultural or historical attraction or a solitary walk in the woods, that you can't find in and around Maryland's largest city.

Maryland is a varied state topographically, packing extraordinary diversity into a relatively small area. Home to mountains in the west, Atlantic coastline in the east, and the country's largest estuary splitting the state in the middle, Maryland offers everything a nature lover could want within a few hours' drive. This diversity led Gilbert Grosvenor, the first editor of *National Geographic*, to nickname Maryland America in Miniature.

This moniker can apply specifically to the Baltimore area. A good-size city (the country's second largest through the first half of the 19th century), Baltimore is endowed with many fine attractions. But surprisingly to many people—even many who live in the city—Baltimore is also home to an abundance of hiking opportunities. This is a pleasant revelation, coming as it does in an area where millions of people make their homes.

As I began working to update the third edition of this book, I was pleasantly surprised to discover so many beautiful hikes I had overlooked, often only a few miles from my home. Some of these trails had such nondescript trailheads that I hardly would have noticed them if I hadn't done some prior research. Other trailheads I'd driven past before, thinking, "I wonder why all of those cars are lining the road." I hope this book gives you the confidence and knowledge to pause at one of these trailheads and decide to dive in and begin exploring the many wonderful hikes that abound in and around Baltimore.

The basic idea in this book is to catalog 60 hikes within 60 miles. As you'll notice when you look at the locations of these hikes, virtually all of them are within 30 miles of Baltimore. This is intentional. First, you don't need to travel very far from the city center to find great places to hike. Further, as anyone who has sat for hours on I-695 knows, traffic can be tough, and 60 miles often does not equal an hour.

It would be an impossible task to include every great hiking destination within 60 miles, and surely at least a few readers will be chagrined to see that their favorite spot was not included. For example, Catoctin Mountain Park and Cunningham Falls State Park, outside Frederick, are within 60 miles of Baltimore and are fantastic places for hiking, but these locations are covered in the excellent *60 Hikes Within 60 Miles: Washington, D.C.* by Renee Sklarew and Rachel Cooper. Because of the thoroughness of that book, most of the hikes in this book are concentrated in the city, north and east of Baltimore, and in the southern and southwestern suburbs. Many hikes in northern Howard and Anne Arundel Counties are represented here. In addition, you'll find trails in Harford, Carroll, and Cecil Counties. While the hikes are categorized primarily by location, I encourage you to also browse the available hikes by difficulty level and accessibility (pages xiv–xvi). I've sought to include footpaths that will appeal to various skill levels and life stages. For example, several new hikes feature paved paths to allow for strollers, wheelchairs, and those who have difficulty with unlevel ground.

The goal in choosing the hikes was to create as much of a spectrum as possible. Each hike has been chosen for its special historical and/or natural interest. The result is 60 hikes that offer a wide array of geographical and topographical diversity.

## Baltimore

**Bustling in the 1700s,** all but leveled in the Great Fire of 1904, and sunk into economic depression for decades after, Baltimore's rise at the tail end of the 20th century is often cited internationally as a leading example of urban renewal. Sparked by the development of the Inner Harbor, as well as the country's first of the now ubiquitous downtown old-style baseball stadiums, many grand old neighborhoods that had fallen into decay have rebounded as well. Not surprisingly, many of these border popular urban green spaces.

Baltimore, which is virtually unmatched in this area, constantly delights visitors with the large amount of green inside this eastern, industrialized city. This didn't happen by accident. From early on, city leaders recognized the need for and value of open spaces. In 1859, they passed a park tax and raised enough revenue to create and preserve a park system, eventually bringing in famed landscape architect Frederick Law Olmsted to design the city's green spaces. Continued attention to these spaces has resulted in the protection and maintenance of more than 7,000 acres of city parkland, much of it in the adjacent parks at Leakin and Gwynns Falls. These two parks make up part of the largest unbroken urban forest in America, no small feat for a city that is one of the country's oldest.

The abundance of so much green space perfectly complements what makes Baltimore so attractive: this eminently walkable city features a patchwork of unique neighborhoods within close proximity of each other. Beyond the glitz of Harborplace, Baltimore's uniqueness can be found in its diverse neighborhoods: the stateliness of Mount Vernon, the history and funkiness of Fells Point and Federal Hill, the grittiness and renewal of Hampden, the beauty and elegance of Guilford and Homeland, the energy of Charles Village, and the cultural attractions (and restaurants) in Little Italy and Greektown. The list goes on. I've heard many first-time visitors exclaim, "I had no idea how charming Baltimore is!"

All of this charm came somewhat slowly, however. For much of Baltimore's history, the city remained first and foremost a maritime destination. Beginning in the 1600s, its deep and wide natural harbor attracted shippers. This attraction grew as Baltimore did, and its position farther inland than any other major Atlantic port allowed for easier delivery to western locations. Likewise, the system of railways and waterways spreading from the city made its allure as a port almost unparalleled for both cargo and people. Indeed, Baltimore Harbor ranked second only to Ellis Island as a port of entry for New World immigrants.

The city played a well-documented and essential role in the War of 1812. The defeat of the British at Fort McHenry prompted Francis Scott Key to pen the words that served as a rallying point for embattled American militiamen and later became our national anthem. Baltimore's proximity to the Chesapeake Bay made it a logical location for canning factories, which packed and exported the bounty of the bay to other parts of the country. Things waxed and waned in Baltimore for years, but recently another renaissance has begun with major development projects spreading out from the Inner Harbor, which remains the city's major compass point.

Enjoy all the city has to offer, but don't forget about the hiking. The numerous opportunities afforded by our watersheds, rural spaces, and many parks in and around the city help put the charm in Charm City.

View of St. Michael the Archangel Ukrainian Catholic Church and the Inner Harbor from Patterson Park (see Hike 8, Patterson Park, page 50)   *Photo by Lauren Brown*

# 60 HIKES BY CATEGORY

| REGION<br>Hike Number/Hike Name | Page # | Mileage | Difficulty | Kid Friendly | Historical Interest | Water Features | Wildlife | Solitude | Accessible by Public Transportation |
|---|---|---|---|---|---|---|---|---|---|
| **CITY OF BALTIMORE** | | | | | | | | | |
| 1 Baltimore Waterfront Promenade | 20 | 5.7/11.4 | E–M | ✓ | ✓ | ✓ | | | ✓ |
| 2 Cylburn Arboretum | 24 | 2.7 | E–M | ✓ | ✓ | | ✓ | | ✓ |
| 3 Gwynns Falls Park | 28 | 4.4 | E | | | ✓ | | | ✓ |
| 4 Gwynns Falls Trail from Leon Day Park to Cherry Hill Park | 32 | 11.2 | M | | ✓ | ✓ | | | ✓ |
| 5 Herring Run Park and Lake Montebello | 37 | 3.7 | E | | | ✓ | ✓ | | ✓ |
| 6 Jones Falls Trail: Druid Hill Park | 41 | 5.4 | E–M | ✓ | ✓ | ✓ | | | ✓ |
| 7 Leakin Park | 45 | 2.7 | M | | | ✓ | ✓ | | ✓ |
| 8 Patterson Park | 50 | 2.0 | E | ✓ | ✓ | ✓ | ✓ | | ✓ |
| 9 Stony Run Trail | 54 | 5.2 | E–M | | | ✓ | ✓ | | ✓ |
| **NORTHEASTERN SUBURBS** | | | | | | | | | |
| 10 Elk Neck State Park | 60 | 12.0 | E–M | ✓ | | ✓ | ✓ | | |
| 11 Gunpowder Falls State Park: Jerusalem Village Trail with Jericho Covered Bridge Trail | 64 | 4.9 | M | | ✓ | ✓ | | | |
| 12 Gunpowder Falls State Park: Pleasantville–Bottom Loop | 69 | 4.7 | M–S | | | ✓ | ✓ | ✓ | |
| 13 Gunpowder Falls State Park: Sweathouse Branch Wildlands | 73 | 9.25 | M–S | | | ✓ | ✓ | | |
| 14 Gunpowder Falls State Park: Sweet Air Area | 77 | 5.5 | E–M | | | ✓ | ✓ | | |
| 15 Rocks State Park | 82 | 3.7 | M | | | | ✓ | | |
| 16 Rocks State Park: Falling Branch Area | 86 | 0.88 | E | ✓ | | ✓ | | | |
| 17 Susquehanna State Park: River Trails | 90 | 7.6 | M | | ✓ | ✓ | ✓ | | |
| 18 Susquehanna State Park: Woodland–Farm Trails | 95 | 8.3 | M–S | | ✓ | ✓ | ✓ | ✓ | |
| **NORTHERN SUBURBS** | | | | | | | | | |
| 19 Cromwell Valley Park | 102 | 3.5 | M | | | | ✓ | | |
| 20 Gunpowder Falls State Park (Hereford Area): Gunpowder North–South Circuit | 106 | 13.2 | M–S | | | ✓ | | | |
| 21 Lake Roland | 111 | 7.2 | M | ✓ | ✓ | ✓ | ✓ | | ✓ |
| 22 Lake Roland: Serpentine–Bare Hills | 115 | 3.7 | E–M | | | ✓ | ✓ | | ✓ |
| 23 Loch Raven Reservoir: Deadman's Cove Trail | 119 | 1.3 | E | | | ✓ | ✓ | ✓ | |
| 24 Loch Raven Reservoir: Glen Ellen–Seminary Road | 123 | 7.0 | M | | | ✓ | ✓ | | |
| 25 Loch Raven Reservoir: Merryman Point | 127 | 7.6 | M–S | | | ✓ | ✓ | | |
| 26 Loch Raven Reservoir: Northwest Area Trails | 131 | 4.8 | M | | | ✓ | ✓ | ✓ | |
| 27 Oregon Ridge Park | 135 | 4.75 | M | ✓ | | ✓ | ✓ | | |
| 28 Torrey C. Brown Rail Trail | 139 | 19.2 | E–S | | | | ✓ | | |

| REGION<br>Hike Number/Hike Name | Page # | Mileage | Difficulty | Kid Friendly | Historical Interest | Water Features | Wildlife | Solitude | Accessible by Public Transportation |
|---|---|---|---|---|---|---|---|---|---|
| **NORTHWESTERN SUBURBS** | | | | | | | | | |
| 29 Hashawha Environmental Appreciation Area at Bear Branch Nature Center | 146 | 2.5 | M | ✓ | | ✓ | | | |
| 30 Liberty Reservoir: Liberty West–Morgan Run | 150 | 7.2 | M | | | ✓ | ✓ | ✓ | |
| 31 Liberty Reservoir: Middle Run Trail | 154 | 3.75 | M | | | ✓ | | ✓ | |
| 32 Morgan Run Natural Environmental Area | 158 | 5.7 | E–M | | | | ✓ | ✓ | |
| 33 Prettyboy Reservoir: CCC Trail | 162 | 3.8 | E | | | ✓ | ✓ | ✓ | |
| 34 Prettyboy Reservoir: Gunpowder Falls | 166 | 3.9 | E | | | ✓ | | | |
| 35 Prettyboy Reservoir: Hemlock Trail | 170 | 2.1 | S | | | ✓ | ✓ | ✓ | |
| 36 Soldiers Delight Natural Environmental Area | 174 | 5.4 | M | ✓ | ✓ | | ✓ | | |
| **WESTERN SUBURBS** | | | | | | | | | |
| 37 Banneker Historical Park and Trolly Line #9 Trail | 182 | 3.9 | E | ✓ | ✓ | ✓ | ✓ | | |
| 38 Patapsco Valley State Park: Alberton and Daniels Area | 187 | 3.5 | E | ✓ | ✓ | ✓ | | | |
| 39 Patapsco Valley State Park: Daniels Area Old Main Line Trail | 191 | 3.4 | E–M | | ✓ | ✓ | | | |
| 40 Patapsco Valley State Park: Hollofield Area | 195 | 3.9 | M | | | ✓ | | | |
| 41 Patapsco Valley State Park: McKeldin Area | 199 | 6.3 | M–S | | | ✓ | ✓ | ✓ | |
| 42 Patapsco Valley State Park: Mill Race Trail | 203 | 3.0 | M–S | | | ✓ | | | |
| 43 Patapsco Valley State Park (Undeveloped Area): Sykesville–Marriottsville | 207 | 10.0 | M | | | ✓ | | ✓ | |
| 44 Piney Run Park | 211 | 3.2 | E | ✓ | | ✓ | | | |
| **SOUTHWESTERN SUBURBS** | | | | | | | | | |
| 45 Centennial Park | 218 | 2.5 | E | ✓ | | ✓ | ✓ | | |
| 46 Lake Kittamaqundi | 222 | 2.25 | E | ✓ | | ✓ | ✓ | | ✓ |
| 47 Middle Patuxent Environmental Area | 226 | 3.5 | E–M | ✓ | | ✓ | ✓ | | |
| 48 Patapsco Valley State Park: Glen Artney Area | 230 | 4.7 | M | | ✓ | ✓ | ✓ | | |
| 49 Patapsco Valley State Park: Hilton Area | 234 | 4.4 | M–S | | ✓ | ✓ | ✓ | | |
| 50 Patapsco Valley State Park: Orange Grove and Avalon Areas | 238 | 6.4 | M | | ✓ | ✓ | | | |

| **DIFFICULTY RATINGS** | | |
|---|---|---|
| E = Easy | M = Moderate | S = Strenuous |

| REGION<br>Hike Number/Hike Name | Page # | Mileage | Difficulty | Kid Friendly | Historical Interest | Water Features | Wildlife | Solitude | Accessible by Public Transportation |
|---|---|---|---|---|---|---|---|---|---|
| **SOUTHERN SUBURBS** | | | | | | | | | |
| 51 Baltimore & Annapolis (B&A) Trail | 246 | 12.7 | M–S | ✓ | ✓ | | | | |
| 52 Beverly–Triton Beach Park | 250 | 2.9 | M | ✓ | | ✓ | | | |
| 53 BWI Trail | 254 | 11.6 | M | ✓ | | | | | |
| 54 Downs Park | 259 | 4.4 | E | ✓ | ✓ | ✓ | ✓ | | |
| 55 Kinder Farm Park | 263 | 2.5 | E | ✓ | | | | | |
| 56 North Point State Park | 266 | 3.4 | E–M | ✓ | ✓ | ✓ | ✓ | | |
| 57 Patuxent Branch Trail | 271 | 10.4 | M | ✓ | ✓ | ✓ | | | |
| 58 Quiet Waters Park | 275 | 5.0 | E | ✓ | | ✓ | | | |
| 59 Savage Park | 279 | 4.4 | E–M | | ✓ | ✓ | | | |
| 60 Wincopin Trails | 283 | 4.2 | E | | ✓ | ✓ | | | |

| **DIFFICULTY RATINGS** | | |
|---|---|---|
| E = Easy | M = Moderate | S = Strenuous |

Welcome to *60 Hikes Within 60 Miles: Baltimore.* If you're new to hiking or even if you're a seasoned trekker, take a few minutes to read the following introduction. We'll explain how this book is organized and how to make the best use of it.

## About This Book

These hikes were chosen for their variety in location and topography, but certain locations feature more than one hike, including the state parks at Patapsco Valley and Gunpowder Falls and the reservoir watershed areas of Liberty, Loch Raven, and Prettyboy. These hiking meccas deserve extra attention from the dedicated hiker.

### PATAPSCO VALLEY STATE PARK

Patapsco Valley State Park (PVSP) extends along 32 miles of its namesake, the Patapsco River, encompassing more than 14,000 acres in four counties with more than 170 miles of trails, enough to satisfy any hiker. Remarkably, many of the trails are empty, and you may see 20 times more deer than people. The park has six developed, maintained sections: Hilton, McKeldin, Hollofield, Avalon, Glen Artney, and Orange Grove (the last three share an entrance). Here you will find ball fields, campgrounds, picnic areas, disc golf, and playgrounds. A network of maintained trails exists in each of these areas, and I have taken all the separate blazed trails to create long hikes, usually a loop, through each area (a combined hike traverses the Orange Grove and Avalon areas). I've also included a hike in an unmaintained section of the park, which I've called Sykesville–Marriottsville for its location between those two towns.

### GUNPOWDER FALLS STATE PARK

Gunpowder Falls State Park (GFSP) extends almost 18,000 acres along the Big and Little Gunpowder Falls and Gunpowder River. This long, narrow park, which is not always contiguous, envelops a stunning array of topography ranging from tidal marshes and wetlands to steep, rugged slopes. Including the 19.7-mile Maryland portion of the Torrey C. Brown Rail Trail, which is maintained by Gunpowder Falls State Park but treated separately in this book, GFSP has more than 100 miles of trails. The park also encompasses three developed areas: Hereford, Central (including Sweet Air, which is popular for equestrian use; Sweathouse Branch Wildlands, popular with bird-watchers and wildflower enthusiasts; and Jerusalem Village, a restored historical town), and Hammerman, plus the Torrey C. Brown Rail Trail and Dundee Creek Marina. With all of these areas to choose from, you can enjoy swimming beaches, picnic areas, historical sites, trails galore, and numerous tubing, paddling, and fishing activities. The five GFSP hikes in this book take in the differing areas of the park and, as a result, provide a fantastic mix of scenery.

## THE RESERVOIRS: LIBERTY, LOCH RAVEN, AND PRETTYBOY

Loch Raven Reservoir, built in 1881 and holding more than 23 billion gallons, provides the drinking water for most of Baltimore County. Its popularity with joggers, hikers, bicyclists, and anglers means that parking areas are often at a premium and the chances for solitude are slim. But once you've hiked here, the reasons for its popularity become obvious: it's an absolute gem and a mere 6 miles north of the city line. The four Loch Raven hikes in this book attempt to bring together the best of what the reservoir watershed has to offer.

Every bit as beautiful as Loch Raven, Prettyboy Reservoir in northwestern Baltimore County lies in what is still a relatively rural area and offers the isolation that is sometimes difficult to experience at Loch Raven.

Anglers routinely catch record-size bass and trout at Liberty Reservoir, which straddles Baltimore and Carroll Counties. People also enjoy bird-watching and horseback riding there, as well as hiking, as the two Liberty treks in this book indicate.

Each of these reservoir watershed areas has many more trails and hiking opportunities beyond what this book describes, and I've tried to present the best of the best. Of course, this is a highly subjective choice, and I encourage you to investigate and discover many more of the trails, which are usually marked with orange cables strung between wooden posts, making them easy to spot.

## CHANGES TO THE THIRD EDITION

A myriad of much-needed updates and upgrades have been made to many of the parks and trails in the past several years. For example, Gwynns Falls Trail, which runs through the city and was in development when the second edition was published, now comprises 15 miles of established trails linking many of Baltimore's historic neighborhoods.

Many previously unmarked trails in and around the city are now clearly blazed (or reblazed a different color), so all have been updated within the hike descriptions. Parks also seemed to go on a renaming blitz in recent years, so several trail names have been revised to reflect their new identities.

Other recent and ongoing maintenance and improvement projects required reroutes to existing trails. In Patapsco Valley State Park, the removal of Bloede's Dam temporarily closed and rerouted some nearby trails. I replaced the original Hilton hike with one that begins in the main Hilton parking area and gives those with children access to the wonderful recycled tire playground and several other amenities. A large-scale Baltimore Gas and Electric pipeline project in Leakin Park also required some reconfiguration to the existing trail, though you'll still pass by all of the original beautiful landmarks within the park.

I've revised or entirely removed several trails or portions of trails that have been neglected over the years. In some cases, this involved only a slight change—for example, the updated Mill Race Trail no longer includes a section of trail in the Pickall Area that had become difficult to navigate. In other cases, I had to replace a hike entirely, though where applicable I tried to find a comparable trail. For example, I replaced a hike in Patapsco Valley State Park's unmaintained area with one that is more clearly marked (though still quiet) and brings you along a beautiful portion of the Patapsco.

I also took the opportunity to add more family-friendly and accessible hikes. Several of these can be found in Anne Arundel County and offer beautiful water views and plenty of amenities (think bathrooms and playgrounds).

*Note:* All hike directions begin at Exit 53 on I-95. Check the directions carefully; depending on where you're coming from, there may be quicker and easier routes. If you see any mistakes or omissions—or if you simply have comments for me—please email me at acaldrich@gmail.com.

## How to Use This Guidebook

The following information walks you through this guidebook's organization to make it easy and convenient for planning great hikes.

### OVERVIEW MAP AND MAP LEGEND

Use the overview map on page iv to assess the general location of each hike's primary trailhead. Each hike's number appears on the overview map, in the table of contents, in the list of hikes at the beginning of each regional chapter, and in the hike profiles themselves. A map legend that details the symbols found on trail maps appears on page viii.

### REGIONAL MAPS

The book is divided into regions, and prefacing each section is a regional map. The regional maps provide more detail than the overview map, bringing you closer to the hikes.

### TRAIL MAPS

A detailed map of each hike's route appears with its profile. On each of these maps, symbols indicate the trailhead, the complete route, significant features, facilities, and topographic landmarks such as creeks, overlooks, and peaks.

To produce the highly accurate maps in this book, the author used a handheld GPS unit to gather data while hiking each route, and then sent that data to the publisher's expert cartographers. However, your GPS is not a substitute for sound, sensible navigation that accounts for the conditions you observe while hiking.

Further, despite the high quality of the maps in this guidebook, the publisher and author strongly recommend that you always carry an additional map, such as the ones noted in each entry's listing for "Maps."

## ELEVATION PROFILES (DIAGRAM)

For trails with any significant elevation changes, the hike description will include this profile graph. Entries for fairly flat routes, such as a lake loop, will not display an elevation profile.

For hike descriptions where the elevation profile is included, this diagram represents the rises and falls of the trail as viewed from the side, over the complete distance (in miles) of that trail. On the diagram's vertical axis, or height scale, the number of feet indicated between each tick mark lets you visualize the climb. To avoid making flat hikes look steep and steep hikes appear flat, varying height scales provide an accurate image of each hike's climbing challenge.

## THE HIKE PROFILE

Each hike contains a brief overview of the trail, a description of the route from start to finish, key at-a-glance information—from the trail's distance and configuration to contacts for local information—GPS trailhead coordinates, and directions for driving to the trailhead area. Each profile also includes a map (see "Trail Maps," page 3) and elevation profile (if the elevation gain is 100 feet or more). Many hike profiles also include notes on nearby/related activities.

## KEY INFORMATION

The information in this box gives you a quick idea of the statistics and specifics of each hike.

**DISTANCE & CONFIGURATION**  Distance notes the length of the hike round-trip, from start to finish. If the hike description includes options to shorten or extend the hike, those round-trip distances will also be factored here. Configuration defines the trail as a loop, an out-and-back (taking you in and out via the same route), a figure eight, or a balloon.

**DIFFICULTY**  The degree of effort that a typical hiker should expect on a given route. For simplicity, the trails are rated as easy, moderate, or strenuous.

**SCENERY**  A short summary of the attractions offered by the hike and what to expect in terms of plant life, wildlife, natural wonders, and historical features.

**EXPOSURE**    A quick check of how much sun you can expect on your shoulders during the hike.

**TRAFFIC**    Indicates how busy the trail might be on an average day. Trail traffic, of course, varies from day to day and season to season. Weekend days typically see the most visitors. Other trail users you may encounter are also noted here.

**TRAIL SURFACE**    Indicates whether the trail surface is paved, rocky, gravel, dirt, boardwalk, or a mixture of elements.

**HIKING TIME**    How long it takes to hike the trail. A slow but steady hiker will average 2–3 miles an hour, depending on the terrain.

**DRIVING DISTANCE**    Listed in miles from the intersection of I-395 and I-95, just south of the city (Exit 53 on I-95).

**ELEVATION GAIN**    Lists elevation at the trailhead and another figure for the highest or lowest altitude on the route. If there is no significant gain, that is also noted.

**ACCESS**    Fees or permits required to hike the trail are detailed here—and noted if there are none. Trail-access hours are also shown here.

**WHEELCHAIR ACCESS**    At-a-glance, you'll see if there are paved sections or other areas for safely using a wheelchair.

**MAPS**    Resources for maps, in addition to those in this guidebook, are listed here. (As previously noted, the publisher and author recommend that you carry more than one map—and that you consult those maps before heading out on the trail in order to resolve any confusion or discrepancy.)

**FACILITIES**    This item alerts you to restrooms, water, picnic tables, and other basics at or near the trailhead.

**CONTACT**    Listed here are phone numbers and website addresses for checking trail conditions and gleaning other day-to-day information.

**LOCATION**    The city (or nearby community) in which the trail is located.

**COMMENTS**    Here you will find assorted nuggets of information, such as whether or not dogs are allowed on the trails.

## IN BRIEF

Think of this section as a taste of the trail, a snapshot focused on the historical landmarks, beautiful vistas, and other sights you may encounter on the hike.

## DESCRIPTION

The heart of each hike. Here, the author provides a summary of the trail's essence and highlights any special traits the hike has to offer. The route is clearly outlined, including landmarks, side trips, and possible alternate routes along the way. Ultimately, the hike description will help you choose which hikes are best for you.

## NEARBY/RELATED ACTIVITIES

Look here for information on things to do or points of interest: nearby parks, museums, restaurants, and the like. Note that not every hike has a listing.

## DIRECTIONS

Used in conjunction with the GPS coordinates, the driving directions will help you locate each trailhead. Once at the trailhead, park only in designated areas.

## GPS TRAILHEAD COORDINATES

As noted in "Trail Maps," page 3, the author used a handheld GPS unit to obtain geographic data and sent the information to the publisher's cartographers. The trailhead coordinates—the intersection of the latitude (north) and longitude (west)—will orient you from the trailhead. In some cases, you can drive within viewing distance of a trailhead. Other hikes require a short walk to the trailhead from a parking area.

In this book, latitude and longitude are expressed in degree–decimal minute format. For example, the coordinates for Hike 1 (page 20) are as follows:

N39° 16.625'   W76° 34.361'

The latitude and longitude grid system is likely quite familiar to you, but here is a refresher, pertinent to visualizing the GPS coordinates:

Imaginary lines of latitude—called parallels and approximately 69 miles apart from each other—run horizontally around the globe. The equator is established to be 0°, and each parallel is indicated by degrees from the equator: up to 90°N at the North Pole, and down to 90°S at the South Pole.

Imaginary lines of longitude—called meridians—run perpendicular to latitude lines. Longitude lines are likewise indicated by degrees. Starting from 0° at the Prime Meridian in Greenwich, England, they continue to the east and west until they meet 180° later at the International Date Line in the Pacific Ocean. At the equator, longitude lines are also approximately 69 miles apart, but that distance narrows as the meridians converge toward the North and South Poles.

To convert GPS coordinates given in degrees, minutes, and seconds to the format shown above in degree–decimal minutes, the seconds are divided by 60. For more on GPS technology, visit usgs.gov.

## Topographic Maps

The maps in this book have been produced with great care and, used with the hike text, will direct you to the trail and help you stay on course. However, you'll find superior detail and valuable information in the U.S. Geological Survey's 7.5-minute series topographic maps. At mytopo.com, for example, you can view and print free USGS topos of the entire United States. Online services such as Trails.com charge annual fees for additional features such as shaded relief, which makes the topography stand out more. If you expect to print out many topo maps each year, it might be worth paying for such extras. The downside to USGS maps is that most are outdated, having been created 20–30 years ago; nevertheless, they provide excellent topographic detail. Of course, Google Earth (earth.google.com) does away with topo maps and their inaccuracies . . . replacing them with satellite imagery and its inaccuracies. Regardless, what one lacks, the other augments. Google Earth is an excellent tool whether you have difficulty with topos or not.

If you're new to hiking, you might be wondering, "What's a topo map?" In short, it indicates not only linear distance but elevation as well, using contour lines. These lines spread across the map like dozens of intricate spiderwebs. Each line represents a particular elevation, and at the base of each topo a contour's interval designation is given. If, for example, the contour interval is 20 feet, then the distance between each contour line is 20 feet. Follow five contour lines up on the same map, and the elevation has increased by 100 feet. In addition to the sources listed previously and in Appendix B, you'll find topos at major universities, outdoors shops, and some public libraries, as well as online at nationalmap.gov and store.usgs.gov.

## Weather

You can hike pretty much year-round in Baltimore. But as any resident knows, there can be uncomfortable extremes during both summer and winter. While it's not that unusual to get a balmy 60-degree day in December or even January, it's also not unusual to have temperatures with windchill readings below zero. A snowfall for an entire winter can sometimes measure a paltry few inches, while several feet of accumulated snow isn't terribly rare either. Likewise, summer days are usually fine for hiking provided you take plenty of water with you. But the sometimes-oppressive humidity that is part of living in the Mid-Atlantic region can make some summer days quite unbearable. With the temperature approaching 100°F with 90% humidity, it's best to leave the hiking for another day. But generally speaking, these extremes are rare, and you can hike in all seasons. Since the Baltimore area is blessed with pleasant spring seasons and absolutely gorgeous autumns, you may find hiking during these months the most enjoyable, although you may also savor the extended light of summer as well as the increased views offered by the leafless winter trees.

The following table lists average temperatures and precipitation by month for the Baltimore region. For each month, "High" is the average daytime high, and "Low" is the average nighttime low.

| AVERAGE DAILY TEMPERATURES | | | | | | |
|---|---|---|---|---|---|---|
| | JAN | FEB | MARCH | APRIL | MAY | JUNE |
| High | 41°F | 45°F | 54°F | 65°F | 74°F | 83°F |
| Low | 24°F | 26°F | 34°F | 42°F | 52°F | 61°F |
| | JULY | AUG | SEPT | OCT | NOV | DEC |
| High | 87°F | 85°F | 78°F | 67°F | 56°F | 46°F |
| Low | 66°F | 64°F | 57°F | 44°F | 35°F | 27°F |

| AVERAGE PRECIPITATION | | | | | |
|---|---|---|---|---|---|
| JAN | FEB | MARCH | APRIL | MAY | JUNE |
| 3.5" | 3" | 3.9" | 3.0" | 3.9" | 3.4" |
| JULY | AUG | SEPT | OCT | NOV | DEC |
| 3.9" | 3.7" | 4.0" | 3.2" | 3.1" | 3.4" |

## Allocating Time

Pay close attention to the elevation profiles that accompany some of the hikes. If you see many ups and downs over large altitude changes, you'll need more time. Inevitably you'll finish some of the hikes long before or after what I have suggested. Nevertheless, use my suggestions as a guide and leave yourself plenty of time for those moments when you simply feel like stopping and taking it all in.

## Water

How much is enough? Well, one simple physiological fact should convince you to err on the side of excess when deciding how much water to pack: a hiker walking steadily in 90° heat needs approximately 10 quarts of fluid per day. That's 2.5 gallons. A good rule of thumb is to hydrate prior to your hike, carry (and drink) 6 ounces of water for every mile you plan to hike, and hydrate again after the hike. For most people, the pleasures of hiking make carrying water a relatively minor price to pay to remain safe and healthy. So pack more water than you anticipate needing even for short hikes.

If you are tempted to drink "found" water, do so with extreme caution. Many ponds and lakes encountered by hikers are fairly stagnant and the water tastes terrible. Drinking such water presents inherent risks for thirsty trekkers. Giardia parasites contaminate many water sources and cause the dreaded intestinal giardiasis that can last for weeks after ingestion. For information, visit The Centers for Disease Control website at cdc.gov/parasites/giardia. The closer you get to the city, the more often you'll see posted warnings regarding contact with the water, which of course would include drinking, so please follow all posted signage.

Effective treatment is essential before using any water source found along the trail. Boiling water for 2–3 minutes is always a safe measure for camping, but day hikers can consider iodine tablets, approved chemical mixes, filtration units rated for giardia, and UV filtration. Some of these methods (for example, filtration with an added carbon filter) remove bad tastes typical in stagnant water, while others add their own taste. As a precaution, carry a means of water purification to help in a pinch and if you realize you have underestimated your consumption needs.

## Clothing

Weather, unexpected trail conditions, fatigue, extended hiking duration, and wrong turns can individually or collectively turn a great outing into a very uncomfortable one at best—and a life-threatening one at worst. Thus, proper attire plays a key role in staying comfortable and, sometimes, in staying alive. Here are some helpful guidelines:

➤ **Choose silk, wool, or synthetics for maximum comfort in all of your hiking attire**—from hats to socks and in between. Cotton is fine if the weather remains dry and stable, but you won't be happy if that material gets wet.

➤ **Always wear a hat, or at least tuck one into your day pack or hitch it to your belt.** Hats offer all-weather sun and wind protection as well as warmth if it turns cold.

➤ **Be ready to layer up or down as the day progresses and the mercury rises or falls.** Today's outdoor wear makes layering easy, with such designs as jackets that convert to vests and zip-off or button-up legs.

➤ **Wear hiking boots or sturdy hiking sandals with toe protection, and pair that footwear with good socks.** Flip-flopping along a paved urban greenway is one thing, but never hike a trail in open sandals or casual sneakers. Your bones and arches need support, and your skin needs protection.

➤ **Don't leave rainwear behind, even if the day dawns clear and sunny.** Tuck into your day pack, or tie around your waist, a jacket that is breathable and either water-resistant or waterproof. Investigate different choices at your local outdoors retailer. If you are a frequent hiker, ideally you'll have more than one rainwear weight, material, and style in your closet to protect you in all seasons in your regional climate and hiking microclimates.

## *Essential Gear*

Today you can buy outdoor vests that have up to 20 pockets shaped and sized to carry everything from toothpicks to binoculars. Or, if you don't aspire to feel like a burro, you can neatly stow all of these items in your day pack or backpack. The following list showcases never-hike-without-them items, in alphabetical order, as all are important:

➤ **Extra clothes** (raingear, warm hat, gloves, and change of socks and shirt)

➤ **Extra food** (trail mix, granola bars, or other high-energy foods)

➤ **Flashlight or headlamp** with extra bulb and batteries

➤ **Insect repellent** (For hikes with stagnant water, this is extremely vital.)

➤ **Maps and a high-quality compass** (Even if you know the terrain from previous hikes, don't leave home without these tools. And, as previously noted, bring maps in addition to those in this guidebook, and consult your maps prior to the hike. If you are versed in GPS usage, bring that device too, but don't rely on it as your sole navigational tool, as battery life can dwindle or die, and be sure to compare its guidance with that of your maps.)

➤ **Pocketknife and/or multitool**

➤ **Sunscreen** (Note the expiration date on the tube or bottle; it's usually embossed on the top.)

➤ **Water** (As emphasized more than once in this book, bring more than you think you will drink. Depending on your destination, you may want to bring a container and iodine or a filter for purifying water in case you run out.)

➤ **Whistle** (This little gadget will be your best friend in an emergency.)

➤ **Windproof matches and/or a lighter, as well as a fire starter**

## FIRST AID KIT

In addition to the aforementioned items, those below may appear overwhelming for a day hike. But any paramedic will tell you that the products listed here—in alphabetical order, because all are important—are just the basics. The reality of hiking is that you can be out for a week of backpacking and acquire only a mosquito bite. Or you can hike for an hour, slip, and suffer a bleeding abrasion or broken bone. Fortunately, these listed items will collapse into a very small space. You also may purchase convenient, prepackaged kits at your pharmacy or online.

➤ **Adhesive bandages**

➤ **Antibiotic ointment** (Neosporin or the generic equivalent)

➤ **Athletic tape**

➤ **Benadryl** or the generic equivalent, diphenhydramine (in case of allergic reactions)

- ➤ **Blister kit** (such as Moleskin/Spenco 2nd Skin)
- ➤ **Butterfly-closure bandages**
- ➤ **Elastic bandages or joint wraps**
- ➤ **Epinephrine in a prefilled syringe** (typically by prescription only, and for people known to have severe allergic reactions to hiking occurrences such as bee stings)
- ➤ **Gauze** (one roll and a half dozen 4-by-4-inch pads)
- ➤ **Hydrogen peroxide** or iodine
- ➤ **Ibuprofen** or acetaminophen

*Note:* Consider your intended terrain and the number of hikers in your party before you exclude any article cited above. A botanical garden stroll may not inspire you to carry a complete kit, but anything beyond that warrants precaution. When hiking alone, you should always be prepared for a medical need. And if you are a twosome or with a group, one or more people in your party should be equipped with first aid material.

## General Safety

The following tips may have the familiar ring of your mother's voice as you take note of them.

- ➤ **Always let someone know where you will be hiking and how long you expect to be gone.** It's a good idea to give that person a copy of your route, particularly if you are headed into any isolated area. Let them know when you return.
- ➤ **Do not count on a cell phone for your safety.** Reception can be spotty or nonexistent on the trail, even on an urban walk—especially if it is embraced by towering trees.
- ➤ **Always carry food and water, even for a short hike.** And bring more water than you think you will need. (That cannot be said often enough!)
- ➤ **Ask questions.** Park employees are there to help. It's a lot easier to solicit advice before a problem occurs, and it will help you avoid a mishap away from civilization when it's too late to amend an error.
- ➤ **Stay on designated trails.** Even on the most clearly marked trails, there is usually a point where you have to stop and consider in which direction to head. If you become disoriented, don't panic. As soon as you think you may be off track, stop, assess your current direction, and then retrace your steps to the point where you went astray. Using a map, a compass, and this book, and keeping in mind what you have passed thus far, reorient yourself, and trust your judgment on which way to continue. If you become absolutely unsure

of how to continue, return to your vehicle the way you came in. Should you become completely lost and have no idea how to find the trailhead, remaining in place along the trail and waiting for help is most often the best option for adults and always the best option for children.

➤ **Always carry a whistle, another precaution that cannot be overemphasized.** It may be a lifesaver if you do become lost or sustain an injury.

➤ **Be especially careful when crossing streams.** Whether you are fording the stream or crossing on a log, make every step count. If you have any doubt about maintaining your balance on a log, ford the stream instead: use a trekking pole or stout stick for balance and face upstream as you cross. If a stream seems too deep to ford, turn back. Whatever is on the other side is not worth risking your life.

➤ **Be careful at overlooks.** While these areas may provide spectacular views, they are potentially hazardous. Stay back from the edge of outcrops, and make absolutely sure of your footing; a misstep can mean a nasty and possibly fatal fall.

➤ **Standing dead trees and storm-damaged living trees pose a significant hazard to hikers.** These trees may have loose or broken limbs that could fall at any time. While walking beneath trees, and when choosing a spot to rest or enjoy your snack, look up.

➤ **Know the symptoms of subnormal body temperature known as hypothermia.** Shivering and forgetfulness are the two most common indicators of this stealthy killer. Hypothermia can occur at any elevation, even in the summer, especially when the hiker is wearing lightweight cotton clothing. If symptoms present themselves, get to shelter, hot liquids, and dry clothes as soon as possible.

➤ **Know the symptoms of heat exhaustion (hyperthermia).** Light-headedness and loss of energy are the first two indicators. If you feel these symptoms, find some shade, drink your water, remove as many layers of clothing as practical, and stay put until you cool down. Marching through heat exhaustion leads to heatstroke—which can be fatal. If you should be sweating and you're not, that's the signature warning sign. Your hike is over at that point—heatstroke is a life-threatening condition that can cause seizures, convulsions, and eventually death. If you or a companion reaches that point, do whatever can be done to cool the victim down and seek medical attention immediately.

➤ **Most important of all, take along your brain.** A cool, calculating mind is the single-most important asset on the trail. It allows you to think before you act.

➤ **In summary: Plan ahead.** Watch your step. Avoid accidents before they happen. Enjoy a rewarding and relaxing hike.

## *Watchwords for Flora and Fauna*

### BLACK BEARS

Though attacks by black bears are uncommon, the sight or approach of a bear can give anyone a start. If you encounter a bear while hiking, remain calm and avoid running in any direction. Make loud noises to scare off the bear and back away slowly. Fortunately, black bears are not typically seen on the hikes featured in this book—they're more commonly found in Garrett, Allegany, Washington, and Fredrick Counties. However, several bears are spotted each year in the more suburban areas, usually due to young males searching for territory of their own. Regardless, most encounters with bears are food related, as bears have an exceptional sense of smell and not particularly discriminating tastes. While this is of greater concern to backpackers and campers, on a day hike, you may plan a lunchtime picnic or munch on an energy bar or other snack from time to time. So remain aware and alert.

### MOSQUITOES

Protect yourself against mosquito bites by applying an effective repellent and/or repellent-impregnated clothing.

The Asian Tiger mosquito, which spreads the West Nile virus, has been seen in Maryland, especially in places with lots of water, including urban areas.

### POISON IVY, OAK, AND SUMAC

Recognizing and avoiding poison ivy, oak, and sumac are the most effective ways to prevent the painful, itchy rashes associated with these plants. Poison ivy (pictured below) occurs as a vine or ground cover, 3 leaflets to a leaf; poison oak occurs as either a vine or shrub, also with 3 leaflets; and poison sumac flourishes in swampland, each leaf having 7–13 leaflets. Urushiol, the oil in the sap of these plants, is responsible for the rash. Within 14 hours of exposure, raised lines and/or blisters will appear on the affected area, accompanied by a terrible itch. Refrain from scratching because bacteria under your fingernails can cause an infection. Wash and dry the affected area thoroughly, applying a calamine lotion to help dry out the rash. If itching or blistering is severe, seek medical attention. If you do come into contact with one of these plants, remember that oil-contaminated clothes, hiking gear, and

Photo: Tom Watson

pets can easily cause an irritating rash on you or someone else, so wash not only any exposed parts of your body but also any exposed clothes, gear, and pets.

## SNAKES

Photo: Breck P. Kent /Shutterstock

Generally speaking, snakes are not a concern in Baltimore, and the prospect of being bitten should never deter a hiker in this area. Maryland has only two native venomous snakes: northern copperheads, which you may see in Baltimore, and timber rattlers, which live in the western, mountainous part of the state. Although the chances of being bitten by a snake on one of the hikes described in this book are slim to none, take proper caution. If you see a snake and it has an hourglass-shaped head, give it a wide berth.

## TICKS

Ticks are often found on brush and tall grass, where they seem to be waiting to hitch a ride on a warm-blooded passerby. Adult ticks are most active April–May and again October–November. Among the varieties of ticks, the black-legged tick, commonly called the deer tick, is the primary carrier of Lyme disease. Wear light-colored clothing to make it easier for you to spot ticks before they migrate to your skin. At the end of the hike, visually check your hair, back of neck, armpits, and socks. During your post-hike shower, take a moment to do a more complete body check. For ticks that are already embedded, removal with tweezers is best. Grasp the tick close to your skin, and remove it by pulling straight out firmly. Do your best to remove the head, but do not twist. Use disinfectant solution on the wound. If you see a bull's-eye rash radiating from a tender red spot, see a doctor right away. If you experience flulike symptoms (intense malaise, fever, chills, and a headache) a day or two after hiking, look very hard for the telltale bull's-eye rash, and see a doctor to alleviate any concerns. Take precautionary measures, but don't let ticks keep you inside. On all of our hikes, my husband and I didn't end up with a single tick.

## Hunting

Separate rules, regulations, and licenses govern the various hunting types and related seasons. You can find a detailed description of hunting rules and regulations by park at dnr.maryland.gov/huntersguide. Though there are generally no problems hiking during game seasons, you may wish to wear orange or instead choose one of the many city hikes where hunting isn't allowed.

## *Regulations*

**Maryland has 72 state parks** offering a variety of outdoor activities, including hiking, biking, horseback riding, and camping, to name a few. Maryland State Parks encourage visitors to practice Leave No Trace principles, which include disposing of waste properly, leaving what you find, respecting wildlife, and being considerate of other visitors. Some of the hikes featured here include trailheads beginning at official state park entrances. Rules, rates, and regulations vary by park and are noted in each hike's profile. Maryland offers an annual State Park and Trail Passport that grants you and those in your vehicle unlimited access to many of these parks.

## *Trail Etiquette*

**Always treat the trail,** wildlife, flora, and your fellow hikers with respect. Here are some reminders.

> ➤ **Plan ahead in order to be self-sufficient at all times.** For example, carry necessary supplies for changes in weather or other conditions. A well-planned trip brings satisfaction to you and to others.

> ➤ **Hike on open trails only.**

> ➤ **In seasons or construction areas where road or trail closures may be a possibility,** use the website addresses or phone numbers shown in the "Contacts" line for each of this guidebook's hikes to check conditions prior to heading out for your hike. And do not attempt to circumvent such closures.

> ➤ **Avoid trespassing on private land and obtain all permits and authorization as required.** Leave gates as you found them or as directed by signage.

> ➤ **Be courteous to other hikers,** bikers, equestrians, and others you encounter on the trails.

> ➤ **Never spook wild animals or pets.** An unannounced approach, a sudden movement, or a loud noise startles most critters, and a surprised animal can be dangerous to you, to others, and to itself. Give animals plenty of space.

> ➤ **Observe the yield signs around the region's trailheads and backcountry.** Typically they advise hikers to yield to horses, and bikers yield to both horses and hikers. By common courtesy on hills, hikers and bikers yield to any uphill traffic. When encountering mounted riders or horsepackers, hikers can courteously step off the trail, on the downhill side if possible. So the horse can see and hear you, calmly greet the riders before they reach you and do not dart behind trees. Also resist the urge to pet horses unless you are invited to do so.

> ➤ **Stay on existing trails** and do not blaze any new trails.

> ➤ **Be sure to pack out what you pack in,** leaving only your footprints. No one likes to see the trash someone else has left behind.

## Choosing the Right Trail

**One of the most important things to consider** when you're deciding how to spend a day in and around Baltimore is to have an idea of what you'd like to get out of the trail. The hikes in this book cover a large variety of landscapes, from urban city walks to isolated trails through deep woods. I'd encourage you to read the trail description, consider the location, and select a hike that best fits your current circumstances and expectations. Some days, I'd like to immerse myself in the wilderness, and so choosing a trail that winds its way around city streets would not fit the bill. Similarly, there are days when the thought of having to drive an extended distance outside of the city would be enough to prevent me going on a hike, so I'd be much happier enjoying a city park. I hope we've included trails diverse enough to meet you where you are and provide an opportunity to get out and explore Baltimore and the surrounding areas, regardless of your circumstances.

## Hiking on Your Own

**When I began updating this guide,** I was often asked whether I planned to hike any of the trails alone. That's a common question for hikers—especially women—and there's a certain risk involved when you set out on your own. However, it's not always possible to find an available trail companion when the mood to hike strikes you (or, in my case, when you need to spend every weekend for months updating hikes). In those cases, setting out on your own can be a lovely way to spend the day in peaceful solitude, and it offers a restfulness that can only be found when you're left with your own thoughts.

If you plan to hike alone, I recommend that you share your plans and estimated schedule with someone you trust and who will follow up if something seems off. When possible, I also check in with a park ranger to confirm the trail and let them know I'll be out there. Though it's personal preference, as a female hiker (and someone who was pregnant for much of this research), I preferred to choose more popular, well-marked hikes when I was traveling alone, and picked hikes in areas I knew to be especially safe. You might also consider taking along a means of protection (besides bug spray!) if you're comfortable using it (such as pepper spray, or whatever you're legally allowed to carry, depending on the locale). Finally, follow your intuition if something doesn't feel right. That all being said, I'm happy to report that in all my hiking so far—especially over the past year when I more often traveled solo—there wasn't a moment when I was concerned about anything more than running out of M&M's in my trail mix.

## Hiking with Children

**A goal of this book** was to include hikes that could be enjoyed by those of all ages—no one is too young for a hike in the woods or through a city park. I was happy to see many parents with children in backpack carriers and off-roading strollers partaking in many of the hikes featured in this book. Of course, you know your child(ren) best, so choose trail lengths and elevations carefully, and be wary on particularly hot or cool days. Use common sense to judge a child's capacity to hike a particular trail, and always rely on the possibility that the child will tire quickly and need to be carried.

When packing for the hike, remember the child's needs as well as your own. Make sure children are adequately clothed for the weather, have proper shoes, and are protected from the sun with sunscreen. Kids dehydrate quickly, so make sure you have plenty of fluid for everyone.

We have indicated which hikes are good for children in the "60 Hikes by Category" table on pages xiv–xvi. Many of these hikes include facilities with water fountains, restrooms, and the best bribe of all—playgrounds! When hiking with children, remember that the trip will be a compromise—a child's energy and enthusiasm alternate between bursts of speed and long stops to examine snails, sticks, dirt, and other attractions.

Allison takes her son on his first hike in Patapsco Valley State Park.

# CITY OF BALTIMORE

# 1 BALTIMORE WATERFRONT PROMENADE

Vista of the Inner Harbor from Fells Point

**JOIN THE THRONGS** strolling around Baltimore's tourist meccas, but begin and end where few tourists venture.

## DESCRIPTION

From the Korean War Memorial, you'll be more or less paralleling Boston Street to your right. But it's often blocked from view, and in any case, the far more lovely scene is to your left: the Patapsco River as it forms Baltimore's Northwest Harbor. As you make your way toward the Inner Harbor, you'll be reminded of just how beautiful and peaceful a major city can be.

Canton's development has been nothing short of remarkable, turning an industrial and neglected waterfront into a series of polished marinas and waterfront housing, mixed in sensibly with existing restaurants and shops. With downtown looming to the east, your view to the south is charming: pleasure craft plying the river, gaggles of ducks paddling around the water, and the iconic Domino's sugar sign; its red glow can be seen at night from almost anywhere in the harbor.

You'll reach Fells Point at 1.7 miles. This historical neighborhood dates back to 1670 but was first incorporated as a town in 1763, becoming part of Baltimore City 10 years later. Houses still exist from that era, and with Broadway Market just a few blocks from the water on South Broadway, you should poke around this wonderful and beautiful cobblestoned neighborhood.

**DISTANCE & CONFIGURATION:** 5.7-mile point-to-point or 11.4-mile out-and-back

**DIFFICULTY:** Easy–moderate

**SCENERY:** Downtown Baltimore, Inner Harbor, Federal Hill, monuments, historical sites

**EXPOSURE:** Sunny

**TRAFFIC:** Heavy

**TRAIL SURFACE:** Asphalt, brick, concrete, cobblestone, wood

**HIKING TIME:** 2.5 hours

**DRIVING DISTANCE:** 6 miles

**ELEVATION GAIN:** 18' at trailhead, with no significant rise

**ACCESS:** Park is open sunrise–sunset. Promenade is always open—use normal caution after dark. No fees or permits are required.

**WHEELCHAIR ACCESS:** Yes

**MAPS:** USGS *Baltimore East*

**FACILITIES:** Food, water, and bathrooms in restaurants and shops along route

**CONTACT:** 410-396-7931, baltimore.org/info/canton-waterfront-park

**LOCATION:** 3001 Boston St., Baltimore

**COMMENTS:** Final plans call for the Waterfront Promenade to extend to Locust Point to connect with the existing promenade in front of the Under Armour complex. For now, however, there is still an unfinished portion between Federal Hill and Locust Point. Additionally, ongoing and future construction projects sometimes require brief detours away from the main route. See planning.baltimorecity.gov/promenade-information for up-to-date information and details.

At 2 miles, in the heart of Fells Point, pass the Broadway (Recreation) Pier. Now a luxury hotel, it was built in 1914 as a commercial pier with recreational facilities, including a ballroom where the young people of Fells would congregate. You will reach the Frederick Douglass–Isaac Myers Maritime Park and Museum (douglassmyers.org) at 2.5 miles, at the intersection of Caroline, Thames, and Point Streets. To continue on, make a left on Point Street. This is the newest addition to the promenade, and this area continues to grow. So while your precise loop may vary, you can continue on the promenade by following Point Street as it becomes Central Avenue. You'll cross Dock Street and then over the harbor, on a bridge constructed in 2018 to provide easier access to the heart of Harbor East. From there, turn left on Lancaster Street.

This area is popular for shopping and dining. You'll pass many restaurants and shops, offering ample opportunities for a break. Reach the Four Seasons at just over 3.5 miles in Harbor East. At 3.8 miles you'll come to a water taxi stop on your left; immediately after, you'll pass Mr. Trash Wheel, the happy-looking water wheel that deposits trash from the Jones Falls River into a waiting dumpster. Installed in 2014, Mr. Trash Wheel collected 38,000 pounds of trash on his busiest day. He's so beloved by the city that he even has his own Twitter handle (@MrTrashWheel). Nearby you'll see a series of Italian flags; you're on the edge of Little Italy.

Take a left over the pedestrian bridge at 3.8 miles and pass the MECU Pavilion (formerly Pier 6) on your left. If there's a concert scheduled, you'll see people begin to line the surrounding Waterfront Pavilion for a free show. Walking in front of the entrance to the concert venue, veer left at McCormick & Schmick's seafood restaurant to stay on the waterfront path. In front of you is the red Seven Foot Knoll Lighthouse. Built in 1856 atop Seven Foot Knoll in the Chesapeake Bay, it was moved to its current location in 1997. For the seasonal hours of the lighthouse and information

## Baltimore Waterfront Promenade

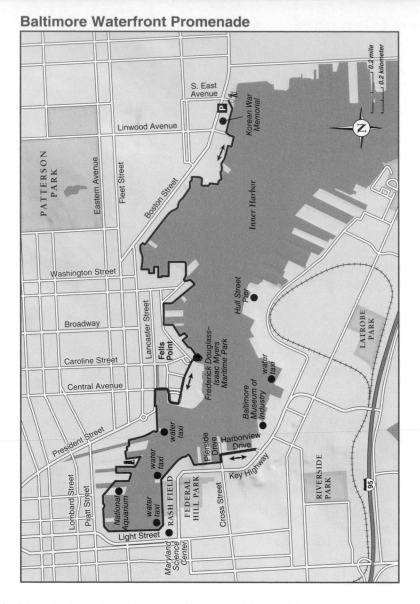

on the historic ships along the waterfront, visit historicships.org. Continue around the peninsula and head north as the National Aquarium comes into view on your left.

In the water in front of you sits the USCG *Cutter Taney,* the only remaining survivor of the attack on Pearl Harbor; you can go on board and check it out. Just before you reach the ship, take a left over the bridge and walk around the aquarium. Cross the pedestrian bridge to your left in front of Dick's Last Resort at 4.4 miles. You'll walk under a portion of the aquarium and pass the entrance. The aquarium has long lines on weekends and holidays, so buy a ticket in advance if you want to visit (aqua.org).

Continuing along the water, you'll come to the World Trade Center, which is the country's tallest regular pentagonal building; the 27th floor offers an unmatched view of Baltimore's harbor and skyline. You can also rent a paddleboat nearby.

At 4.5 miles you'll reach the heart of the Inner Harbor. The wide-open waterfront area features an outdoor stage for a variety of performances and is also one of the pickup locations of the Baltimore Water Taxi. Looking toward the water, you'll see the USS *Constellation,* the last sail-only warship built in 1854 by the U.S. Navy. Continuing on, you'll have unobstructed views of the aquarium to the left across the harbor. To the right is the Baltimore Visitor Center. About a half mile straight up Conway Street to the right of the visitor center stands Oriole Park at Camden Yards, widely regarded as one of the nicest stadiums in Major League Baseball.

The popular Maryland Science Center (mdsci.org), with its massive *Tyrannosaurus* in the window, looms straight ahead. When you reach the Science Center at just under 5 miles, head left, keeping the water on your left. Pass a merry-go-round on the right. In summer you'll see hordes of people playing volleyball to your right at Rash Field. The promenade continues after the Rusty Scupper Restaurant, weaving in front of luxury apartments and condos. Here, the tourist crowds thin. At 5.5 miles the path makes an abrupt left turn and heads uphill, dropping you at Pierside Drive. Make a left, then an immediate right onto Harborview Drive to continue past some beautiful town homes, with the water and a lovely marina on your left. Key Highway is where our trail concludes at 5.7 miles. From here, you can explore some of the sights in this area—Federal Hill, American Visionary Art Museum (avam.org), Baltimore Museum of Industry (thebmi.org)—or retrace your steps back to your starting point. As a nice alternative, the Baltimore Water Taxi (baltimorewatertaxi.com) picks up just to the left down Key Highway, offering a nautical shortcut back to your car.

## NEARBY/RELATED ACTIVITIES

Your best bet is to stop at the **Baltimore Visitor Center,** open daily 10 a.m.–5 p.m., except Mondays in January and February. Before heading back to your car, walk up to Federal Hill, which offers great views of the city.

• • • • • • • • • • • • • • • • • • • • • • • •

**GPS TRAILHEAD COORDINATES**  N39° 16.625'   W76° 34.361'

**DIRECTIONS**  Take I-95 N 4 miles, heading through the Fort McHenry Tunnel, to Exit 57 toward Boston Street/O Donnell Street. Turn left onto Interstate Avenue and then continue onto Boston Street. Go just over 1 mile and turn left onto S. East Avenue. Park in the lot and head right toward the water. The promenade begins at the fishing pier at the south end of Canton Waterfront Park.

One of the shady trails that winds around Cylburn Arboretum

**TAKE IN A** stunning array of flowers and trees on the grounds of a beautiful 19th-century mansion.

## DESCRIPTION

Construction on the Italianate Cylburn Mansion began in 1863 and was completed in 1888 by Jesse Tyson, a wealthy Baltimore businessman. Construction took so long because of the Civil War, the death of Jesse's mother, and the not-so-easy task of moving such large stones by oxen from their mines. In 1888 Jesse moved into the home full-time with his much younger bride, Edyth Johns. After he died in 1906, Edyth married a military officer stationed at Fort McHenry, and she and her husband lived in Cylburn until her death in 1942, when the house became the property of Baltimore City. For several years, it served as a home for children, and in 1954, the Board of Recreation and Parks created the Cylburn Wildflower Preserve and Garden Center, which was later renamed Cylburn Arboretum.

The grounds of Cylburn are pretty any time of year but are especially glorious in mid- to late spring. There are no fewer than 13 separate gardens that range from Victorian-designed formal spaces to backyard vegetable gardens and a plot devoted to alpine plants. All of this flora goes a long way toward attracting birds. More than 170 species have been spotted at Cylburn, including bald eagles.

**DISTANCE & CONFIGURATION:** 2.7-mile loop

**DIFFICULTY:** Easy–moderate

**SCENERY:** Trees and flowers, an Italianate mansion

**EXPOSURE:** Mostly shade

**TRAFFIC:** Light on trails; heavy in gardens and mansion, especially in spring and summer

**TRAIL SURFACE:** Dirt, asphalt

**HIKING TIME:** 1 hour, longer for poking around gardens and mansion

**DRIVING DISTANCE:** 12 miles

**ELEVATION GAIN:** 400' at trailhead, with no significant rise

**ACCESS:** Spring–fall, Tuesday–Sunday, 8 a.m.–8 p.m; winter, Tuesday–Sunday, 8 a.m.–5p.m. No fees or permits required.

**WHEELCHAIR ACCESS:** Mansion, Vollmer Center, and paved paths

**MAPS:** USGS *Baltimore West*

**FACILITIES:** Restroom and water in the mansion and Vollmer Center

**CONTACT:** 410-367-2217, cylburn.org and bcrp.baltimorecity.gov/Cylburn

**LOCATION:** 4915 Greenspring Ave., Baltimore

**COMMENTS:** To schedule a trail, garden, and/or museum tour, call 410-367-2217.

From the parking area, cross the entrance road in front of the Vollmer Center (restrooms available inside). Facing the Vollmer Center, walk down the paved path on the right. Pass the loading dock and Vollmer Center on your left, following the treeline, and come to the trailhead for the Circle Trail, which you'll recognize as a path leading across a small wooden bridge and into the woods. The Circle Trail is the main path encircling the grounds of Cylburn Arboretum.

At just over a quarter of a mile, you'll come to an intersection with signs pointing hard left to the mansion, left (northeast) to the Circle Trail, and straight (south east) to the Ravine Trail, which descends gradually into the ravine and eventually brings you back to the Circle Trail. Head straight, making your way through the deer exclusion fence. At just over half a mile, a nice stream comes into view on your right. Soon after, the trail splits; veer left, staying on the well-trodden trail. Despite being in the city, this trail feels quite remote, the only reminder the distant hum of traffic, though it's often drowned out by the birds.

At just under 1 mile, the Ravine Trail intersects the Vista and Spicebush Trails. Stay straight to take the Spicebush Trail (the Vista Trail was closed due to storm damage during my hike). The Spicebush Trail heads uphill, with some small switchbacks. At just under 1.25 miles, you'll reach the deer exclusion fence and the Circle Trail on the other side, with some stone benches on your right for a rest. Continue right on the Circle Trail. At 1.3 miles a trail leads to the left, but you should stay on the Circle Trail. Soon you'll see the Etta Stem Wedge Trail, a pleasant little diversionary trail that runs parallel to the Circle Trail but deeper into the woods. Take that to the right, and when you rejoin the Circle Trail from the Etta Stem Wedge Trail at just under 1.5 miles, head right. Soon after, take another detour to the right onto the Azalea Trail.

At the next junction, continue right on the Azalea Trail, walking north through the deer exclusion fence. At 1.75 miles a sign points you toward the Ridge Trail, a steeper detour worth taking. You'll reach the wide, gravel Woodland Trail at just

## Cylburn Arboretum

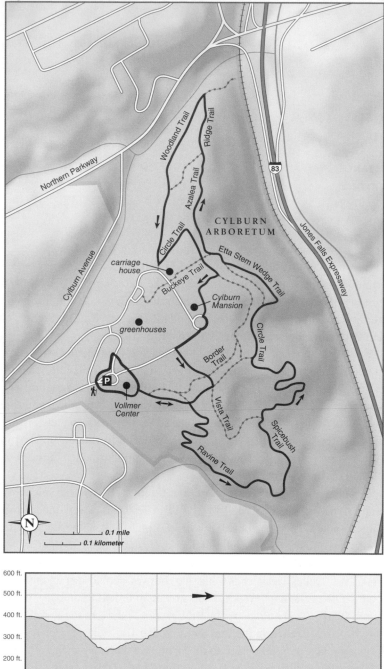

under 2 miles; take it left, heading southwest. In 0.1 mile a sign points left to the Azalea Trail, but stay straight on the Woodland Trail. Continuing south at just over 2.2 miles, you'll reach the deer exclusion fence. Walk through it to a junction right before the road and head left to jump back on the main Circle Trail. Continue on the Circle Trail, bypassing the Azalea Trail on your left, and continue straight through the four-way junction. At the second junction, turn right, following the sign for the mansion. Continue straight and make a left through the two lions head pillars. Head south along the lawn, with the mansion on your right, to the main drive. Walk along the road, passing beautiful gardens on your left, where you're likely to see many painters if it's a nice day.

Walking southwest along the road leading from the mansion, a sign labeled TRAILS points you to the left. Take this grassy trail past some benches and a grove of bamboo. There, you'll see several trail options, two leading into the bamboo. Take the trail on your right, heading south. You'll quickly intersect with the Circle Trail, running left and right, with the Vista Trail directly in front of you. Turn right onto the Circle Trail to head back toward your car. You'll soon reach the original trail junction where you took the Ravine Trail. Turn right and stay on the Circle Trail to return to your car.

## NEARBY/RELATED ACTIVITIES

Just down I-83 is **Druid Hill Park,** where you'll find tennis and basketball courts, a public swimming pool, a disc-golf course, the **Rawlings Conservatory** (displaying thousands of plants and flowers in a lovely glass pavilion), and the **Maryland Zoo.** Go south on I-83 to Exit 7 and head west on Druid Hill Park Drive to the park entrance, off Swann Drive.

• • • • • • • • • • • • • • • • • • • • • • • • •

**GPS TRAILHEAD COORDINATES** N39° 21.085'    W76° 39.286'

**DIRECTIONS** From I-95, take Exit 53 for I-395 N and continue 1.2 miles. Turn slightly right onto W. Conway Street, and then 0.3 mile later, turn left onto Light Street. In 0.2 mile turn right onto E. Pratt Street. In another 0.2 mile turn left onto S. Gay Street; after 0.4 mile take I-83 north 5.6 miles to Exit 10 (Northern Parkway West). In 0.4 mile take the first left onto Cylburn Avenue and continue 0.5 mile to Greenspring Avenue. Turn left onto Greenspring Avenue, and then take another immediate left into Cylburn Arboretum. Follow the road to the parking area on the left.

A portion of the nearly 25-mile-long Gwynns Falls stream

**ADJACENT TO AND** connected with Leakin Park, this section of the Gwynns Falls Trail runs through one of the largest unbroken urban forests in the United States. Follow the falls several miles through its most scenic sections to Leon Day Park and back.

## DESCRIPTION

Begin the Gwynns Falls Trail on the southeast end of the Windsor Mill Road parking lot. This portion of the trail is known as the Mill Race Trail. The Windsor Mill area is named for the old Windsor Mill, just one of many flour and textile mills built along the Dead Run and Gwynns Falls in the early 1800s. The trail surface becomes crushed stone on the Mill Race Trail, named for the waterwheels that once conveyed water 5 miles downstream to Calverton (present-day Rosemount). You'll see the Jastrow Trail stairway immediately to the left, but stay straight—you'll return on the Jastrow Trail. An informational sign points out the three distinct tree levels along the trail: oak, hickory, tulip poplar, beech, and black walnut form the canopy; redbud, dogwood, serviceberry, and spicebush form the midlevel; and laurel, rhododendron, azalea, multiflora rose, may applejack-in-the-pulpit, and fern fill the understory.

This is a very pleasant section. Even though Windsor Mill Road is not far away, the falls below easily drowns out traffic noise. To the left, the thickly wooded hill

**DISTANCE & CONFIGURATION:** 4.4-mile out-and-back with 2 loops

**DIFFICULTY:** Easy

**SCENERY:** Gwynns Falls, mixed hardwoods

**EXPOSURE:** Half and half

**TRAFFIC:** Light–moderate

**TRAIL SURFACE:** Packed dirt, crushed rock, and asphalt

**HIKING TIME:** 2 hours

**DRIVING DISTANCE:** 7.5 miles

**ELEVATION GAIN:** 206' at trailhead, with no significant rise

**ACCESS:** Sunrise–sunset; no fees or permits required

**WHEELCHAIR ACCESS:** No

**MAPS:** USGS *Baltimore West,* gwynnsfallstrail .org/images/pics/GFTMapForWeb.pdf

**FACILITIES:** None (restrooms and water at Winans Meadow Trailhead section of Gwynns Falls Trail—see Leakin Park hike, page 45)

**CONTACT:** gwynnsfallstrail.org, email: info@gwynnsfallstrail.org

**LOCATION:** Windsor Mill Rd., Baltimore

**COMMENTS:** For a hike along the Gwynns Falls Trail from Leon Day Park to the trail's terminus, see page 32.

rises precipitously; here the beech and walnut trees are especially enormous and old, somewhat amazing considering the lumber needs of the growing city over the last few centuries.

Occasionally, views open up on the right and all you can see are the tops of trees—no roads and no buildings, despite being in the middle of the city. At 0.65 mile you'll reach a paved street with several trail options: Jastrow Levin area (with accompanying Jastrow Trail) to the left, Gwynns Falls Stream Trail to the right, and Gwynns Falls Trail straight ahead. Go straight.

For almost the next mile, the scenery doesn't change much, but it's consistently beautiful; every time it opens up, you'll have phenomenal views of the stream valley below, especially in winter. In summer the woods are a riot of green, and in autumn yellow, orange, and red dominate. However, depending on recent storms in the area, you may have to squeeze past some downed trees—trail maintenance crews can't seem to clear them as quickly as they fall down. At just under a mile on your left, a nice waterfall and rock landscaping appear. This is one of a few attempts along the path to help with erosion and path stability.

At 1.4 miles you'll hit asphalt as the trail turns right and parallels Morris Road and Hilton Parkway on your left. Unfortunately, you'll lose the forest here, but it's not an unpleasant walk.

When you reach the intersection of Morris and Franklintown Road, turn left and go under the Hilton Parkway Bridge. Follow the signs to Leon Day Park. You'll see a GWYNNS FALLS TRAIL sign to the left just before you go under the bridge. Cross Franklintown Road at just over 1.7 miles and pick up the asphalt on the other side; Gwynns Falls sits in a buffer of trees to the right. At 1.85 miles you'll come to Leon Day Park, named in honor of the West Baltimore resident and Negro League baseball star who was inducted into the Baseball Hall of Fame in 1995. A loop circles the park, so you can go in either direction. On the far side of the park you'll see a railroad bridge

## Gwynns Falls Park

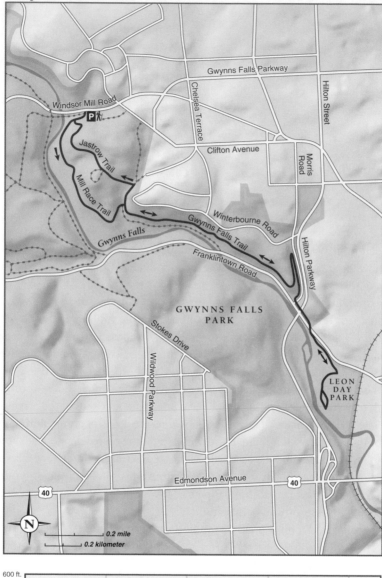

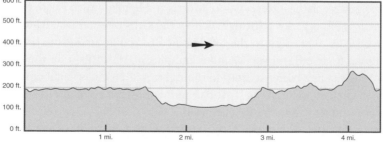

and a small truss bridge. The Gwynns Falls Trail continues here and is the trailhead for Gwynns Falls Trail from Leon Day Park to Cherry Hill Park (pages 32–36).

However, instead of continuing on the Gwynns Falls Trail, finish your loop around the park and retrace your steps back to the three-way trail intersection at 3.8 miles. This time, turn right toward the Jastrow Levin area, walking up the road. Be on the lookout for the Jastrow Trail on your left and take it.

The Jastrow Trail rises uphill above the stream valley to the left. You'll soon pass the Jastrow Levin campsite, a 1930s-era Girl Scout campground. The trail here is much tighter and wilder, with lots of midlevel growth, and you'll have to duck under vines a few times. We came upon two fawns just after the campground. At 4.3 miles head down a wooden staircase to the main trail and turn right onto Mill Race Trail to reach the Windsor Mill parking area.

## NEARBY/RELATED ACTIVITIES

Within 10 miles, plenty of other hiking and recreation opportunities abound. Head south on Hilton Parkway from Gwynns Falls Park to MD 40 west and continue to **Patapsco Valley State Park.** Go east on Hilton Parkway to Liberty Heights to **Druid Hill Park,** home of the Maryland Zoo, among other attractions. Also on Hilton Parkway, just before Liberty Heights, is **Hanlon Park** and **Lake Ashburton;** although it's not a hiking destination, the view of downtown over the lake is fantastic—and something of a local secret.

• • • • • • • • • • • • • • • • • • • • • • • • • •

**GPS TRAILHEAD COORDINATES** N39° 18.730'   W76° 41.263'

**DIRECTIONS** Take I-95 S 3 miles to Exit 49B (I-695 W) toward I-70 W/Towson. In 5 miles take Exit 16 to merge onto I-70 E, and then in 2 miles take Exit 94 to merge onto Security Boulevard. In 0.2 mile turn right onto N. Forest Park Avenue. In just under a mile, turn right onto Windsor Mill Road. The trailhead parking will be 1.2 miles ahead on your right, marked by a sign labeled GWYNNS FALLS TRAILHEAD AT WINDSOR MILL ROAD.

The USS *Constellation*—the U.S. Navy's last sail-only warship—keeps watch over the Inner Harbor.
Photo by Lauren Brown

**FOLLOW A GREENWAY** trail through West Baltimore. Bracketed by wooded and waterfront parks on both ends, the middle section is entirely urbanized, running through some of Baltimore's lesser known but more interesting neighborhoods.

## DESCRIPTION

The Gwynns Falls Trail is part of the East Coast Greenway and the Chesapeake Bay Gateways Network. It is a focal point for city activities; check out the website for a calendar of happenings.

John Smith mapped the Gwynns Falls in 1608, though the Susquehannock and Algonquian Indians had been nearby for centuries. Smith said the stream tumbled over "felles," or falls, which explains the sometimes confusing local practice of naming streams and rivers as "falls" (see Jones Falls, Gunpowder Falls). The stream itself was named for Richard Gwinn, who established a trading post here in 1669. In 1904 the Olmsted brothers laid out a series of parks and open spaces to be included in their plan for the Greater Baltimore Public Grounds. The Gwynns Falls Trail (GFT) resurrects much of that plan.

This portion of the hike begins at Leon Day Park. Go 0.3 mile to the other end of Leon Day, where you'll cross under a steel bridge and enter CSXT property, which for the next 1.5 miles is nicely wooded with the Gwynns Falls to the right down the

**DISTANCE & CONFIGURATION:** 11.2-mile point-to-point

**DIFFICULTY:** Moderate

**SCENERY:** Gwynns Falls, city neighborhoods, waterfront parks

**EXPOSURE:** More sun than shade

**TRAFFIC:** Moderate–heavy

**TRAIL SURFACE:** Asphalt, cement

**HIKING TIME:** 4 hours

**DRIVING DISTANCE:** 5 miles

**ELEVATION GAIN:** 118' at trailhead, with no significant rise

**ACCESS:** Many of the parks along the route are open sunrise–sunset. The trail is always open

but best avoided after dark. There are light-rail stops as well as bus service at many points along the route. For a schedule, call 410-539-5000 or 866-RIDE-MTA, or visit mta.maryland.gov.

**WHEELCHAIR ACCESS:** Yes

**MAPS:** USGS *Baltimore West, Baltimore East, Curtis Bay;* printable trail map available at gwynnsfallstrail.org

**FACILITIES:** Many establishments along the route offer food, shelter, a phone, and restrooms.

**CONTACT:** gwynnsfallstrail.org, email: info@gwynnsfallstrail.org

**LOCATION:** 1200 N. Franklintown Rd., Baltimore

**COMMENTS:** Often running along city sidewalks through neighborhoods, substations, and even industrial parks, this hike is for urban adventurers.

hill and large rock outcrops up the hill to the left. Though you won't see it, beyond the hill is Western Cemetery, more than 250 years old and incorporated in 1846. Cross under a bridge at 0.6 mile and look for the informational sign and benches at 0.8 mile. The sign will tell you that this section was once known as "Baltimore's Niagara Falls." You'll be tempted to laugh at the hyperbole, but the water pouring over the rocks is nice nonetheless. Though with this pleasing scene, there's no mistaking the strange dichotomy around you: the pretty Gwynns Falls, set in thick woods full of beautiful sweet gum, hickory, and maple, is sometimes despoiled by a dumped furnace or plastic tubing.

Cross over Baltimore Street, following the Ellicott Driveway, once a millrace then a vehicular road, now closed to traffic and crowded with thick woods. At 1.8 miles take a right at Frederick Avenue (GFT signs are at all sections where it's not abundantly clear which way to go). Cross over the CSX line and Gwynns Falls and head left at Dukeland. Cross Hurley at 2.2 miles and turn left, crossing the falls once again. It soon becomes quite wooded again, and you'll reach a scenic section of trail: a series of three steel bridges crisscrossing old stone abutments of the former Brunswick Street Bridge. A fourth bridge appears soon after, and you'll head under the wagon pass of the old Carrolton Aqueduct, the B&O's first bridge, constructed in 1829. The trail soon skirts the outer edge of Carroll Park Golf Course and becomes very urban soon after, passing the renovated Montgomery Business Park on the left and paralleling Washington Boulevard.

At 3.7 miles enter Carroll Park, known as the home of Mount Clare Mansion, circa 1760, Maryland's first house museum and one of the oldest colonial Georgian houses in Baltimore. When you see three wooden poles in the path, take a right crossing Washington and onto Bush Street. The trail is delineated as a well-marked

## Gwynns Falls Trail from Leon Day Park to Cherry Hill Park

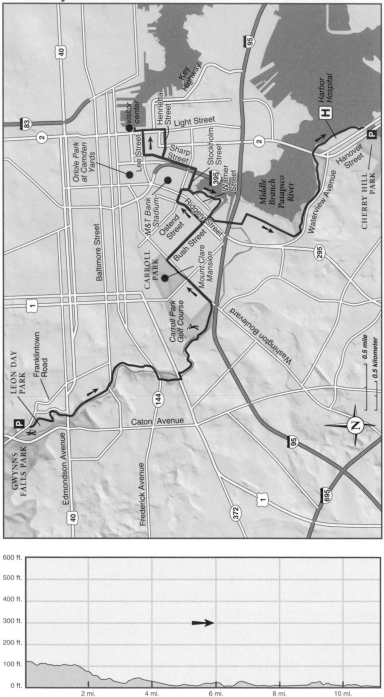

bike route in the street. Obviously, if you're walking, use the parallel sidewalk. *Warning:* This will no longer feel like a hike but rather a city stroll. If you follow the length of the GFT, it will remain urbanized for quite a while. Nevertheless, you'll pass through some historic and interesting city neighborhoods.

First up is the Camden-Carroll Industrial Area. Follow the BIKE ROUTE signs to a left onto and then straight up Ridgely Street. Cross railroad tracks and turn right onto West Ostend Street, again following BIKE ROUTE and GFT signs. You're on the edge of downtown, passing M&T Bank Stadium, home of the Ravens, on the left. Turn right onto Warner Street across from the stadium. Once you cross the railroad tracks, you'll see signs for the GFT pointing straight as well as left. If you've had enough of the city and want a return to green, go straight. If you want to do the whole trail, head left. Assuming you've headed left, pass under I-395 and through Solo Gibbs Park, a small community park in Sharp-Leadenhall, a neighborhood that is more than 200 years old and home to the city's first African-American enclave.

Take a right on Henrietta Street, and then a left on Williams Street to Key Highway. Cross Key Highway at the crosswalk and follow the bike path left to Light Street, around the Maryland Science Center. Follow the path right to turn onto Light Street, which takes you past the Baltimore Visitor Center at the Inner Harbor at mile 6.4 on your right, where you can find out anything and everything about what to see and do.

The Jones Falls Trail continues through the harbor, but for this urban hike, turn around on the GFT and cross Light Street to make a right on Lee Street. Then, turn left on Sharp Street, going through Otterbein. A mid-19th-century neighborhood of orderly row houses and flower boxes, it's a true success story. Locals might remember Otterbein as the site of the $1 houses, sold to those willing to settle and revitalize. Follow Sharp Street straight past the Otterbein Swim Club and tennis courts, under the Hamburg Street overpass, and back through Solo Gibbs Park (veering right at the park to pick up Sharp Street on the other side). Turn right onto Stockholm Street and go once again under I-395 to a left back onto Warner Street. Just before the Horseshoe Casino, you'll see a bike trail on your left, with a painted sign indicating the Jones Falls Trail. Turn left, following the BIKE ROUTE signs.

Immediately go over a steel bridge, crossing short tentacles of the Middle Branch of the Patapsco River. Cross another bridge; you'll see the Greyhound bus terminal nearby, but you're waterside, sort of "underneath" the city. If you've done any downtown driving and have entered the city from I-95 on the I-395 ramp, you'll be familiar with the view. It's an odd feeling watching a large great white heron lope off across the Patapsco, bounded by a grove of wildflowers, underneath the swirl of interstate ramps.

When you pass under I-95, you'll be crossing the Gwynns Falls again, near where it empties into the Middle Branch of the Patapsco River. Take a left onto Clare Street, then a right onto Kloman Street when you hit the railroad tracks. Pass the Westport Light Rail stop and turn left when you reach Waterview Avenue. If you've had enough urban adventuring, you'll be relieved as you enter Middle Branch Park. There's a wildlife observation boardwalk to the left that ends at a viewing deck at 9.5 miles. Turn left onto the asphalt from the wooden boardwalk and pass another observation deck soon, then the Middle Branch Marina, home of the Baltimore Rowing Club. Follow the path as it winds along the water and go under the Hanover Street Bridge. The Broening Park Boat Ramp is just beyond, yielding to a lovely little section that winds along the edge of the Patapsco.

The trail ends at the fishing piers near Hanover Street. A path leads under the road, and there are plans to link it with the BWI and B&A Trails to the south as a continuation of the East Coast Greenway. Parking is available at MedStar Harbor Hospital (3001 South Hanover Street) to make the GFT a point-to-point.

## NEARBY/RELATED ACTIVITIES

You'll find enough nearby activities to keep you occupied for a long time. On your route, you'll pass near **Checkerspot Brewing Company** (checkerspotbrewing.com) if you want to pop in for a beer. Additionally, nearby **Nick's Fish House** (2600 Insulator Drive, nicksfishhouse.com) offers live music, water views, and easy parking.

• • • • • • • • • • • • • • • • • • • • • • • •

**GPS TRAILHEAD COORDINATES** N39° 18.004'    W76° 40.301'

**DIRECTIONS** Take I-95 S 1.6 miles to Exit 50B (Caton Avenue). Veer right to take Caton Avenue north. In just over a mile, veer left to take S. Hilton Street for 1 mile, and then turn right onto Edmondson Avenue. In 0.2 mile turn left onto Ellicott Drive, go 0.4 mile, and then make a left onto N. Franklintown Road. You'll see Leon Day Park immediately on your left.

Herring Run meanders through Baltimore City before eventually emptying into Back River.

**STROLL AROUND THE** busy urban retreat of Lake Montebello and then plunge into the thick woods surrounding Herring Run, a forested marvel surrounded by dense population.

## DESCRIPTION

Begin your walk around Lake Montebello by heading back to where you entered on Lake Montebello Drive. When you reach the entrance, head down the walking path on your right and cross Harford Road at the crosswalk at the intersection of Harford Road and Chesterfield Avenue (you'll see St. Francis of Assisi Church across the street). Once you've crossed, head left down the hill on the trail (a bit gravelly to begin, but then fully paved). Father Hooper Fields, ringed by mature trees, opens up to your right. This path continues to descend until Harford Road is high above you to the left. At 1 mile you'll come to a T-intersection, with the Harford Road Bridge (or construction on a new bridge) to the left; take a right. You'll immediately come to another trail intersection. You'll return over the bridge on the left; for now, stay straight, going southeast. Herring Run is on your left inside a stand of woods. The water of Herring Run has been deemed unclean by the Baltimore City Department of Health; walking near the water poses no threats, but stay out of the water itself.

**DISTANCE & CONFIGURATION:** 3.7 miles, 2 loops connected by an out-and-back

**DIFFICULTY:** Easy

**SCENERY:** Lake Montebello, Herring Run

**EXPOSURE:** More sun than shade

**TRAFFIC:** Heavy around lake, light at Herring Run

**TRAIL SURFACE:** Asphalt, grass

**HIKING TIME:** 2 hours

**DRIVING DISTANCE:** 6 miles

**ELEVATION GAIN:** 175' at trailhead, with no significant rise

**ACCESS:** Sunrise–sunset; no fees or permits required

**WHEELCHAIR ACCESS:** Yes, trails are paved.

**MAPS:** USGS *Baltimore East*

**FACILITIES:** Restrooms, water

**CONTACT:** 410-396-7900, bcrp.baltimorecity.gov /parks/herring-run

**LOCATION:** Harford Rd. and Lake Montebello Dr., Baltimore

**COMMENTS:** A long-awaited new Harford Road Bridge over Herring Run is expected in the coming years. City plans indicate that pedestrian traffic won't be impacted, but it's possible your approach to Lake Montebello and the walk to Herring Run Park may have some slight detours. Follow signage if the project is underway.

The water soon comes into better view, but unfortunately trash can sometimes spoil the scene, especially after a heavy rain, which speaks to the fragile nature of such urban runs as Herring. Even so, the water sounds soothing.

At 1.3 miles you'll enter the woods, well away from city traffic. Hearing swiftly moving water to the left and seeing thick woods on either side is heavenly. Soon you'll arrive at a little stone bridge. To the right are some beautiful rock formations, creating natural cavelike shelters. Just beyond to the left is a sign informing you that you are in Fox Den. Old oaks and maples dominate this truly magnificent, isolated, idyllic stretch of forest. The trail remains wide and paved, with lots of underbrush and trees towering above on either side, as well as the occasional well-placed bench if you'd like to sit and enjoy the peace.

At 1.5 miles you'll enter a section appropriately called Deep Forest. At 1.9 miles the trail begins to head left with woods in front of you. Row houses come into view behind the woods as you enter Orlinksy Grove. Here the trail follows the natural curve of the run itself and then opens up as a field comes into view on the right. Straight ahead is Belair Road. When you reach Belair Road, turn left and cross over Herring Run. Look for the paved trail on your left at just under 2 miles, and take a left, heading northwest. (You'll first pass a dirt path on your left, which rejoins the main trail shortly.)

Back in the woods on the other side of Herring Run, you'll soon cross a raised bridge over a small tributary. Just after the bridge, a trail appears on your right labeled PRIOR AVENUE. As you might guess, this takes you to Prior Avenue; however, continue straight on the paved trail.

This section of the trail is called Second Tributary, and the path opens up at just over 2.3 miles as it swings around to the right, passing Eastwood Field to your left. A series of brick duplexes to the right pops up in the clearing up the hill. At this point,

## Herring Run Park and Lake Montebello

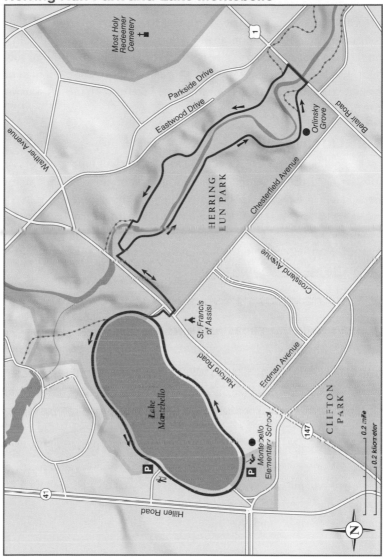

you can't see Herring Run, though you're still paralleling it to your left. At 2.6 miles the metal pedestrian bridge you passed earlier comes into view. Take the path over the bridge (bypassing the one that leads to your left). A series of rocks in the water gives off a pleasing sound, almost loud enough to drown out the sound of traffic, which you'll hear again as soon as you approach Harford Road.

At the intersection at 2.75 miles, turn right, and then make an immediate left to backtrack toward the lake, this time paralleling Harford Road on your right. Cross over Harford Road and make it back to the lake at just over 3 miles. Head right to finish your loop around Lake Montebello before heading back to your car. On your right you'll pass a disc golf course. Soon after, you'll see tidy Baltimore row houses to the right. Just before reaching your car, a series of evergreens planted in neat rows appears on the right, while cattails dominate the lakefront on the left. Loads of birds and butterflies shuttle between these two oases.

## NEARBY/RELATED ACTIVITIES

A city-owned public golf course is in **Clifton Park,** just a half mile south of Lake Montebello on Harford Road. For good eats and a bit of shopping, head to the revitalized **Belvedere Square.** On summer Friday nights, enjoy live music outside from 6 to 9 p.m. For more information, visit belvederesquare.com. Also nearby is **Waverly Brewing Company** tap room (1625-C Union Avenue, waverlybrewingcompany.com). If you're in the area on Saturday morning, you should also consider checking out the **32nd Street Farmers Market,** open year-round, 7 a.m.–noon (400 E. 32nd St.).

• • • • • • • • • • • • • • • • • • • • • • • • •

**GPS TRAILHEAD COORDINATES** N39° 19.930'    W76° 34.774'

**DIRECTIONS** Take I-395 N 1.2 miles to W. Conway Street and turn right. In 0.2 mile turn left onto Light Street, and then, in another 0.2 mile, turn right onto E. Pratt Street. Take Pratt Street for 0.4 mile, and then make a left onto South President Street, which turns into I-83 N. Take I-83 to Exit 9 (Cold Spring Lane East). Follow Cold Spring Lane to Harford Road (0.5 mile past Morgan State University) and turn right; soon after, turn right onto Lake Montebello Drive. Once you've entered the park, you can only head left; there's plenty of parking on the side of the street as well as a parking lot with a playground roughly one-quarter of the way around the lake.

The Rawlings Conservatory was designed by George A. Frederick and offers five greenhouses to explore.
*Photo by Steven Sturm*

**THIS HIKE FOLLOWS** a portion of the Jones Falls Trail through wooded Druid Hill Park and then makes a loop around Druid Lake.

## DESCRIPTION

The Jones Falls Trail (JFT), Baltimore's newest greenway, stretches 11 miles from the Baltimore Visitor Center at the Inner Harbor in the south all the way to Cylburn Arboretum in the north. The trail more or less follows the course of Baltimore's main north–south waterway, Jones Falls.

Begin this hike in Baltimore's Woodberry neighborhood, an attractive and historical mill area with some great restaurants as well as the Clipper Mill development, which beautifully mixes historical mill structures with new environmentally sound homes. Entering Druid Hill Park at the end of Parkdale Avenue, you'll quickly come to a trail intersection and turn right. At 0.2 mile walk through the series of switchbacks, which were installed to help the park meet accessibility standards for people in wheelchairs. It's an impressive display, and beautifully constructed. At the next junction at 0.3 mile, turn left, following the foot signs. The trail winds through a picturesque hardwood forest, some particularly lovely sections of which are crowded with mature tulip, oak, poplar, and maple trees. The area can be an eye-opener to residents who remember the old days when this part of Druid Hill was something of a no-go zone.

41

**DISTANCE & CONFIGURATION:** 5.4-mile out-and-back with lake loop

**DIFFICULTY:** Easy–moderate

**SCENERY:** Druid Lake, Druid Park (Maryland Zoo, Rawlings Conservatory)

**EXPOSURE:** More sun than shade

**TRAFFIC:** Moderate–heavy

**TRAIL SURFACE:** Asphalt

**HIKING TIME:** 2.5 hours

**DRIVING DISTANCE:** 5 miles

**ELEVATION GAIN:** 190' at trailhead, a little over 300' at high point

**ACCESS:** Sunrise–sunset. No fees or permits required. The Woodberry Light Rail Station is just past the I-83 overpass on Union Ave. (see Directions below). MTA buses run to Druid Hill Park; for a schedule, call 410-539-5000 or 866-RIDE-MTA, or visit mta.maryland.gov.

**WHEELCHAIR ACCESS:** Yes, trails are paved.

**MAPS:** USGS *Baltimore East* and *Baltimore West;* trail map available at jonesfallstrail.us

**FACILITIES:** Restrooms, water, playground, gazebos, picnic tables, pool, tennis and basketball courts

**CONTACT:** 410-396-0730, jonesfallstrail.us or bcrp.baltimorecity.gov/parks/druid-hill

**LOCATION:** Druid Park Dr. and Parkdale Ave. (drive south to end of Parkdale), Baltimore

You'll come to the outer edges of a disc-golf course, one of the more popular courses in the area (watch for errant discs). At just under 0.5 mile, you'll reach another trail junction; keep left to stay on the trail (heading right leads to the disc-golf course). At 0.8 mile look for an old circular stone shelter on the right. This is the Grove of Remembrance Pavilion, designed by architect E. L. Palmer to remember First Lieutenant Merrill Rosenfeld, a prominent Baltimore attorney of German Jewish heritage, killed while serving in the military during World War I. The surrounding grove was planted on October 8, 1919, to honor those who died in World War I.

At just under 1 mile, you'll skirt around a parking lot to the right, where the trail continues. The trail then swings around near the entrance to the Maryland Zoo (410-396-7102, marylandzoo.org) and then the Rawlings Conservatory at 1.4 miles. The conservatory (open Wednesday–Sunday, 10 a.m.–4 p.m.) is one of the city's better-kept secrets; an 1888 glass pavilion offers a chance to see exotic plants and flowers.

In the 19th and early-20th centuries, Monument City was a popular nickname because of the city's profusion of commemorative sites. Name the person, and there is probably a monument somewhere to him or her in Baltimore. As you begin to make your way toward Druid Lake, passing basketball courts and portable toilets, you'll see four of these monuments in quick succession, and their eclectic nature truly is a testament to Baltimore's love of monuments. First, look for a memorial to George Washington. It will be facing away from you, but you will see PRESENTED BY THE FAMILY OF NOAH WALKER etched in the back. When you reach this monument, at 2.35 miles, veer right to walk around the lake counterclockwise, rather than veering left to continue following the JFT. Make a loop around the lake.

As you continue around the lake, you'll also pass a very impressive statue of a man in chain mail, shield by his side, sword raised above his head—this is William Wallace, "Guardian of Scotland." He stands atop five massive granite boulders. The statue was originally presented by William Wallace Spence on November 30, 1893,

## Jones Falls Trail: Druid Hill Park

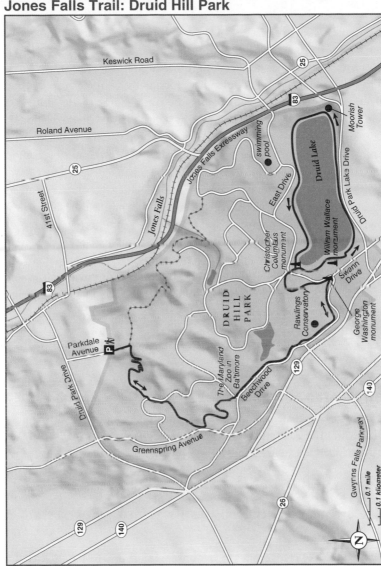

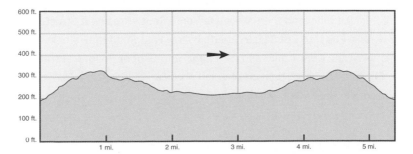

and was rededicated on August 22, 1993, by Baltimore's Society of St. Andrew. You'll also see a memorial to artist Eli Siegel, founder of aesthetic realism. His likeness is cast onto a bronze plate that has been set into a large rock.

Druid Lake is a pretty and popular place for city residents to get some exercise on its 1-mile loop. Ringed with aquatic plants, the lake is home to a multitude of ducks, geese, and red-winged blackbirds. Founded in 1860 and listed on the National Register of Historic Places, 674-acre Druid Hill Park was created with revenue collected from a penny tax on nickel horsecar fares. In the 19th and early-20th centuries, couples in love would head out onto the lake in rowboats. A lot has changed since those days, but the lake remains just as lovely. Still used for city drinking, the water looks clean and fresh.

Continuing around the lake, you'll reach the iconic Moorish Tower, a squat white-marble structure with club-shaped windows. From here you can see Wyman Park, the bell tower of Gilman Hall on the Johns Hopkins University campus, and the old brick Stieff Silver building, among other notable landmarks. Late March and early April yield a special treat: the hill below is completely covered in yellow tulips.

After making a complete circuit of the lake, I recommend turning right at the Columbus monument to get back on the JFT to retrace your steps through the park and back to your car. The JFT continues, but it parallels Fallsway past a not terribly pleasant collection of industrial buildings until it emerges onto Maryland Avenue near Penn Station.

## NEARBY/RELATED ACTIVITIES

Apart from the cultural attractions and disc-golf course mentioned previously, you'll also find a swimming pool and tennis and basketball courts in Druid Hill Park. **Johns Hopkins University** and the **Baltimore Museum of Art** are also nearby.

• • • • • • • • • • • • • • • • • • • • • • • •

**GPS TRAILHEAD COORDINATES** N39° 19.780'    W76° 38.872'

**DIRECTIONS** Take I-395 N 1.2 miles to W. Conway Street and turn right. In 0.2 mile turn left onto Light Street, and then, in another 0.2 mile, turn right onto E. Pratt Street. Take Pratt Street for 0.4 mile, and then make a left onto South President Street, which turns into I-83 N. Take I-83 N to Exit 8 (Falls Road). Follow Falls Road for 2 blocks and turn left onto Union Avenue. Go 0.4 mile and turn right onto Clipper Road. Make an immediate left onto Clipper Park Road, then another left onto Parkdale Avenue. Park on the street. The trailhead is at the end of Parkdale.

Duck as you walk under some low-hanging branches, and keep an eye out for outdoor art installations.

**YOU'LL HAVE SEVERAL** "I can't possibly be anywhere near a city" moments along this amazingly wild and isolated trail through one of the largest unbroken urban forests in the United States.

## DESCRIPTION

Begin your hike at Winans Meadow, named after Thomas Winans, a Baltimorean who returned from Russia a wealthy man after helping to build a railroad between Moscow and St. Petersburg in the 1840s. Here, you'll see where the Gwynns Falls and the Dead Run meet. In colonial times, the Gwynns Falls marked the boundary between the Iroquois and Algonquian tribes. At this time, around 1800, Baltimore was the nation's third-largest city, and growth and industrialization came quickly. This swath of natural beauty miraculously managed to survive. Unfortunately, Leakin Park eventually became synonymous with crime (it was featured on *The Wire* and in the *Serial* podcast), but it has been restored, is vigorously maintained, and is now a true urban retreat.

Despite this, you might initially have a sour taste in your mouth as you head right on the Gwynns Falls Trail from the parking area—you're likely to see a lot of trash on either side of the trail as well as in Dead Run to your left.

Soon after you begin your hike, you'll see a footbridge over Dead Run to the left, but head straight. Despite the trash in the river, Dead Run actually sounds nice because

**DISTANCE & CONFIGURATION:** 2.7-mile loop

**DIFFICULTY:** Moderate

**SCENERY:** Mature forest, Dead Run and Gwynns Falls, historical structures

**EXPOSURE:** Mostly shade

**TRAFFIC:** Light on Leakin Park trails, moderate on Gwynns Falls Trail, moderate–heavy near parking area and pavilion in park

**TRAIL SURFACE:** Packed dirt, exposed roots, rocks, asphalt

**HIKING TIME:** 2 hours

**DRIVING DISTANCE:** 7 miles

**ELEVATION GAIN:** 160' at trailhead, 365' at high point

**ACCESS:** Sunrise–sunset. No fees or permits required. MTA runs buses along Windsor Mill that bring you close to several trailheads. For a complete schedule, call 866-RIDE-MTA or visit mta.maryland.gov.

**WHEELCHAIR ACCESS:** Gwynns Falls Trail portion

**MAPS:** USGS *Baltimore West;* Leakin Park trail maps are available at the Winans Meadow parking area.

**FACILITIES:** Restrooms, water at Winans Meadow parking area

**CONTACT:** 410-396-0808, carriemurraynaturecenter.org and bcrp.baltimorecity.gov/parks/gwynns-falls

**LOCATION:** 4500 N. Franklintown Rd., Baltimore

**COMMENTS:** For information on Leakin Park happenings, visit friendsofgwynnsfallsleakinpark.org.

it is swift and full of rocks. At 0.35 mile cross over a pretty steel bridge and come upon Wetheredsville Road, which is closed to traffic. Grass and weeds have begun their job of reclaiming the road. Just after crossing, look left for a staircase heading uphill into the woods marked STREAM TRAIL. Take the stairs, heading west, and then turn right onto the Stream Trail. At the next two trail junctions, head right to take Old Spring Trail and bypass Stream Trail and Ridge Trail, which more closely parallel Dead Run.

When you come out of the woods at the intersection of two paved roads, head left toward the sign for the Carrie Murray Nature Center—you're now on Hutton Avenue, which is also closed to traffic. Walking up Hutton Avenue, you'll be mostly in the shade and see lots of rocks and moss on either side of the cracked asphalt.

At just over a mile into the hike, you'll see a sign for the Wetland Trail and Nature Center on your left. Head into the woods and over a wooden footbridge on the Wetland Trail, walking along the boardwalk through a stand of smaller, newer trees—mostly oaks and beeches. You'll be thankful you're on a raised boardwalk as you cross over small streams, marshy aquatic plants, mud, and poison ivy.

Soon the boardwalk ends and the now white-blazed trail becomes dirt and moss. Here comes one of those moments that, if you were dropped here from a plane, you would never guess you were in the middle of an industrialized city. All you can see are sky and trees; portions of the movie *The Blair Witch Project* were shot here, and the thick forest makes it easy to see why.

The trail then leads uphill and becomes a loose collection of exposed roots and rocks. You begin to zigzag up and down—mostly up—until you come to a clearing and the Carrie Murray Nature Center at 1.3 miles. The nature center was named for the mother of Orioles Hall of Famer Eddie Murray. If it's open, it's worth going

# Leakin Park

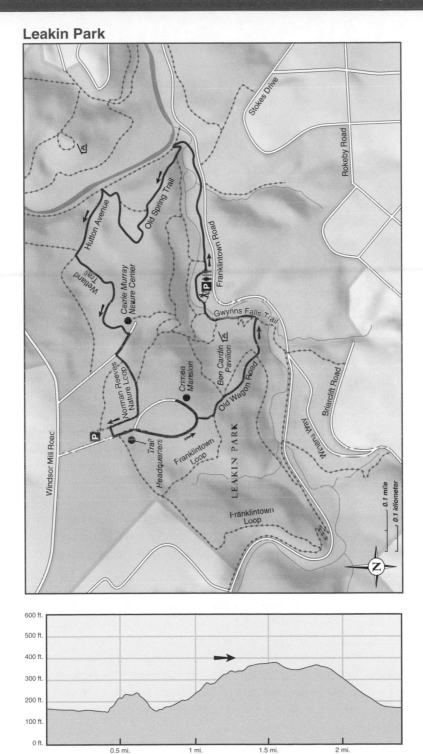

inside. Most interesting is the rehabilitation center for injured birds of prey; the center also provides a nice display of reptiles and has a restroom and water fountain.

Moving away from the nature center, turn right at the paved trail and go up and over the hill. You'll see a small parking area to the right and a dirt footpath across from it on the left labeled NORMAN REEVES LOOP TO MANSION. Follow the path, which is very dense and well shaded, mostly by tall oaks, and again you'll feel as if you can't possibly be anywhere near Baltimore.

At just under 1.7 miles, you'll come to an intersection with a sign pointing left to Heide's Trail (formerly the Ridge Trail), but head right going northwest. If you're fortunate, you'll pass some art installations along this portion of the trail. To the left you'll see pavilions, picnic benches, a parking area, a playground, a volleyball net, and tennis courts. You'll also see Winans Chapel to the left; colorful wildflowers surround it in spring and summer.

When the trail emerges from the woods onto paved Eagle Drive, turn left, heading away from the tennis courts, and pass Winans Chapel on your left. The chapel was built in 1859 at the request of Thomas Winans's wife, a devout Catholic. Unfortunately, she died soon after it was completed and the chapel was never consecrated for use.

When the road splits, veer right and walk toward the old stone building with the red roof, once the honeymoon cottage of the Crimea Mansion and now the Outward Bound headquarters. Continue looping around and take note of the parking area on your right—there's a path at the far end that you'll take on your return. For now, though, continue just a little farther on the paved path to take a look at the Orianda House—also known as the Crimea Mansion—ahead on your right. Crimea was built in the mid-1800s by Thomas Winans. He called the estate Crimea after the Russian peninsula of the same name. The Winans, who were known Southern sympathizers, tried to discourage Union troops from entering their estate by constructing a faux fort with fake cannons. It didn't work; the troops of General Benjamin Butler cut up the orchard for firewood, arrested Winans's father, Ross, and locked him away in Fort McHenry.

When you're ready, backtrack to the parking area and find the trailhead for Old Wagon Road at just under 2 miles. Head left on the trail. At 2.4 miles the trail splits, with the Franklintown Loop to your right and Old Wagon Road straight ahead. Follow Old Wagon Road as it heads downhill on this rocky portion of trail. You'll quickly come upon another trail junction; turn right to stay on Old Wagon Road.

At just over 2.5 miles, you'll arrive at a big clearing. To your left you'll see a road and some bike paths. The trail continues straight across the gas line cut and veers left. Soon you'll be walking on the edge of the clearing, along the treeline downhill. At the bottom, you'll reach an asphalt path—the Gwynns Falls Trail. Straight ahead, you'll see a sign for the continuation of Old Wagon Road trail. Continue straight, following the path as it leads you through the woods to a large iron waterwheel that once pumped water to the estate.

Continuing on, you'll meet back up with the paved Gwynns Falls Trail. Head right on the Gwynns Falls Tail and pass the Ben Cardin picnic grove on your left, named after the Baltimore congressman and now Maryland senator. Turn right again and you'll see the Winans Meadow parking area to your right, over a cement bridge.

## NEARBY/RELATED ACTIVITIES

On the second Sunday of each month from April to November, the **Chesapeake and Allegheny Steam Preservation Society** runs trains for passenger pleasure rides from 11 a.m. to 3 p.m. For information, call 410-448-0730 or visit calslivesteam.org.

• • • • • • • • • • • • • • • • • • • • • • • •

**GPS TRAILHEAD COORDINATES** N39° 18.280'   W76° 41.622'

**DIRECTIONS** Take I-95 S 3 miles and merge onto I-695. Take I-695 for 5 miles to Exit 16 (I-70 E) toward Local Traffic. Loop around the park, continuing as if to I-70 W, and take Exit 94 for Cooks Lane/South-City. Merge onto Security Boulevard and continue onto Cooks Lane. Turn left onto Briarclift Road and then veer left onto Winans Way to enter the park. Turn right at Franklintown Road, and you'll see the Winans Meadow parking lot on your left. Facing away from Franklintown Road and the restrooms, you'll see the paved Gwynns Falls Trail straight in front of you.

The Patterson Park marble fountain was erected in 1865 and designed by George A. Frederick, who also designed the Rawlings Conservatory you see in Druid Hill Park (see page 41). *Photo by Lauren Brown*

**ENJOY A RENEWED** urban oasis, 137 acres in Baltimore's oldest public park.

## DESCRIPTION

Often referred to as "Baltimore's Backyard," Patterson Park has hosted residents since 1669. It started as a small 6-acre park in 1827 and was formally recognized as a public space in 1853 when it was expanded to 35 acres. Previously, it served an important defense function. During the War of 1812, as the British were burning the nation's capital, entering North Point, and bombarding Fort McHenry, they were stopped at Patterson Park's Hampstead Hill, where the sight of 100 cannons and 20,000 troops made them head back toward the harbor and their waiting ships. After the park's formation, it became a fortification yet again, during the Civil War.

The park ran into some hard times again during the 1980s and early 1990s when it became synonymous with drug activity. Neighborhood revitalizations and booms in the housing markets of nearby Highlandtown and Canton, however, renewed interest in the park as a place of recreation, and a true urban oasis has been created. The Friends of Patterson Park organization gets the primary credit for the park's renaissance.

Begin your urban hike by passing the Friends of Patterson Park white brick headquarters on your left as you head into the park from the trailhead. *Note:* The

**DISTANCE & CONFIGURATION:** 2-mile loop

**DIFFICULTY:** Easy

**SCENERY:** East Baltimore, historic structures, duck pond

**EXPOSURE:** Sunny

**TRAFFIC:** Moderate–heavy

**TRAIL SURFACE:** Asphalt

**HIKING TIME:** 45 minutes–1 hour

**DRIVING DISTANCE:** 3 miles

**ELEVATION GAIN:** 108' at trailhead, with no significant rise

**ACCESS:** Sunrise–sunset. No fees or permits required. MTA buses run on streets bordering the park on all four sides; for a complete schedule, call 866-RIDE-MTA or visit mta.maryland.gov.

**WHEELCHAIR ACCESS:** Yes, paved trail

**MAPS:** USGS *Baltimore East;* online park map at pattersonpark.com/learnmore

**FACILITIES:** Dog park, ball fields, tennis and basketball courts, playgrounds, swimming pool, skate center

**CONTACT:** 410-276-3676, pattersonpark.com and bcrp.baltimorecity.gov/parks/patterson-park

**LOCATION:** 28 S. Patterson Park Ave., Baltimore

**COMMENTS:** The Pagoda is open Sundays mid-April–mid-October, noon–6 p.m., with free music throughout the week during the summer.

park is a popular spot for the new-to-Baltimore rentable electric scooters; they should yield to you, but keep an eye out for new drivers while you're on the path.

You'll see a fountain straight ahead; turn left where the giant shade trees tower over the benches. Baltimore's ubiquitous row houses ring the park, and you will have views of East Baltimore from several points in the park, especially the higher ground near the trailhead. Open, well-maintained fields border the first part of the trail. At 0.25 mile turn left when you see the Virginia S. Baker Recreation Center, and then take a quick right onto the narrow paved path, which runs alongside mature maple and white oak trees. (For activities at the rec center, call 410-396-9156.)

At just under 0.4 mile, take a left and another quick left 50 feet later, heading down a sycamore-studded hill. You'll see ball fields to the right farther down the hill. Take the next right onto a narrower path, which descends slowly until it becomes level with the fields. You'll see a bench here, surrounded by more shade trees, and at 0.5 mile you'll come to tennis courts on the left. Stay on the inner path. When you see the red Tudor-style building straight ahead, turn left; you'll pass by playgrounds, swing sets, and an Olympic-size pool (it's a bargain to swim here—just $30 to join for the whole summer and only $2 for a day pass; call 410-396-3838 for info).

Next you'll arrive at the Dominic "Mimi" DiPietro Family Skating Center (a blue building)—for info on skating admissions and lessons, call 410-396-9392. Take a left here. When you reach the grass buffer near the street, across from the tennis courts, turn right; you'll pass the Utz Twardowicz Field on the right and a dog park on your left.

At 0.8 mile you'll come to a ring of iron bars protecting an impressive concrete monument to the "Father of the American Cavalry," General Casimir Pulaski, fronted by an enormous American flag and flanked by tall evergreens; turn right here. At 0.9 mile you'll reach another water fountain. On the next pretty, serene stretch you'll walk uphill past lots of mature trees. At 1 mile head up three concrete

## Patterson Park

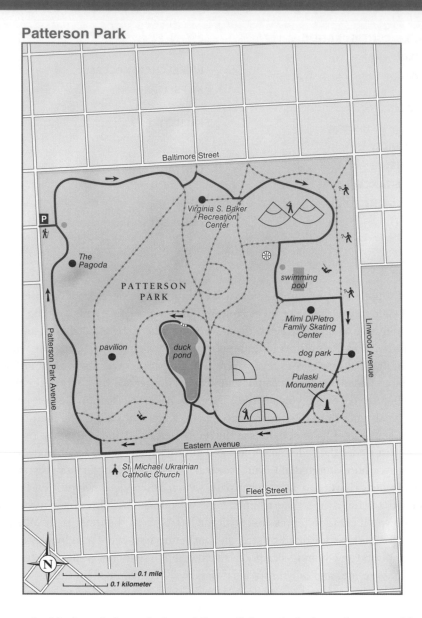

steps to the black asphalt marked as a bike trail that winds through trees and heads toward the interior of the park.

You'll soon reach the Patterson Park Boat Lake, a catch-and-release duck pond; it requires a fishing license for those over age 16. Take a right to circle the pond. While many ducks and geese congregate here, more than 50 bird species, and another 100 varieties, have been spotted in Patterson Park, mostly members of the thrush, warbler, and sparrow families, but also some birds rarely spotted in the area, such as the gadwall, blue-winged teal, and merlin. Visit the park's website and baltimorebirdclub .org for more information on birding at Patterson Park.

Cross over the pond on the boardwalk, winding through a large concentration of cattails and lily pads. The boardwalk, which is just under a tenth of a mile long, ends at the stone wall that encircles the pond. At 1.3 miles, when you've made a full circuit of the pond, turn right and then head straight toward the white asphalt and row houses. At 1.4 miles turn right and you'll soon be standing in front of the gold-tipped onion domes of St. Michael the Archangel Ukrainian Catholic Church. Follow the path to the right as it heads uphill and take a left when you reach the wider path. You will see playgrounds and a pavilion to the right.

At 1.7 miles you'll pass a monument to German composer Conrad Kreutzer on the left and see the octagonal, four-story Chinese Pagoda up the hill on the right. Charles Latrobe designed the structure, which was originally known as the Observation Tower, in 1890. This striking hybrid of Oriental and Victorian design, graced by beautiful stained glass, sits on Hampstead Hill and provides scenic views of downtown and the harbor. These views help explain the line of cannons, marked 1814, in front of the Pagoda. These cannons delineate the chain of fortifications that once ran from the harbor all the way to Johns Hopkins Hospital and helped drive back the British. After walking around the Pagoda, head left and you will see the concrete pillars where you began your hike straight ahead. Note the lovely fountain to the right.

## NEARBY/RELATED ACTIVITIES

The **Inner Harbor,** with its multitude of things to see and do, is just a half mile to the west via Eastern Avenue or Lombard Street. Take Eastern Avenue to Albemarle Street to taste the great food available in **Little Italy** and **Greektown,** which is just east of Patterson Park and Highlandtown. Just south is **Fells Point,** which is on the National Register of Historic Places and was first incorporated in 1773; you'll find plenty of shopping, food, history, and people-watching in this fascinating neighborhood.

· · · · · · · · · · · · · · · · · · · · · · · ·

**GPS TRAILHEAD COORDINATES** N39° 17.445'  W76° 35.070'

**DIRECTIONS** Take I-395 N 1.2 miles to W. Conway Street and turn right. In 0.2 mile turn left onto Light Street, and then, in another 0.2 mile, turn right onto E. Pratt Street. Take Pratt Street for 1.7 miles until it ends at Patterson Park. The trail starts between the two concrete pillars where Lombard Street ends at Patterson Park Avenue.

The footpath runs under University Parkway and crosses Stony Run on a footbridge.

**BEGIN NEAR THE** campus of America's oldest research institution. Then escape the city without leaving it as you hike through a wooded riparian buffer in historic Roland Park.

## DESCRIPTION

The hike begins just to the west of Johns Hopkins University. Park along the street and you'll see a sign with a trail map and history of the trail. Take the asphalt trail downhill to meet up with Stony Run Trail, which runs along the stream of the same name. It begins to the south on Wyman Park Drive and continues up to the Gilman School. The trail follows the old Maryland & Pennsylvania (Ma & Pa) Railroad Line for 3 miles, connecting surrounding neighborhoods with many points of interest, including the Jones Falls Trail (see page 41 for a nearby hike). Friends of Stony Run has been instrumental in creating a continuous walking path and continues to help maintain the trail with stream cleanups, tree plantings, and other activities.

When you reach Stony Run Trail at 0.1 mile, turn left to walk under Remington Avenue. You'll be walking upstream with Stony Run on your right. In 0.25 mile you'll come to a grove of bamboo on your right, and just after, you'll see a trail leading uphill to your left. Continue straight. At just under 0.5 mile, you'll see a retaining wall on your left—constructed as part of a recent Baltimore City stream restoration

**DISTANCE & CONFIGURATION:** 5.2-mile out-and-back

**DIFFICULTY:** Easy–moderate

**SCENERY:** Mature hardwoods, Stony Run, Johns Hopkins University

**EXPOSURE:** A bit more shade than sun

**TRAFFIC:** Moderate

**TRAIL SURFACE:** Dirt, asphalt, cement

**HIKING TIME:** 2.5 hours

**DRIVING DISTANCE:** 5 miles

**ELEVATION GAIN:** 183' at trailhead, about 350' at high point

**ACCESS:** Sunrise–sunset; no fees or permits required. The MTA bus runs several stops along the southern portion of the route; for a complete schedule, call 866-RIDE-MTA or visit mta.maryland.gov.

**WHEELCHAIR ACCESS:** No

**MAPS:** USGS *Baltimore West* and *Baltimore East*

**FACILITIES:** Playground, ball field

**CONTACT:** 410-396-3100, bcrp.baltimorecity.gov /parks and stonyrun.org

**LOCATION:** Remington Ave. and W. 33 St., Baltimore

**COMMENTS:** Portions of the trail in Wyman Park can be muddy. Efforts to improve trail conditions are underway, but wear sturdy shoes, especially if it has been raining.

project. At just over 0.5 mile, you'll reach a water retention area, where the trail becomes gravel and slightly elevated. Cross over the stream to continue on the trail.

On your right, you'll be passing the Johns Hopkins campus. At just under 0.7 mile, a trail on the right offers access to the campus, and you'll see a field on your left. Continue straight, following Stony Run upstream, and you'll reach University Parkway in another 0.1 mile. The trail continues under it and leads to a footbridge (constructed in 2017 as part of Friends of Stony Run's efforts to create a continuous walking path), which enables you to cross over Stony Run and reach Linkwood Road at 0.9 mile.

You may be disappointed when you see that Stony Run is a small trickle contained within cement in this section of the trail, but don't despair—it gets better soon. Turn left on Linkwood Road and follow it until you see a footbridge crossing a stream to your left, where your trail continues.

You've now entered Roland Park, one of Baltimore's most distinctive neighborhoods. It's an eclectic mix of Queen Anne, English Tudor, Georgian, and Shingle architecture. Developed in the 1890s by City Beautiful designer George E. Kessler and Frederick Law Olmsted, the neighborhood continues today as an oft-studied example for urban planners on how to create a community that naturally conforms to its geological contours. Part of Roland Park's charm is its vast amount of greenery, with gardens, centuries-old trees, and, of course, Stony Run, which travels through its heart.

The trail soon appears on your left, with a nice buffer of woods—oak and tulip poplar mostly—shading both sides of the water. Cross Stony Run on the footbridge and follow the trail as it winds out of the woods and through a thick stand of bamboo. Crows, sparrows, jays, vireos, blackbirds, and an oriole or two flitter overhead. Rabbits, squirrels, and chipmunks scurry over the trail, and abundant ducks, frogs, and snakes live at the water's edge. Be on the lookout for blue herons on the water.

# Stony Run Trail

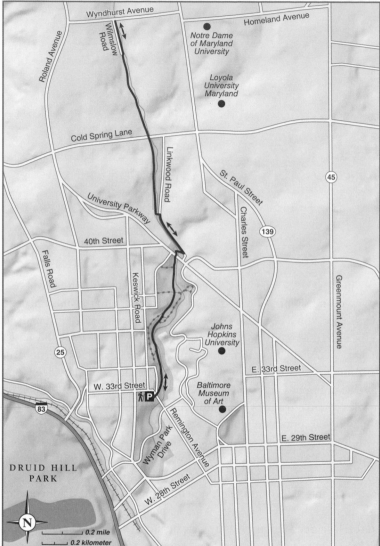

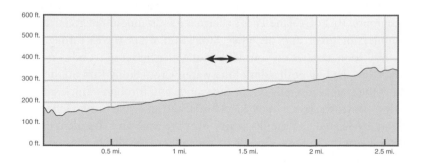

To the left you'll see a series of private houses and community gardens, all immaculately maintained. Cross Overhill Road and pick up the trail on the other side, where it winds along the edge of the treeline, blocking the houses from view. At 1.5 miles a popular playground sits to the right. Linkwood Road to the east is sufficiently far away, across a green field, and thick trees shield Wickford Road, to the west, entirely from view, making this a pleasant spot for kids to play and families to picnic.

Pass the playground and soon come to a chain-link fence and Cold Spring Lane beyond it. Walk west on Cold Spring Lane to cross at the pedestrian crossing at 1.8 miles and continue north on the path, passing a stationary trail map kiosk. Pick up the trail in the woods at the far end of the little parking area. Oak, maple, hickory, poplar, sassafras, ash, and a few walnut trees shade the trail here. You'll also see a thriving understory of berry bushes, morning glories and trumpet vines, honeysuckle, and staghorn sumac, among other vegetation. Stony Run flows to the right. Birds, rabbits, and squirrels shuttle between the woods and the water's edge.

You'll parallel Wilmslow Road on a narrow, unpaved path until you come to Wyndhurst Avenue at 2.6 miles. Here, the trail continues briefly up to Friends School (the oldest continuously operating school in Baltimore, founded in 1784) and then concludes at the Gilman School. However, this is where you begin your return. Turn around and retrace your steps back to your car. If you'd like a slightly different return trip, rather than walking back under University Parkway on the pedestrian path, continue straight and cross Northern Parkway into Johns Hopkins campus. You can walk through the campus, eventually make a right onto Wyman Park Drive, and then, in 0.1 mile, turn right onto Remington. The trailhead, and your car, will be on the left in 500 feet.

## NEARBY/RELATED ACTIVITIES

Take a couple of hours to enjoy the beautiful (and free) **Baltimore Museum of Art.** If you're hungry, check out **R. House,** a popular food hall in Remington. If you're thirsty, you have your choice of several Baltimore breweries: **Peabody Heights, Waverly,** and **Union Craft** are all nearby.

• • • • • • • • • • • • • • • • • • • • • • • • •

**GPS TRAILHEAD COORDINATES** N39° 19.613'   W76° 37.561'

**DIRECTIONS** Take I-395 N 1.2 miles to W. Conway Street and turn right. In 0.2 mile turn left onto Light Street, and then, in another 0.2 mile, turn right onto E. Pratt Street. Take Pratt Street 0.4 mile, and then make a left onto S. President Street, which turns into I-83 N. Take I-83 N 2 miles to Exit 6-7A-7B for 28th Street; in 0.7 mile turn right onto W. 28th Street. In 0.6 mile turn left onto Remington Avenue and follow it 0.5 mile until you see the intersection with Gilman Terrace and W. 33rd Street. Park along the street. The trailhead is marked by a sign.

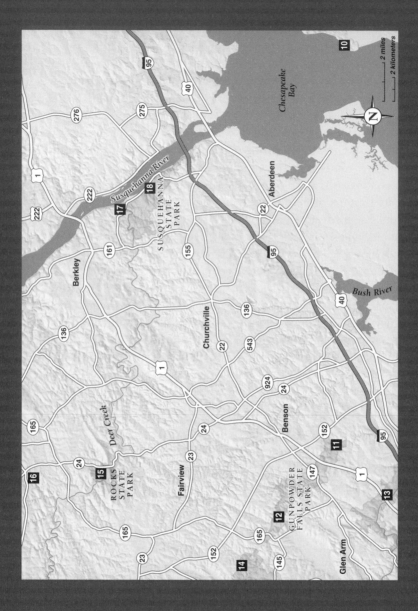

# NORTHEASTERN SUBURBS

From the base of Turkey Point Lighthouse, the Chesapeake Bay stretches out before you.

**DO IT ALL** at Elk Neck State Park in one long day of hiking. If it's summer, leave time for swimming as well.

## DESCRIPTION

Head straight away from the parking area on the wide, packed Turkey Point Lighthouse Trail. Great views of the Chesapeake Bay are yours by just peering to the right. Eventually, thick woods crowd out the views. At the junction at 0.6 mile, go left, where there's a raptor-viewing area. Depending on the season, you'll see vultures, eagles, ospreys, buteos, hawks, harriers, kites, kestrels, merlins, and falcons.

At 0.8 mile you'll reach the Turkey Point Lighthouse. The highest of the bay's 74 lighthouses, it was built in 1833 and is open to climbers on weekends May–October, 10 a.m.–2 p.m. Sheer cliffs fall away from the lighthouse ahead, dropping into the bay. Though many signs warn of danger, you can go right to the edge. (For more information on the lighthouse, visit tpls.org.) With the lighthouse behind you, head right and back into the woods onto a narrow trail that eventually comes to water level. Walk along the water for a few hundred feet and then turn back into the woods at a little beach, following the trail back to the parking area.

Drive or bike north on Turkey Point Road and turn right on Rogues Harbor Road after about a mile (look for signs to the boat launch). Follow it to the parking

**DISTANCE & CONFIGURATION:** 12 miles total, 4 loops

**DIFFICULTY:** Easy–moderate

**SCENERY:** Beach, Elk River, Chesapeake Bay, forests, marshes

**EXPOSURE:** Varies

**TRAFFIC:** Light–moderate

**TRAIL SURFACE:** Packed dirt; some sand and gravel on Wapiti Pond Trail and Beaver Marsh Loop

**HIKING TIME:** 1 hour each for Mauldin Mountain Loop and Turkey Point Lighthouse Trail; 1.5 hours each for the Beaver Marsh Loop and Wapiti Pond Trail

**DRIVING DISTANCE:** 59 miles

**ELEVATION GAIN:** 150' at trailhead; 250' at high point on Mauldin Mountain Loop; no significant rise on others

**ACCESS:** 9 a.m.–sunset; $3/car on weekdays and $3/person on weekends in-season

**WHEELCHAIR ACCESS:** No

**MAPS:** USGS *Earleville* and *Spesutie;* a detailed trail map is available at the Elk Neck State Park headquarters, the camp store, and online at dnr.maryland.gov/publiclands/Documents/ENSP_map.pdf.

**FACILITIES:** Picnic pavilions, campsites, playgrounds, boat launch

**CONTACT:** 410-287-5333, dnr.maryland.gov/publiclands/Pages/central/elkneck.aspx

**LOCATION:**
End of Turkey Point Rd., North East

**COMMENTS:** None of the trails intersect; bringing a bike makes going from one to another easy and pleasurable.

lot on the left. Go all the way to its farthest end and you'll see the trailhead for the Beaver Marsh Loop. At the first junction soon after starting, go left. When you reach the edge of a marsh, look for herons. The Beaver Marsh Loop is an extraordinarily beautiful trail—wooded with poplar, hickory, and oak trees and full of wildlife such as deer, squirrels, and owls. It feels quite isolated until it runs near a campground—because of thick woods, you'll rarely see the campground, but it can be noisy during summer. When you reach the beach at 2 miles, turn right and walk along the beach toward the rock jumble in the distance. Be careful—during high tide this may involve walking in several inches of water! Climb along the rocks and reenter the woods just before the junction where you turned left coming in. Now go straight ahead to the parking area.

Drive or hop on your bike and ride back out to Turkey Point Road and turn right. Take the next right, following signs to the camp store. When you get to the camp store, walk behind it to pick up the Wapiti Pond Trail. Take a left. Don't worry about the lack of blazes—you're actually on a secondary path that connects to the green-blazed Wapiti Pond Trail. When you reach a junction, turn right; otherwise, you'll end up on a park road. You'll soon reach the wide Wapiti Pond Trail; head right on it. After 0.4 mile, once you're on the trail, you'll come to a beaver pond stocked with bass and sunfish. A Maryland non-tidal freshwater fishing license is required to fish here. Look for mallards, black ducks, and teal at the pond.

Veer left at the Y junction at the end of the pond. Follow it to the camp loop and go left until the end of the loop. There's a little path heading to a beach from there. This beach abuts the Elk River, just north of Thackery Point. Backtrack and when you reach the pond again, go left. The trail becomes very tight and close. When you

## Elk Neck State Park

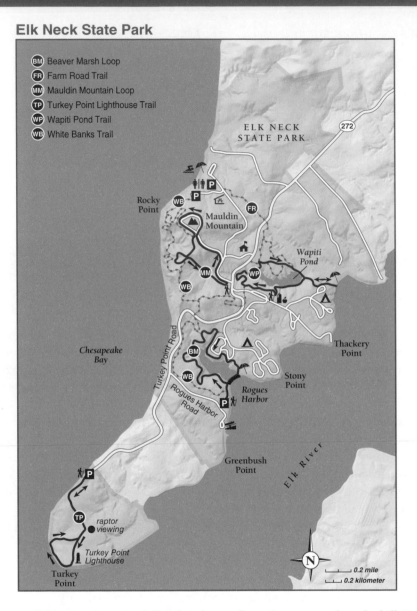

BM Beaver Marsh Loop
FR Farm Road Trail
MM Mauldin Mountain Loop
TP Turkey Point Lighthouse Trail
WP Wapiti Pond Trail
WB White Banks Trail

ELK NECK STATE PARK

272

Rocky Point

Mauldin Mountain

Wapiti Pond

Chesapeake Bay

Turkey Point Road

Rogues Harbor Road

Thackery Point

Stony Point

Rogues Harbor

Greenbush Point

Elk River

raptor viewing

Turkey Point Lighthouse

Turkey Point

N

0.2 mile
0.2 kilometer

come to a T intersection, turn left to head away from the water and up the hill. You'll quickly come to the back of the camp store.

Head back out to Turkey Point Road and turn right. Almost immediately, take a left. The trailhead for the Mauldin Mountain Loop is just ahead on the left. This trail follows the contours of the N.E. Beach Access Road until it splits toward a picnic area. The trail loops around the picnic area, passing the Mauldin House near the top of Mauldin Mountain (really a hill, to be more precise), which rises almost 300 feet above the surrounding land.

The red-blazed Mauldin Mountain Loop is listed as moderate on the Elk Neck park map because of its ups and downs, but it's nothing too strenuous. However, if this is the last hike of the day after doing all the others above, you'll feel it. Nevertheless, the tall canopy of locust, beech, maple, poplar, hickory, and oak trees won't fail to inspire. With a thriving understory, including wildflowers (and springtime blooms from dogwoods), the trail is truly beautiful. Among the foliage, look for red-breasted nuthatches, cedar waxwings, and pileated woodpeckers. You'll reach your car in 1.5 miles.

## NEARBY/RELATED ACTIVITIES

Besides enjoying a swim at Elk Neck State Park, the town of North East is a pleasant place to spend a few hours. Among the attractions is the **Upper Bay Museum** (upper baymuseum.org), two big buildings on the North East River, housing an extensive collection of hunting, boating, and fishing artifacts. Heading back to I-95, if you continue past the exit, you can follow the signs to **Plumpton Park Zoo** (410-658-6850, plumptonparkzoo.org) in Rising Sun. It is home to a collection of indigenous animals as well as African creatures.

• • • • • • • • • • • • • • • • • • • • • • • •

**GPS TRAILHEAD COORDINATES** N39° 27.577'    W76° 00.367'

**DIRECTIONS** Take I-95 N 47 miles to Exit 100 (MD 272). Take MD 272 south 12 miles through the town of North East until it ends at Elk Neck State Park. This is the trailhead for the Turkey Point Lighthouse Trail.

Turkey Point Lighthouse is open May–October for those who want to climb to the top for fantastic views of Chesapeake Bay.

The Jericho Covered Bridge over Little Gunpowder Falls was built in 1865 and connects Baltimore and Harford Counties.

**LEAVE FROM HISTORIC** Jerusalem Village and follow the floodplain of Little Gunpowder Falls before returning for a trip to the Jericho Covered Bridge.

## DESCRIPTION

You can spend hours in historic Jerusalem Village alone, and the fact that some fantastic hiking opportunities abound is a wonderful bonus. The gristmill, now Gunpowder Falls State Park headquarters, was built in 1772 and continued operations until the last miller died in 1961. Miller's House, located behind the mill, once served as a gun/cooper shop, where employees produced walnut gunstocks for the Maryland militia during the Revolutionary War. Spread out from the mill, all within easy walking distance, stand many buildings, including the tenant house, Lee's Mansion, McCourtney's Store, Springhouse, and the stone blacksmith shop, also built in 1772, where the hike begins. Each historic building tells a fascinating story.

Pick up the trailhead at the edge of the woods behind the blacksmith shop. Initially, the white-blazed Little Gunpowder Trail has a surface of cedar chips and packed dirt as it winds through a stand of oak. Soon after you begin your hike, a trail leads to your left, but continue up to the right until you reach a gravel path. Turn left on the path toward Little Gunpowder Falls, which you'll follow upstream. Look for

**DISTANCE & CONFIGURATION:** 4.9 miles, 2 loops

**DIFFICULTY:** Moderate

**SCENERY:** Little Gunpowder Falls, wetlands, mixed hardwoods, historic sites

**EXPOSURE:** Shady

**TRAFFIC:** Moderate

**TRAIL SURFACE:** Packed dirt

**HIKING TIME:** 2 hours

**DRIVING DISTANCE:** 25 miles

**ELEVATION GAIN:** 150' at trailhead, 375' at high point

**ACCESS:** 7 a.m.–sunset; no fees or permits required

**WHEELCHAIR ACCESS:** The mill visitor center, blacksmith shop, and McCourtney's Store are accessible, but the trails are not.

**MAPS:** USGS *White Marsh;* trail maps at bulletin board at parking area

**FACILITIES:** Restrooms in park headquarters, open Monday–Friday, 8 a.m.–4 p.m.; visitor center open Saturday and Sunday, 1–4 p.m.; portable bathroom at parking area

**CONTACT:** 410-877-3560, jerusalemmill.org

**LOCATION:** 2813 Jerusalem Rd., Kingsville

ruins of the millrace at 0.1 mile. The path is very well maintained, but it feels nicely isolated because it's ridged on both sides.

When the trail splits at just under 0.3 mile, with white blazes to the left and blue blazes to the right, stay on the white-blazed Little Gunpowder Trail but take note of the blue-blazed Jerusalem Mill Trail, as it will be your return route. The river soon comes into view; it's shallow, very rocky, and roughly 150 feet across. You'll see big chunks of granite, interspersed with ferns, sycamore, and sumac on the hill on the right. Even though the river is not far away on the left, the trail often winds away from it, but the many path offshoots make a quick trip to the river possible.

At 0.5 mile cross a wooden bridge over a little creek. Beech, hickory, tulip poplar, and red and white oak trees abound here. As the trail winds uphill, you'll have good views of the river, especially in winter. The trail is very well maintained; huge trees fall on the path but are quickly cut and pulled to the side. You will see some of them on the edge of the trail, covered in lichen and mosses and sprouting white, flaming red, and orange fungal growth.

At 0.75 mile you'll come to a power line cut and continue straight. At just over 0.9 mile, the trail splits, but both paths are blazed white and reconnect shortly thereafter. This happens again at just under a mile; pass the cutoff path leading left toward the water and continue on the white trail as it heads uphill. Once you reach the top at 1.2 miles, you can either head right on the blue trail to return to your car or turn left on the white trail to continue the hike. Take a left, and at 1.7 miles, you'll reach Gunpowder Falls. Make a right, staying on the white-blazed trail.

At 1.85 miles you'll reach Wildcat Branch; the water runs clear and swift toward the Little Gunpowder on your left. If you would like to add an extra 1.5 miles (round-trip) to your hike, you can cross Wildcat Branch using the large rocks. Paths to the right and left lead to eventual dead ends, but you can go left for a scenic trail along Little Gunpowder Falls until it eventually dead-ends at Belair Road.

## Gunpowder Falls State Park: Jerusalem Village Trail with Jericho Covered Bridge Trail

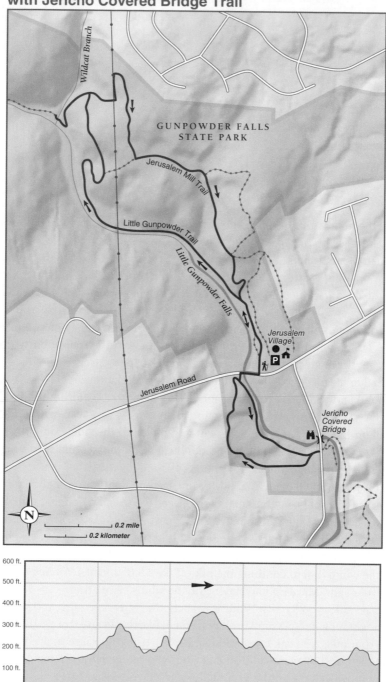

Whether you're returning from your detour or just continuing on, from the original side of Wildcat Branch, look up and find the white-blazed tree. Head up the hill, going northeast, and you'll begin to see double white blazes. At 2 miles (mileage does not include the optional addition) you'll come to a subtle trail junction. Going right will take you back on the original path to the Jerusalem Mill Trail junction, but continue straight uphill, heading southeast, for a nice alternative. In just 0.1 mile you'll reach a power line cut; cross over and continue. When you reach the gravel road, turn left heading north. At just over 2.2 miles, just before one of the large power line poles, head right down the dirt path, and then immediately veer right, and then right again. This unmarked but well-maintained trail parallels the power line cut and brings you through an oak forest. At 2.5 miles you'll reach a trail intersection with the blue-blazed Jerusalem Mill Trail; head left.

Cross a little stream at 2.8 miles and then, when the trail splits, go straight to follow the blue blazes. At 3.15 miles you'll reach another trail junction; turn right to stay on the Jerusalem Mill Trail.

Shortly after, the river comes into view on the right. At 3.35 miles a trail heads left into the meadow, but you should continue straight on the blue-blazed Jerusalem Mill Trail. Almost immediately after, you'll rejoin the white-blazed Little Gunpowder Trail and head left toward the parking area. This time, however, instead of returning to your car, go straight toward the mill and cross Jerusalem Road. Turn right, cross the bridge on Jerusalem Road, and reach the Jericho Covered Bridge Trailhead just to the left on the other side, down the cement steps.

When you reach the trail junction at 3.9 miles, with a white-blazed tree in front of you, turn left, heading southeast. The trail initially follows the river downstream, with thick woods on the hill on the right. When the trail splits again at the bend in the river, the path climbs the hill up to your right, giving you a great view. Go over a wooden footbridge at 4 miles, and the red covered bridge will soon come into view on your left. Soon after, you'll see a post indicating that the covered bridge is to your left, and the yellow-blazed horse trail is to your right. You'll return on this trail, but for now, take a left to check out the covered bridge on Jericho Road. Built in 1865, it's the last remaining covered bridge in either Baltimore or Harford County.

On the way back, take the yellow-blazed horse trail heading southwest. You'll pass through a stand of tall, thin oaks, and at the top of the hill, red cedar takes over the landscape. The route follows the inside edge of the treeline about 10 feet from the field. White-tailed deer love this border area, and you'll see lots of pine, fir, red cedar, and sumac.

At 4.75 miles you'll come to Jerusalem Road and see a sign pointing you to Jerusalem Village. To avoid walking on the road, head right to take the gravel path through the woods back to the trailhead.

## NEARBY/RELATED ACTIVITIES

To visit the nationally recognized **Ladew Topiary Gardens** (410-557-9466, ladewgardens .com) go north from Jerusalem Village to Mountain Road (MD 152) and turn left. Follow MD 152 northwest to the dead end at MD 146 (Jarrettsville Pike) and go left. Ladew Gardens is approximately 1 mile ahead on your left.

• • • • • • • • • • • • • • • • • • • • • • • • • •

**GPS TRAILHEAD COORDINATES** N39° 27.779'  W76° 23.417'

**DIRECTIONS** Take I-95 N 21 miles to Exit 74 for MD 152 and go north toward Fallston. Go 2 miles and turn left onto Jerusalem Road; continue 1 mile to the parking area on the right (overflow parking is just before this lot, on your left). The trail starts at the edge of the woods behind the blacksmith shop and across an open field, to the left of the parking area.

Lee's Merchant Mill was constructed around 1772 and produced white silk flour. It now serves as the visitor center and museum.

# 12 GUNPOWDER FALLS STATE PARK:
## Pleasantville–Bottom Loop

This hike follows Little Gunpowder Falls for much of the way.

**HIKE ALONG LITTLE** Gunpowder Falls, then ascend to the exceedingly beautiful railbed of the defunct Maryland and Pennsylvania Railroad.

## DESCRIPTION

Initially heading downstream, make your way through a rather narrow yellow-blazed trail. This is the Ma & Pa Trail, named after the Maryland (Ma) & Pennsylvania (Pa) Railroad, formed from the merger of the Baltimore and Lehigh Railway with the York Southern. The Ma & Pa was in operation from 1901 to the middle of the 20th century. According to the Maryland & Pennsylvania Railroad Preservation Society, the rail line covering the distance between Baltimore and York, Pennsylvania (45 highway miles apart), was 77 miles, reflecting the meandering nature of the line. But here it's flat and straight—and simply beautiful.

You'll immediately pass a trail on your left heading uphill, but continue straight. Several paths to your right lead to the water, if you'd like to take a closer look. After a few hundred feet, take a left uphill, continuing on the yellow-blazed trail.

Uphill now, you'll cross a beautiful little horseshoe stream on a wooden bridge at just over 0.5 mile. Many white-tailed deer congregate here. Though you're now well above the water, you'll quickly descend to water level. When the trail splits at just under 1 mile, head left, following the yellow blazes uphill.

**DISTANCE & CONFIGURATION:** 4.7-mile loop

**DIFFICULTY:** Strenuous in summer, moderate otherwise

**SCENERY:** Riverine and upland forest

**EXPOSURE:** Shady

**TRAFFIC:** Light

**TRAIL SURFACE:** Packed dirt, rocks

**HIKING TIME:** 2.5 hours

**DRIVING DISTANCE:** 24 miles

**ELEVATION GAIN:** 295' at trailhead, 380' at high point

**ACCESS:** Sunrise–sunset; no fees or permits required

**WHEELCHAIR ACCESS:** No

**MAPS:** USGS *Jarrettsville*

**FACILITIES:** None

**CONTACT:** 410-592-2897, dnr.maryland.gov /publiclands/Pages/central/gunpowdercentral .aspx

**LOCATION:** 2998 Pleasantville Rd., Fallston

**COMMENTS:** You can start this hike on Bottom Rd. (parking is limited on Pleasantville Rd.). To get there, take I-95 N 11 miles to I-695 W. Take I-695 W 3 miles Exit 31 (Harford Rd. NW). Go 8 miles, turn left on Fork Rd., then go 1.6 miles and turn right on Bottom Rd. Go 2 miles to the parking spots near the river. In summer, wear long pants. There's poison ivy galore, plus sticker bushes, devil's tear thumb, and nettles.

At 1.2 miles you'll reach a trail junction and head right on the yellow-blazed trail. At 1.75 miles ignore the trail junction and continue on the yellow-blazed trail. At just under 2 miles, you'll come to yet another junction—this time with three options—and continue straight on the yellow trail. The river flows a couple hundred feet below to the right, across valleys and hills filled with birdsong and shaded by mature forest. The trail sits on a riser with gorges on both sides, interspersed with sudden uprisings of rock.

At just under 2.2 miles, begin heading downhill to a junction: the left path leads to Laurel Brook Road, while the path straight ahead leads into the forest. Head left to Laurel Brook Road, and then turn right on Laurel Brook. Go straight onto Bottom Road. Take care walking along the road, as there's no wide shoulder. Cross the steel bridge over Little Gunpowder Falls. You'll soon see a white-blazed trailhead along the shoulder. However, this trail has become eroded and ends at the river. Instead, continue up the bend in the road, and at 2.7 miles take the next white-blazed trail you see to your right down into the forest. You're now on the Little Gunpowder Trail.

At the junction at 3.2 miles, turn right to continue on the white-blazed Little Gunpowder Trail. At 3.6 miles follow the white blazes to the left. Soon after, cross a small stream and head uphill. Once you reach the top of the hill, the trail splits again; take a right. This seems to be a popular place for deer, as I kept spotting them throughout my trek. At 4 miles you'll parallel the river off in the distance to your right and continue straight, still on the white-blazed Little Gunpowder Trail.

At 4.3 miles the trail cuts right toward the river. Both routes lead to Pleasantville Road, so choose your course. I continued straight, but heading right drops you off a bit closer to your car. Regardless, when you reach Pleasantville Road at 4.4 miles, head right on the road (again, be careful because there isn't much of a shoulder) and cross the steel bridge to reach your car.

## Gunpowder Falls State Park: Pleasantville–Bottom Loop

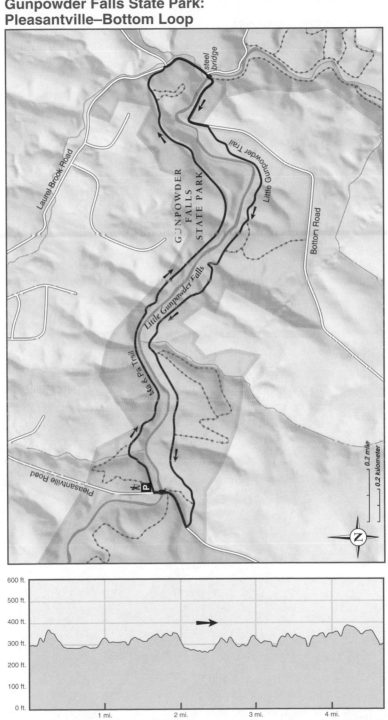

## NEARBY/RELATED ACTIVITIES

**Boordy Vineyards** (410-592-5015, boordy.com), Maryland's oldest family-run winery, is a short distance away and offers daily tours at 2 and 3:30 p.m. Head south on Harford Road and turn right on Long Green Pike. Follow the signs.

• • • • • • • • • • • • • • • • • • • • • • • • • • •

**GPS TRAILHEAD COORDINATES** N39° 30.453'   W76° 27.551'

**DIRECTIONS** Take I-95 N 11 miles to I-695 W. Stay on I-695 W for 3 miles to Exit 31 (Harford Road NW). Go 8 miles and turn left onto Fork Road. Go 2.5 miles and make a hard right onto Pleasantville Road. Go 1 mile and cross the bridge over Little Gunpowder Falls to a small parking area immediately on the right. The trail heads downhill toward the river from the parking area.

In addition to deer, we shared the trail with a box turtle.          *Photo by Steven Sturm*

Big Gunpowder Falls is a freshwater river that begins in Pennsylvania and runs nearly 57 miles before joining Gunpowder River and emptying into the Chesapeake Bay.

**STROLL THROUGH THE** floodplain along Big Gunpowder Falls, taking in an abandoned millpond, sawmill ruins, and swimming holes.

## DESCRIPTION

Doing the west trails first, begin by walking under the US 1 tunnel and entering the Sweathouse Branch Wildlands Area. After 500 feet, turn right onto the pink-blazed Wildlands Trail. It initially runs alongside US 1, so it can be a bit loud, but the trail soon heads away through a beautiful area of mature trees, many easily 50–60 years old, among them some fantastically large beeches. By 0.75 mile the sound of US 1 is gone and you're left only in pristine woods filled with birdsong.

At 0.8 mile the trail gets sandy and crosses a stream soon after; you're likely to scatter a few frogs as you cross. Cross a smaller stream at 1 mile. Here the hill is covered with lichen-stained rocks. At 1.1 miles you'll come to a trail junction just after a pink-blazed tree; head left to see a big pine plantation. While these pines do crowd out other tree species, the plantation is quite beautiful.

At just over 1.3 miles, turn right onto the blue-blazed Stocksdale Trail, skirting the edge of the pine plantation. Soon you'll see lots of ferns. Take notice of the posts telling hikers to keep left, as there is private land to the right. At just over 1.8 miles, you'll cross over another small stream, and the path becomes quite rocky.

**DISTANCE & CONFIGURATION:** 9.25 miles, loop and out-and-back with loops

**DIFFICULTY:** Moderate–strenuous

**SCENERY:** Big Gunpowder Falls and branches, upland forest, ruins

**EXPOSURE:** Mostly shade

**TRAFFIC:** Light–moderate on west side of US 1 (Stocksdale, Sweathouse, Wildlands); moderate on east side (Lost Pond, Sawmill)

**TRAIL SURFACE:** Dirt, rock, sand

**HIKING TIME:** 4 hours

**DRIVING DISTANCE:** 19 miles

**ELEVATION GAIN:** 98' at trailhead, 384' at high point

**ACCESS:** Sunrise–sunset; no fees or permits required

**WHEELCHAIR ACCESS:** No

**MAPS:** USGS *White Marsh;* large stationary map on the bulletin boards in the parking area

**FACILITIES:** None

**CONTACT:** 410-592-2897, dnr.maryland.gov /publiclands/Pages/central/gunpowdercentral .aspx

**LOCATION:** 11205 Belair Rd., Kingsville

**COMMENTS:** Because the parking area sits in the middle of this hike, you can easily do either just the west (of US 1) trails or the east trails. The hike described here does both sides. Bikes are not allowed on the west side Wildland trails.

At the junction at 2.1 miles, turn right onto the yellow-blazed Sweathouse Trail. There's another pine plantation at 2.2 miles. The forest floor here has been affected by the pines crowding out sunlight. But while this spot is not very diverse, it is lovely, especially in spring and summer, with its carpet of green and wildflowers. Walk along the ridge; the hills fall quite a bit to your left.

Start descending into the valley below and you'll soon hear the gurgle of water. Small rock ledges are piled along the trail to guard against erosion. This is just another example of how lovingly (but unobtrusively) maintained these trails are. At 2.5 miles you'll reach the Sweathouse Branch and hike alongside it, traveling downstream.

At 2.85 miles cross the stream using the rocks to stay dry. Once you've crossed, move away from the water and head uphill, continuing to follow the yellow-blazed trail (disregard any offshoot paths). At 3.3 miles keep left, and then cross Sweathouse Branch, a pretty stream full of frogs and fish. The trail widens as you begin paralleling Big Gunpowder Falls. Box elders and sycamores hug the banks. Quite a few paths lead to the water, providing lots of opportunities to search for great blue herons and belted kingfishers, as well as ducks and geese. Plenty of beavers and muskrats live nearby too.

At 3.8 miles you'll see the other end of the Stocksdale Trail to the left. Continue straight. Many limestone boulders decorate the trail to the left. At 4.4 miles the other end of the Wildlands Trail is to the left, followed soon by more beautiful rock formations and a little grotto. Reach the US 1 tunnel at 4.8 miles; the parking area is just on the other side.

To continue hiking and take in the Lost Pond and Sawmill Trails, take the blue-blazed Lost Pond Trail that leads into the woods, keeping the river to your right.

You'll see beech trees with their roots spread over a rock outcrop. At 5.3 miles head left on the yellow-blazed Sawmill Trail. Descend and follow Broad Run to the site of the early-19th-century Carroll Sawmill ruins and millrace.

## Gunpowder Falls State Park:
## Sweathouse Branch Wildlands

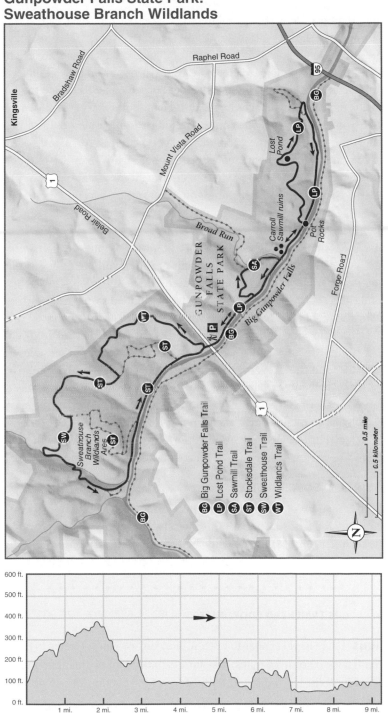

Rejoin the Lost Pond Trail by taking a left after you cross a stream at 6 miles. As you continue along the blue-blazed trail, you'll hear the wonderful sound of rapids on the right from the large rocks in the river. At 6.3 miles you'll see a sign for POT ROCKS or OVERLOOK AND LOST POND. Head left toward the overlook and Lost Pond as the trail leads through an upland forest of mature mixed hardwoods. You'll see the Pot Rocks on your return. Soon you'll reach the beautiful overlook spot, perfect for a picnic.

When you've had your fill, continue along the blue-blazed Lost Pond Trail (bypassing the split at just under 6.5 miles by keeping right). At 7.6 miles you'll reach an unmarked trail junction and see water to your right. Take the trail that heads toward the water and descend to a stream, crossing it in 0.1 mile.

The trail passes the site of the long-gone Long Calm, a fort on the Big Gunpowder used in the late 17th century. The fort was still in use during the Revolutionary War, when Lafayette and his troops camped there.

Continue walking until you reach Lost Pond at 7.8 miles. If you were expecting water, you'll be disappointed. What's left of this abandoned pond is merely the shape and indentation of an oval body of water. Still, it's an interesting sight: a grassy marshland sitting in the middle of the woods surrounded by tall trees.

It gets a bit confusing here. There appears to be a well-maintained trail up the hill to the left of the pond, but that quickly peters out. Instead, head around the pond indent, keeping it to your right; when you come out on the other side, head east away from the pond. You'll eventually come to an overgrown trail on your right at 8.3 miles; take this path down to the Lost Pond Trail and turn right. If you miss this trail, you'll soon reach a small stream that requires you to cross it twice (the second time is quite difficult) to loop around and join the Lost Pond Trail. Take the well-used Lost Pond Trail back to your car. Along your return trip, you'll pass the Pot Rocks, so called because of the deep potholes created in the bedrock from the river erosion.

## NEARBY/RELATED ACTIVITIES

Several other sections of the noncontiguous Gunpowder Falls State Park are nearby. **Rocks State Park** in Harford County is also nearby; to get to the park, continue north on US 1, turn left onto MD 24 N, and the park entrance is about 5 miles north of Forest Hill. You'll find plenty of places to eat in all price ranges in Bel Air, off US 1.

• • • • • • • • • • • • • • • • • • • • • • • •

**GPS TRAILHEAD COORDINATES** N39° 25.652' W76° 26.608'

**DIRECTIONS** Take I-95 N 11 miles to I-695 W. Stay on I-695 for 1.4 miles to Exit 32 (US 1/ Belair Road) and go north 5.5 miles; look for the parking lot on the right after you cross Big Gunpowder Falls. The trails start at the edge of the parking lot behind the first bulletin board closest to the road.

Little Gunpowder Falls, so named because it's much smaller than the neighboring Big Gunpowder Falls, runs just over 25 miles before joining Gunpowder River.

**THIS RELATIVELY SHORT** hike features an amazing amount of variety the scenery changes every mile or so.

## DESCRIPTION

It's almost a crime that this exceedingly beautiful 1,250-acre section of Gunpowder Falls State Park is so lightly used. But what a treat that is for hikers seeking solitude. The bulk of traffic in the Sweet Air section is from equestrians.

From the trailhead, follow the path as it merges into a wide farm road. You'll soon pass an open field to the left. There's a cornfield straight ahead where, at 0.1 mile, you'll come to the first junction. Head left to stay on the yellow-blazed Barley Pond Loop. Follow the treeline around the cornfield, turning right at a YOU ARE HERE sign at 0.3 mile and reaching the edge of the woods at 0.6 mile. There's a sign here pointing left to a red-blazed hikers-only trail and right to the Barley Pond Loop—continue to the right. (The red-blazed trail is a good option if bikers and horses are afoot—it eventually links up to the hike described here.) Several varieties of ferns cover the ground, and mostly oak, maple, and tulip poplar with spicebush and mountain laurel round out the midlevel growth.

At the junction at 0.83 mile, continue straight on the Barley Pond Loop, which soon narrows and zigzags, turning into a foot trail and crossing over a tiny stream with skunk

**DISTANCE & CONFIGURATION:** 5.5-mile loop

**DIFFICULTY:** Easy–moderate

**SCENERY:** Upland forest, Little Gunpowder Falls, Barley Pond, pine plantations

**EXPOSURE:** Mostly shade

**TRAFFIC:** Light

**TRAIL SURFACE:** Packed dirt, mowed grass

**HIKING TIME:** 2 hours

**DRIVING DISTANCE:** 29 miles

**ELEVATION GAIN:** 485' at trailhead, 350' at low point

**ACCESS:** Sunrise–sunset; no fees or permits required

**WHEELCHAIR ACCESS:** No

**MAPS:** USGS *Phoenix* and *Jarrettsville*; stationary trail map at parking area; available online at dnr.maryland.gov/publiclands/Documents /GFSP_SweetairMap.pdf

**FACILITIES:** None

**CONTACT:** 410-592-2897, dnr.maryland.gov /publiclands/Pages/central/gunpowdersweetair .aspx

**LOCATION:** Dalton Bevard Rd., Marshall

cabbage and lilies. (The left trail heads to Little Gunpowder Falls, but you'll be there soon.) The scenery is typical of piedmont northeastern Baltimore/Harford County. At just over 1.1 miles, at the top of the hill, you'll reach Barley Pond. It's a beautiful spot, and the pond has great visibility. Be on the lookout for red foxes, which inhabit the area.

Head left around the pond—look for water snakes, frogs, and small fish, mostly bluegills. At the trail junction immediately after the pond, head left to stay on the Barley Pond Loop. At 1.3 miles you'll come to a post with a blue trail to your right and the white-blazed Little Gunpowder Trail to your left. Go left. You'll come to another junction at just under 1.5 miles, directing horses to the left and a little wooden bench. Continue straight on the gravel path.

Little Gunpowder Trail is twisty and full of green. Little streams wind through-out the landscape amid rolling hills studded with red maples. These riparian streams offer perfect cover for many birds, evidenced by a chorus of song.

You'll reach the river at 1.6 miles. There's a little wooden resting area to your right with a bench. The hike is entirely in Harford County, but the river is the divid-ing line between Harford and Baltimore Counties. Head left along the river. Many long, flat rocks extend into the water where you can vie with the snakes and turtles for a spot to sit and sun yourself.

Cross a footbridge at 1.9 miles and veer right following the white blazes to arrive at an intersection. The trail quickly widens out to a fire road. You'll see the Boundary Trail to the right across the river and Little Gunpowder Trail going straight. Con-tinue on the Little Gunpowder Trail, but pause at the bench below the John Muir quotation. In the river is a fallen sycamore, where water eddies into a pool. The syca-more has sprouted five new trees, testament to nature's regenerative power. Many of the trees in this area are covered in moss, with wildflowers strewn about, including asters, bloodroot, boneset, jack-in-the-pulpit, jewelweed, joe-pye weed, and wood-land sunflower. Across the river sits a striated rock outcrop supporting some oaks.

## Gunpowder Falls State Park: Sweet Air Area

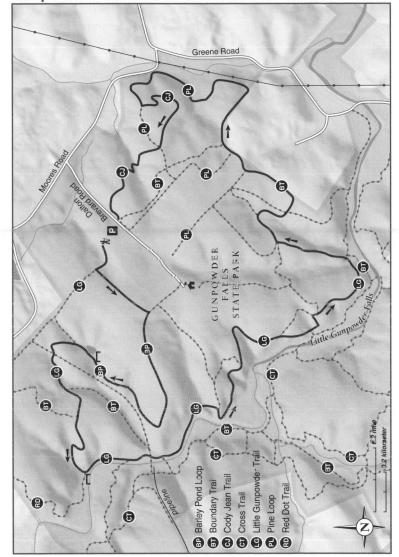

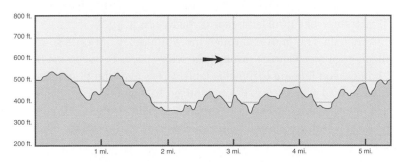

As you continue, you'll pass several orange-blazed paths running vertically along the hills. These are connector paths between the upland and river trails, which you can ignore.

At 2.3 miles you'll come upon a red trail and the yellow connector. Head straight, downhill toward the river. Still following the white-blazed Little Gunpowder Trail, you'll reach a bench with a nice overlook of the river in 0.3 mile, a nice spot to pause and rest. At just over 2.8 miles, come to a "let us probe the silent places" quote and a bench, with a trail leading up to a cornfield. Rather than taking that trail, continue right, following the white and blue blazes.

At 3.5 miles go over a wooden footbridge and come to a four-way intersection. The Gunpowder Trail goes straight, while the blue-blazed Boundary Trail runs left and right. Turn left on the Boundary Trail. Along with the trees already mentioned, you'll find some locust and ironwood as well. At 3.8 miles come to a picnic table and trail junction. Turn right to continue following the blue blazes, hiking northeast. The trail turns to grass, and in 0.1 mile you'll see a junction with grassy trails heading right and left. Go right toward the wooden fence, and the blue blazes will lead you back into the woods on the right. At just over 4 miles, you'll see the white Little Gunpowder Trail to your right, but continue straight on the grassy trail, following the blue-blazed Boundary Trail alongside the fence.

As you walk along the fence and trees, look for the trail heading slightly to the left, with a blue marker on a tree. In early spring or winter, the grass path may be the same height as the field surrounding it and can be hard to spot.

Head right at the cornfield where dogwood and pine line the edge. At 4.35 miles you'll see signs for the Pine Loop (to the left) and the blue Boundary Trail (straight ahead)—go straight. The trail soon splits—the Boundary Trail goes left, while the yellow Pine Loop heads right. Take the yellow Pine Loop, and you'll soon see the reason for the name. At just under 4.6 miles, turn left to continue on the yellow-blazed Pine Loop. Skunk cabbage lines the trail, and you'll find a bench to take a rest.

At 4.8 miles you'll come to a road. On your hard left you'll see a horse trail, and just to the right of it, you'll see a trail with wooden erosion logs. Head northwest up the hiker's trail. In 0.1 mile head right, still following the yellow-blazed Pine Loop going north. Then, in another 0.2 mile, turn left on the green-blazed hikers-only Cody Jean Trail. If you continue straight on the Pine Loop, they'll eventually link up, but you'll miss some beautiful landscape if you bypass it.

The Cody Jean Trail moves through the white pines but does so from the top of the hill, giving a nice vantage through the wide spaces between the trees. At just under 5.5 miles, you'll come to a picnic table. Cross over the Pine Loop to stay on the Cody Jean Trail as it zigzags through mixed hardwoods, crosses a stream, and heads back into the pines, where it becomes especially aromatic. Emerge onto the opposite side of where you turned right earlier to park and you'll see blue and yellow trailheads to the left. Cross Dalton Bevard Road, passing the training area for Chesapeake search dogs to the left, and find your car on the other side.

## NEARBY/RELATED ACTIVITIES

**Ladew Topiary Gardens** (410-557-9466, ladewgardens.com), dubbed the "most outstanding topiary garden in America" by the Garden Club of America, earns its place on the National Register of Historic Places. It's a fascinating and inspiring destination. To reach it from GFSP, reverse the alternate directions below to a right on Jarrettsville Pike and follow the signs to Ladew on the right.

• • • • • • • • • • • • • • • • • • • • • • • •

**GPS TRAILHEAD COORDINATES** N39° 32.167'   W76° 30.294'

**DIRECTIONS** Take I-95 N 21.5 miles to Exit 74 (MD 152 N) and stay on MD 152 for 10 miles. Turn left onto MD 165 S, and in 0.3 mile turn right onto Greene Road. In 1.2 miles turn right onto Moores Road. In 0.5 mile turn left onto Dalton Bevard Road. The gravel parking area is up to the right. At the leftmost point of the parking area is a sign for the Barley Pond Loop. That is the trailhead for the hike described here.

A sentiment of John Muir, an early advocate for preserving America's wilderness, dots the landscape. You'll pass several quotes along the trail.

Visit King and Queen Seat at the beginning of this hike for breathtaking views.

**EXPLORE 885 ACRES** of dense forest and massive boulders rising above Deer Creek, including the main attraction: King and Queen Seat, a 190-foot rock outcrop that was once the ancestral meeting place of the Susquehannock and Mingo Indians.

## DESCRIPTION

In 1951 the State of Maryland began purchasing land surrounding the Deer Creek Valley. Originally envisioned as Deer Creek State Park, the name was later changed to the unceremonious but apt Rocks State Park. An amble through the area quickly bears out that decision.

To begin, head northeast, following the red-blazed gravel trail toward the King and Queen Seat. You'll quickly reach this feature in less than 0.2 mile. A natural 190-foot rock outcrop overlooking Deer Creek Valley, King and Queen Seat provides a stunning vista of the rolling farmlands of northern Harford County sprawling out and Deer Creek running below. Be very careful here—people have fallen off these vertical rock faces.

In spring and summer, you can see an almost unbroken ribbon of green, and the autumn foliage puts on a spectacular show. In winter, when you should use extreme

**DISTANCE & CONFIGURATION:** 3.7-mile loop

**DIFFICULTY:** Moderate

**SCENERY:** Rural northern Harford County, mature upland forest, rock columns

**EXPOSURE:** Shady

**TRAFFIC:** Light on trail, moderate–heavy at King and Queen Seat

**TRAIL SURFACE:** Packed dirt, rock

**HIKING TIME:** 2 hours

**DRIVING DISTANCE:** 40 miles

**ELEVATION GAIN:** 600' at trailhead, 300' at low point

**ACCESS:** March–October, 8 a.m.–sunset; November–February, 10 a.m.–sunset;

$3 per person service charge on weekends and holidays at the picnic areas

**WHEELCHAIR ACCESS:** No

**MAPS:** USGS *Fawn Grove;* trail maps available at park entrance; downloadable map at dnr.maryland.gov/publiclands/Documents /Rocks_Map.pdf

**FACILITIES:** Tables, grills, restrooms, and playground equipment at picnic areas

**CONTACT:** 410-557-7994, dnr.maryland.gov /publiclands/Pages/central/rocks.aspx

**LOCATION:** Rock Ridge Picnic Area, St. Clair Bridge Rd., Jarrettsville

**COMMENTS:** Rock climbing is allowed, but use caution. Regardless of whether you're climbing or merely hiking, wear sturdy boots.

caution if you're hiking in snow and ice, the leafless view stretches even farther than it does in summer. In short, it's an amazing spot.

After you've taken it all in, backtrack just a bit and head right (north) on the white-blazed trail. Continue downhill, and at 0.3 mile you'll see a trail junction for the purple trail, which takes you to Rocks Road. Instead, turn left (northwest), continuing on the white-blazed trail.

You'll appreciate the fairly level, wide, well-maintained packed dirt trail surrounded by ferns and sassafras at the top of the hill. After 100 feet you'll come to another T-intersection, with white blazes in both directions. Take a right, and you'll see a bench immediately on the left. The trail heads downhill and then levels out at 0.5 mile. Walk along the middle of a flat ridge, which falls off about 20 feet on both sides. At 0.7 mile don't take the green-blazed trail straight ahead (it will take you to the Wilson's Picnic Area on Saint Clair Bridge Road); turn left instead. The white blazes return as you gradually head uphill; you'll see lots of nice spongy moss along the trail, and a rock outcrop to the right provides good views of Deer Creek below. (You can tube and swim in the creek, but be aware that there are no lifeguards; you can also fish here if you have a freshwater fishing license and trout stamp.)

Squirrels, chipmunks, wild turkeys, and white-tailed deer accompany you as you continue uphill, winding among the huge slabs of rock along the path. Moss and lichen cover the rocks, and the area is awash in ferns. At just over 1.3 miles, you'll come to the small asphalt road you took up to the Rock Ridge Picnic Area. Cross the road and pick up the white-blazed trail in the woods on the other side. At 1.45 miles look for an oak tree with its trunk growing over a rock; it looks like spilled wax. Just after, you'll arrive at the Collier Pit. A sign indicates that it was once used as the source of charcoal for the furnaces at La Grange Iron Works.

## Rocks State Park

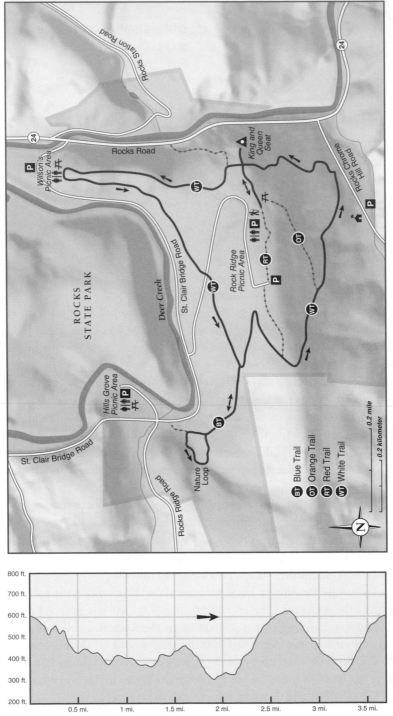

At 1.6 miles the trail splits; head right onto the blue-blazed trail going west, which runs a little lower down the hill and closer to Deer Creek. The red oaks crowding above provide welcome shade on hot days. You'll continue to see a profusion of rocks covered with moss and spilled tree roots. At 1.85 miles you'll reach the Nature Loop. The blue trail goes right and left; turn right (northeast), where ferns carpet the ground.

Along the Nature Loop, you'll come to an open, grassy area where the trail isn't immediately clear. Heading straight will take you to the Hills Grove Picnic Area. Instead, go left. At just over 2 miles, pass over a wooden footbridge and come to a bench on your right, and then another wooden footbridge. Soon after, you'll reach the end of the Nature Loop; turn right onto the blue trail.

When the trail splits at 2.35 miles, with blue pointing in both directions, take a right to return via a higher elevation, and you'll see white blazes right away.

The trail runs as a switchback, ascending quickly over the ubiquitous rock. A well-placed bench on the left at just under 2.6 miles provides a welcome resting place. You'll soon reach an intersection with a rather confusing sign pointing in various directions. Head southwest, following the white blazed trail (diagonally to your right). At just under 3 miles, you'll come to another intersection. Here you can cut left on the orange trail to head back to the Rock Ridge Picnic Area or stay straight to remain on the white trail, which becomes quite level as it winds through mature upland forest. Unless you'd like to cut your hike short, continue straight.

At 3.3 miles you'll see a sign for the white trail heading left (north) toward the King and Queen Seat. Turn left, go up the hill, which is a moderate climb, and when you reach the top, at 3.63 miles, make a left on the red trail to return to your car.

## NEARBY/RELATED ACTIVITIES

Rocks State Park includes two more tracts: the Hidden Valley Natural Area, located 5 miles north at the intersection of Madonna, Telegraph, and Carea Roads; and the Falling Branch Area (see the next hike in this book), home to Maryland's second-highest vertical waterfall, Kilgore Falls.

• • • • • • • • • • • • • • • • • • • • • • • • •

**GPS TRAILHEAD COORDINATES** N39° 38.281'   W76° 24.761'

**DIRECTIONS** Take I-95 N 24 miles to Exit 77B (MD 24) north toward Bel Air. Continue through the towns of Bel Air, Rock Spring, and Forest Hill. Turn left on St. Clair Bridge Road, and then make another left into the park at the Rock Ridge Picnic Area. Follow the road up and park in the first parking lot on your left. The trailhead for King and Queen Seat begins at the paved path on the edge of the parking lot.

The 17-foot-high Kilgore Falls is a popular spot for swimming.

**TAKE A SHORT** hike with a grand payoff: Kilgore Falls, Maryland's second-highest vertical waterfall.

## DESCRIPTION

The relatively small 67-acre Falling Branch Area of Rocks State Park was once a meeting place for Susquehannock Indians. Local hikers and nature enthusiasts didn't know about it for many years because it sat on private property. Fortunately, in 1993, the state, with the help of many local activists (including Harford County public schoolchildren), bought the land and turned it over to Rocks State Park officials for administration. It has become one of the most attractive parcels for many miles around.

Just after the trailhead, you'll see a path leading left, but that goes to private property. Continue to your right and stay on the main trail, winding through a well-exposed section of the route with thick underbrush of mostly goldenrod and spicebush; a stand of pines provides shade. The path soon runs downhill. You'll see lots of poison sumac on mature red oak trees, as well as an abundance of tulip poplars, beeches, sassafras, hollies, and mountain laurels.

You'll reach a wooden boardwalk and footbridge over a little stream at 0.1 mile. The trail turns to packed dirt on the other side, and red cedars abound as the trail

**DISTANCE & CONFIGURATION:** 0.88-mile out-and-back

**DIFFICULTY:** Easy

**SCENERY:** Kilgore Falls, hardwoods

**EXPOSURE:** Shady to the waterfall but mostly sunny on the extension along Falling Branch

**TRAFFIC:** Moderate

**TRAIL SURFACE:** Packed dirt after an initial small section of crushed rock

**HIKING TIME:** 30 minutes

**DRIVING DISTANCE:** 44 miles

**ELEVATION GAIN:** 465' at trailhead, with no significant rise

**ACCESS:** 8 a.m.–sunset; no fees or permits required; also see Comments below

**WHEELCHAIR ACCESS:** No

**MAPS:** USGS *Fawn Grove;* trail maps available at Rocks State Park central office (see Directions)

**FACILITIES:** Portable bathroom at trailhead; restrooms and water at Rocks State Park central office (see Directions)

**CONTACT:** 410-557-7994, dnr.maryland.gov /publiclands/Pages/central/Rocks/Falling-Branch .aspx

**LOCATION:** 1026 Falling Branch Rd., Pylesville

**COMMENTS:** The trailhead parking fills up quickly on nice days, and there is no overflow parking available. Arrive early, but have a backup plan if the lot is full.

rises above a little valley on the left. This area, as well as the woods on the other side of Falling Branch, provides prime habitat for red fox, white-tailed deer, and a multitude of woodland birds, including wild turkey. You'll soon hear the rumble of Kilgore Falls; Falling Branch comes into view on the left, and you'll parallel it upstream.

At 0.25 mile you'll pass a bench. Soon after, the trail splits; head left toward Falling Branch. (On the return, you'll head up this path to walk above the waterfall.) You'll see other trail cuts here and there, but avoid these; with the exception of the trail described here, all of them invariably lead to private property.

Cross over Falling Branch on the stepping-stones and head right toward the falls. Be extra careful crossing in winter; the stones are not set very high out of the water, and ice and snow can make them very slippery. Heavy rains will also cover and/or make the stones slippery. In general, though, the water remains pretty shallow.

At just under 0.4 mile you'll reach Kilgore Falls, which sits in an absolutely gorgeous spot—a rock amphitheater made up of erosion-resistant Prettyboy schist. The falls, at 19 feet tall, is the second-highest natural vertical waterfall in Maryland. Be sure to sit down and take in the view of the falls. While it certainly can't compare to Niagara or Angel Falls, if you're lucky enough to have it to yourself, you'll find the wildness of the area very inspiring. Over the schist, the water spills into a deep pool, where actress Sissy Spacek swam in the movie *Tuck Everlasting.*

Before you head back, you can extend the hike just a bit by taking the trail we passed earlier. Cross back over Falling Branch and make a left at the junction. This trail brings you above the waterfall, and, although the views are obscured, you'll have a nice soundtrack in the background, plus a break from the crowds if it's a warm day. When you're ready, turn around and head back to your car.

## Rocks State Park: Falling Branch Area

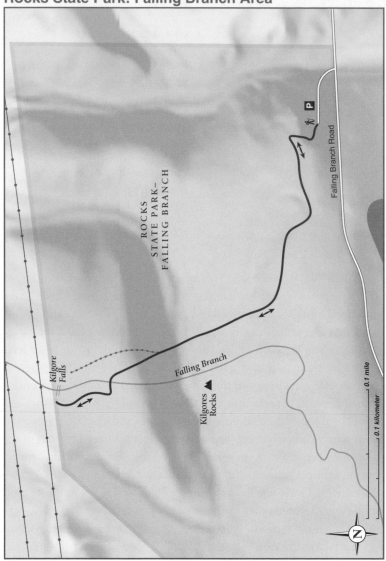

## NEARBY/RELATED ACTIVITIES

In addition to the main section of Rocks State Park (page 82), you may want to visit nearby **Eden Mill Park and Nature Center** (1617 Eden Mill Road, Pylesville; 410-836-3050; edenmill.org). It offers many short hiking trails perfect for small children, picnicking, and canoeing and fishing on Deer Creek. The nature center, which is housed in a restored gristmill, features a hands-on area for children.

• • • • • • • • • • • • • • • • • • • • • • • • • •

**GPS TRAILHEAD COORDINATES**  N39° 41.402'    W76° 25.387'

**DIRECTIONS**  Take I-95 N 24 miles to Exit 77B (MD 24) north toward Bel Air. Continue through the towns of Bel Air, Rock Spring, and Forest Hill. After 13.4 miles on MD 24, you'll see a sign for Rocks State Park. Keep going another half mile; you'll see signs pointing to the park office to the left, but to reach the Falling Branch Area, pass the office sign and proceed another 4.2 miles and turn left onto Saint Mary's Road. Go another 0.4 mile and turn right onto Falling Branch Road; park on the right at the ROCKS FALLING BRANCH AREA sign. Please see Comments above for a note about parking. The trail starts at the left end of the parking lot.

The Susquehanna River is the longest river on the East Coast of the US and one of the oldest existing rivers in the world.

**FOLLOW THE MIGHTY** Susquehanna River upstream to Conowingo Dam—then return via an obscure wooded foot trail, concluding with a woodland loop.

## DESCRIPTION

If any area outdoors enthusiast needs a reminder of why he or she is lucky to live in this area, Susquehanna State Park provides it. First, the Susquehanna River's impressive numbers: 444 miles, a 13-million-acre drainage basin, the second-largest watershed in the eastern United States. The river begins as an overflow of Otsego Lake in New York and runs through three states before draining into the Chesapeake Bay, just south at Havre de Grace, Maryland, pouring 19 million gallons of freshwater into the bay every minute.

John Smith explored the Susquehanna in 1608. Of course, the native Susquehannock Indians had already been hunting and fishing in the area for centuries. Smith's assessment of the area is applicable even today: "Heaven and earth seemed never to have agreed better to frame a place for man's . . . delightful habitation." European establishments on the river date to 1622 as successful trading posts. By 1658, the settlement that would become Havre de Grace had been established.

Begin your hike on the opposite side of Stafford Bridge, taking a right on the Lower Susquehanna Heritage Greenway Trail. Stafford Flint Furnace, just off the

**DISTANCE & CONFIGURATION:** 7.6-mile out-and-back with loop

**DIFFICULTY:** Moderate

**SCENERY:** Susquehanna River, Deer Creek, historical sites, hardwoods

**EXPOSURE:** Shady

**TRAFFIC:** Moderate–heavy on Lower Susquehanna Heritage Greenway Trail, light on alternate Greenway Route and Woodland Trails

**TRAIL SURFACE:** Gravel, packed dirt, some asphalt

**HIKING TIME:** 3 hours

**DRIVING DISTANCE:** 40 miles

**ELEVATION GAIN:** 25' at trailhead, 170' at high point

**ACCESS:** 9 a.m.–sunset; no fees or permits required

**WHEELCHAIR ACCESS:** The Greenway Trail from Conowingo to Stafford Road is accessible.

**MAPS:** USGS *Conowingo Dam* and *Aberdeen;* trail map available at dnr.maryland.gov/publiclands /Documents/SSP_map.pdf

**FACILITIES:** Within the park (not at trailhead) you have access to restrooms, water, campground, Steppingstone Museum, picnic area, boat launch, and phone.

**CONTACT:** 410-557-7994, dnr.maryland.gov /publiclands/Pages/central/susquehanna.aspx

**LOCATION:** Craigs Corner and Stafford Rds., Havre De Grace

trail to the right, wasn't one of the area's original structures, even though it has been around for quite a while. It is, however, all that remains of the once-thriving town of Stafford, established in 1749 and destroyed by an ice gorge in 1904. The wide gravel trail, lined with wild strawberries, parallels Deer Creek. Fishing in freshwater Deer Creek requires a nontidal freshwater fishing license. The creek serves as habitat for the federally endangered Maryland darter and the short-nosed sturgeon. It's also popular for swimming and tubing. Several paths head down to this pretty waterway.

Continuing on, you'll be struck by the wealth of understory flora all about you. There are literally hundreds of species of shrubs, including honeysuckle, invasive multiflora rose, raspberry, staghorn sumac, swamp rose, winterberry, and trumpet vine. Up the hills, trillium abounds, recognizable by its three-petaled flowers and three-leafed bodies. You'll also see Dutchman's-breeches (rare for Maryland), Virginia bluebells, dogtooth violet, windflower, and spring beauty. Rare and endangered plants include sweet-scented Indian plantain and valerian.

Cross a footbridge at just over 0.5 mile, and then another larger one right after. You're going over the site of what was once the Susquehanna Tidewater Canal, built from 1835 to 1839 and linking Havre de Grace with Wrightsville, Pennsylvania. Make note of the little footpath to the right of the bridge, as you'll take it on the return trip. For now, continue left on the wide Heritage Greenway Trail.

At just under a mile, you'll see the first right cut to the banks of the Susquehanna. Head down there; you'll see fishermen standing on one of the many decent-size rocks that dot the river near its banks. Many regard the Susquehanna as the best fishing grounds on the East Coast. It's a striking river, and standing on its banks—alternating as sand, mud, and rocks—is inspiring. As if the river isn't enough, the woods behind you present one of the most biologically diverse ecosystems in North America. In

# Susquehanna State Park: River Trails

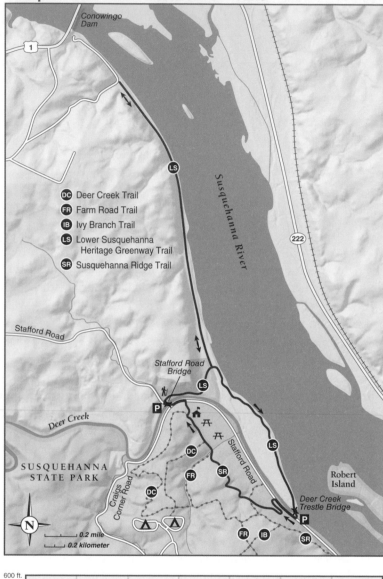

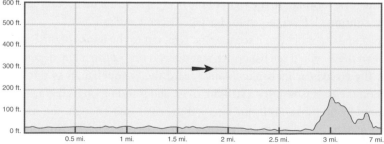

addition to the flora listed above, you'll see yellow poplar, birch, red oak, black oak, white oak, chestnut oak, American beech, black cherry, white ash, black gum, hickory, sycamore, and red maple dominant in the overstory. Among the creatures making homes here are the wood frog, eastern painted turtle, river otter, raccoon, white-tailed deer, white-footed mouse, eastern chipmunk, and red fox.

If birds are more your fancy, the river hosts many of them, mostly kingfishers, gulls, osprey, heron, and bald eagles. (For a much more comprehensive list of the bird types—well over 100—that have been spotted in and around the area of Conowingo Dam, see harfordbirdclub.org/conowingo.html.) In the woods behind, dominant species include the red-headed woodpecker, wild turkey, pileated woodpecker, winter wren, house wren, wood thrush, sapsucker, downy woodpecker, and screech owl.

There's a very long boardwalk at 1.2 miles, which helps to protect especially sensitive wetlands; river floods often reach this area, as it's barely above sea level. The hills to the left rise very steeply and abruptly; these are gneiss columns, many of them 90 degrees. The trail soon runs alongside railroad tracks, part of the defunct Philadelphia Electric Railroad Company, and ends near 3 miles at a gate. The Conowingo Dam is just ahead. The dam, constructed in 1926, is almost 4,500 feet long and 100 feet high. Full capacity flows approach 40 million gallons per minute. If you're lucky enough to catch a release, it's an extraordinary sight.

Turn around and head back, taking advantage of one of the paths to the river if you haven't already headed there. When you get back to the trail junction you passed earlier (this time at 4.6 miles), keep straight and then take the packed dirt foot trail to the left (east). This is a stunning and beautiful trail, crowded with vegetation and close to the banks of the river. As for that close vegetation, be aware of not only poison ivy but also nettles, which can give you what feels like an intense jellyfish or bee sting and can last up to half an hour. If water levels aren't too high, at just over 5.2 miles there's a path down to the Susquehanna to a great little beach.

At 5.8 miles you'll see the train tracks reappear and cross the Deer Creek Trestle Bridge. Once over the bridge, take the stairway on your right down to the parking area and head right toward the water for a nice view of the trestle bridge and Deer Creek entering the Susquehanna. Head back up and turn right to walk along Stafford Road. Take care walking, as there isn't a wide shoulder. At 6.2 miles you'll see a parking area on your left. At the back of the lot, you'll find the blue-blazed Mason Dixon Trail. This trail is marked by little round blue medal tokens attached to trees, with a hiker icon.

Head southeast on this trail, backtracking above the road. At 6.4 miles the Mason Dixon Trail abruptly switchbacks to the right and links to the red-blazed Susquehanna Ridge Trail. This portion of the hike is a bit tough, but worth it as it winds uphill through mixed hardwoods and a chorus of birdsong. Cross over a little stone bridge at 6.75 miles.

Hit a cleared area at just over 7 miles with a trail junction. Continue right on the more well-trod trail. At 7.2 miles the trail intersects with the Farm Road Trail to your left, but continue right (north) on the Susquehanna Ridge Trail. Soon after, cross over the wooden footbridge on your left and come to another trail junction. Turn left, and you'll soon come to a four-way intersection with a sign indicating Deer Creek Trail to both your left and straight, and a parking area to your right. Continue straight (northwest).

At 7.4 miles you'll come to another trail junction and head left. At the final junction, at just over 7.5 miles, you'll see a sign pointing you straight to Deer Creek Trail, but you should turn right to go down to Craigs Corner Road. Emerge from the woods at the Stafford Bridge and make a left to follow Craigs Corner to the parking area.

## NEARBY/RELATED ACTIVITIES

**Steppingstone Farm Museum** (410-939-2299, steppingstonemuseum.org) is located within the park. It demonstrates the rural arts and crafts of the 1880–1920 period. Also nearby is the historic town of **Havre de Grace** (take MD 155 east) with museums, lighthouses, and its famous promenade, extending 2,400 feet along the Chesapeake Bay from the City Marina to the Concord Point Lighthouse.

• • • • • • • • • • • • • • • • • • • • • • • • • •

**GPS TRAILHEAD COORDINATES** N39° 37.386'  W76° 09.875'

**DIRECTIONS** Take I-95 N 36 miles to Exit 89 (MD 155). Go west 2.9 miles and turn right onto MD 161. Go 0.4 mile and turn right onto Rock Run Road. In 1.1 miles make a slight left onto Craigs Corner Road. At 1.4 miles turn left to stay on Craigs Corner Road. When you begin to parallel Deer Creek on your left, look for parking. Park on your left, just before the Stafford Bridge. Walk across Stafford Bridge and take a right to reach the trailhead of the Lower Susquehanna Heritage Greenway Trail.

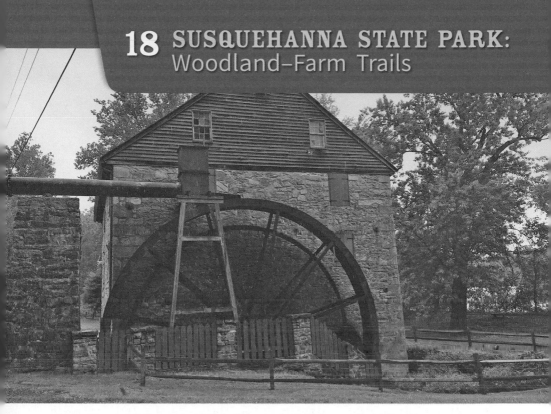

The Rock Run Gristmill ground wheat into flour, much of which was sold to the Caribbean.

**THIS IS THE** wilder side of Susquehanna State Park: there's not much walking along the river, but it's full of old growth and blissful solitude.

## DESCRIPTION

Before you begin the hike, you might want to first walk down to the river, just behind the mill. In addition to being physically beautiful, the river is quite impressive: for the numbers, see page 90 of the previous hike in this book. From behind the mill, you can see narrow Wood Island in front of you. The larger Roberts Island sits behind it, and Spencer Island is to the right. Beyond is Cecil County.

The mill was built in 1794 and operated well into the 20th century. It's open May–September on weekends and holidays, 10 a.m.–4 p.m., with grinding demonstrations from 1 p.m. to 4 p.m. A bridge once spanned the river near the mill, but it was destroyed by ice floes in 1856. The toll keeper's house, however, still remains in its position to the left of the mill. It now houses an information center for the park. The building across the road was once the Rock Run miller's house.

The red-blazed Susquehanna Ridge Trail is a narrow foot trail that runs along a western ridge facing the Susquehanna, a few hundred feet above the river. It is noted for birding and wildflower-viewing. Quickly, you'll cross a tiny stream and see a little cairn next to it with a hiker icon. The area is loaded with raspberry bushes. If you

**DISTANCE & CONFIGURATION:** 8.3-mile loop

**DIFFICULTY:** Moderate–strenuous

**SCENERY:** Susquehanna River, Rock Run, historical sites

**EXPOSURE:** More shade than sun

**TRAFFIC:** Moderate–heavy at historical area, picnic area, campgrounds, and river; light on trails

**TRAIL SURFACE:** Dirt, gravel, asphalt

**HIKING TIME:** 3–3.5 hours

**DRIVING DISTANCE:** 40 miles

**ELEVATION GAIN:** 23' at trailhead, 345' at high point

**ACCESS:** 9 a.m.–sunset; no fees or permits required

**WHEELCHAIR ACCESS:** No

**MAPS:** USGS *Conowingo Dam* and *Aberdeen;* you can purchase the Susquehanna State Park Trail Guide at dnr.maryland.gov/publiclands/Pages/central/susquehanna.aspx.

**FACILITIES:** Within park (not at trailhead) you have access to restrooms, water, campground, Steppingstone Museum, picnic area, boat launch, and phone.

**CONTACT:** 410-557-7994, dnr.maryland.gov/publiclands/Pages/central/susquehanna.aspx

**LOCATION:** 761 Stafford Rd., Havre De Grace

**COMMENTS:** This hike stitches together major portions of each of the trails in Susquehanna State Park except the Lower Heritage Greenway Trail, which is described in the previous hike. Length can be varied by taking spur trails, as noted in the Description.

want to see the berries, visit in summer. The river will be difficult to see then, but it's a fine price to pay for the thickness of the woods.

At 0.6 mile you'll cross an intact stone wall. This is evidence of once cleared land, not surprising since the community of Lapidum is close by. This settlement traces its history to 1683. When you see the white-blazed Land of Promise Trail at 0.9 mile, you'll notice the Susquehanna Ridge Trail continuing straight ahead. It ends soon at Lapidum Road, entrance point for the Lapidum Boat Launch. Instead of hitting the dead end, turn right on the Land of Promise Trail, an isolated trail that more or less follows that same stone wall.

At 1.1 miles, skirt around the edge of a cleared field, still walking astride the wall. Emerge into a field, a favorite of songbirds, as the trail moves through chest-high grass. More raspberry bushes await when you reenter the woods at 1.4 miles before quickly coming back out into the field. At 1.5 miles cross a tree-lined road; to the right is the Steppingstone Farm Museum. It demonstrates the rural arts and crafts of the 1880–1920 period (steppingstonemuseum.org, 410-939-2299). Across the road, you'll soon notice a little stream down the hill to the left. At about 2 miles, there's a fascinating area full of grapevine, trumpet vine, honeysuckle, and some invasive *Ailanthus altissima* trees. The admixture of these Chinese trees and all the vines creates a little scene that appears downright semitropical.

At 2.1 miles turn left on the yellow-blazed Rock Run Trail, noted for its grapevines, raspberry bushes, and briar patches. Make sure to take the rightward split in the pine plantation when you see the 1A sign—otherwise, you'll end up at Quaker Bottom Road. The trail serves as the access point to where Rock Run meets the Susquehanna at the historical area. To avoid going back to where you began, take the left at Rock Run, crossing over at 2.7 miles (take care on the loose rocks), and link up

## Susquehanna State Park: Woodland–Farm Trails

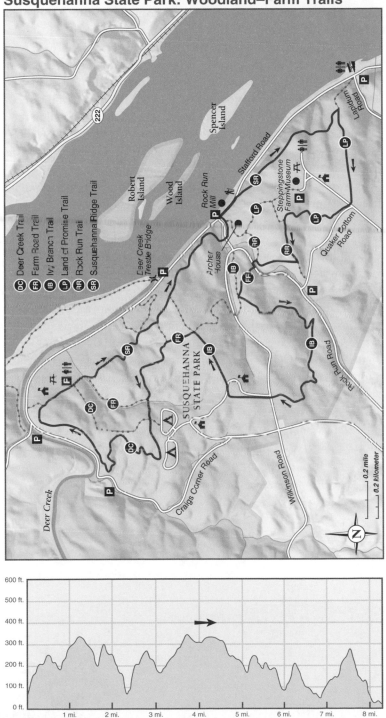

with the blue-blazed Farm Road Trail. The area around Rock Run is full of mountain laurel and mature beech trees.

Once across the run, take a right. You're likely to see many brown wood frogs, characterized by black "raccoon masks" around the eyes. Cross over the stone wall and immediately turn left. At 2.8 miles emerge onto Rock Run Road and go left for about 50 feet and then back up into the woods to the right. The trail is recognizable by a series of log steps and a log handrail. Pass an orange-blazed trail to the right; in another 10 feet, you'll see the same orange-blazed trail to the left. Turn left here on the Ivy Branch Trail. (Taking the first Ivy Branch to the right will lead you directly to the road going to the historical area, where you parked.)

There's a multitude of enormous trees along the Ivy Branch Trail; it's stunningly beautiful and very peaceful, especially around 3.5 miles. Pass a bog—again, many frogs—full of skunk cabbage. Cross a rocky stream shaded with hay-scented and Christmas fern; their combined aromas are reminiscent of cedar. Up the hill, you'll see a trail junction: Spur #5 heads left and dead-ends at Rock Run Road. Go right to stay on the Ivy Branch Trail. Cross a little footbridge. Skirt around a pine plantation to the right and reach Wilkinson Road at 3.8 miles. Straight ahead is the maintenance complex. Keep it to your right and walk along the treeline at the edge of the farm field. Continue in the same direction as the little gravel road at 3.9 miles and pass the entrance to the maintenance complex. Be on the lookout for when the groove in the grass, which is the trail, cuts to the left, away from the treeline. The top of the gradual hill affords a wonderful view of undeveloped land for miles.

At 4.5 miles turn left on the blue-blazed Farm Road Trail once again. You'll also see a trail going right here. This is Spur #4, which you can take if you're short on time, tired, or want to see an abandoned barn, silo, and stable—all looking very spooky in their dark, overrun state. The other end of the trail spur links to the red

Even on a cloudy day, the Susquehanna River is impressive.

Susquehanna Ridge Trail, which you can follow right, back to the parking area. But to continue hiking, skip the spur and continue on the Farm Road Trail (you can see the barn later when you're on the Susquehanna Ridge Trail).

The Farm Road Trail cuts straight across an open field in waist-high grass full of grasshoppers, dragonflies, and green beetles in summer. Reenter the woods for good at 4.8 miles and take note of the little stream to the left. Take Spur #3 at 5.2 miles, crossing over the stream, to link to the green-blazed Deer Creek Trail. This trail winds through mature forest, noted mostly for what the trail guide calls "two giant specimens of native trees, the white oak and American beech." Indeed, the girth of some of them is very impressive.

At the trail junction at 6 miles, keep heading right, up the hill. Going left will take you to Craigs Corner Road. Deer Creek runs on the other side of Craigs Corner, and you'll hear it for a while until you turn away and pass Spur #2. Next, continue past Spur #1, across from the Deer Creek Picnic Area through the woods to the left, and soon the trail links up with the red Susquehanna Ridge Trail again, this time at 6.9 miles.

Cross a footbridge and a forest buffer, where a clear-cut area has been allowed to grow back naturally. Along the Susquehanna Ridge Trail, a profusion of wild mint and honeysuckle offers a very nice aroma in summer. If you're hiking in winter and miss it, the tradeoff is great river views around the wide girthed trees. If you didn't check it out earlier, look for Spur #4 to the right to see the abandoned barn.

You'll reach Rock Run at 8 miles. Cross it and take a left when you reach the park road. You're now reentering the Rock Run Historic Area, passing to the right of the Rock Run House, the 1804 home of Brigadier General James Archer, who resigned from the U.S. Army to join the Confederacy. He was wounded and captured at Gettysburg in 1863. Several rooms in the mansion have been restored and stocked with period antiques; call the park for information on tours. Take a right, and the parking area is straight ahead.

## NEARBY/RELATED ACTIVITIES

See Susquehanna State Park: River Trails on page 90 for many nearby activities.

• • • • • • • • • • • • • • • • • • • • • • • •

**GPS TRAILHEAD COORDINATES**   N39° 36.424'   W76° 08.453'

**DIRECTIONS**   Take I-95 N 36 miles to Exit 89 (MD 155). Go west 2.5 miles and turn right on MD 161. Go 0.3 mile and turn right on Rock Run Road to follow it into the park. Follow the signs to the historic area until the road ends at the parking area to the left of Rock Run Mill. Walk up Stafford, keeping Rock Run Mill on your left. The trailhead is 600 feet ahead, leading into the woods to the right.

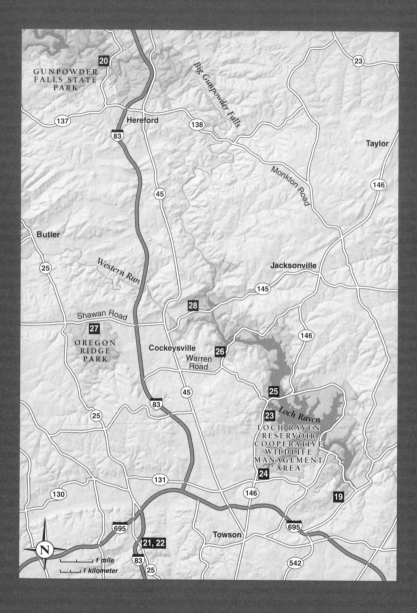

# NORTHERN SUBURBS

The English manor–style Sherwood House was built in 1935 for approximately $37,000.
*Photo by Evan Balkan*

**KEEP YOUR EYES** open for abundant wildlife on this pleasant hike within 371-acre Cromwell Valley Park.

## DESCRIPTION

Cromwell Valley Park (CVP), first settled some 300 years ago, has a long history. Today, thanks to conservation efforts by the county and state, as well as the generosity of families who owned the farms that now make up CVP, it exists mostly as an educational park, focusing primarily on farming, history, and nature. Programs demonstrating animal husbandry and organic farming provide educational opportunities year-round. This means that the park is often busy, but the trails remain largely uncrowded.

From the parking area, walk toward Cromwell Bridge Road and take the bridge back over Minebank Run, which eventually flows into Loch Raven Reservoir not far to the east. Take a right on Minebank Run Trail, which parallels its namesake. Near the water, look for belted kingfishers and great blue herons.

You'll pass many mature trees, including maple, walnut, tulip poplar, locust, oak, and sassafras. Staghorn sumac, Queen Anne's lace, and goldenrod flank an old property-line fence to the left. As the park is actually composed of three separate farms, you'll see divisions such as the fence, as well as a grove of beautiful willow

**DISTANCE & CONFIGURATION:** 3.5-mile loop

**DIFFICULTY:** Moderate

**SCENERY:** Mature woods, Minebank Run, plentiful wildlife

**EXPOSURE:** More shade than sun

**TRAFFIC:** Light

**TRAIL SURFACE:** Packed dirt, short stretches of asphalt and gravel

**HIKING TIME:** 1.5–2 hours

**DRIVING DISTANCE:** 20 miles

**ELEVATION GAIN:** 187' at trailhead, 440' at high point

**ACCESS:** Sunrise–sunset; no fees or permits required; vehicles in the park after sunset may be locked in overnight.

**WHEELCHAIR ACCESS:** No

**MAPS:** USGS *Towson;* trail maps are available at the information kiosk across from the Willow Grove parking lot and the Sherwood Farm parking lot near the Sherwood House or online at cromwellvalleypark.org.

**FACILITIES:** Restrooms and water in Willow Grove Nature Center (open Tuesday–Sunday, 9 a.m.–4 p.m.)

**CONTACT:** Willow Grove Nature Center, 410-887-3014; Cromwell Valley Park Office, 410-887-2503, cromwellvalleypark.org

**LOCATION:** 2175 Cromwell Bridge Rd., Parkville

**COMMENTS:** There are plenty of adjoining hikes in the Loch Raven Watershed property if you'd like to extend this hike.

trees. All of the foliage here makes the area a haven for birds. In all, CVP hosts hundreds of bird species; for a complete list, visit cromwellvalleypark.org/birding.

At 0.5 mile turn right onto Sherwood Road and follow signs for Sherwood Farm. You'll pass the Cromwell Valley Community Supported Agriculture (CSA) site, an organic farm that sells shares to its produce (for more information visit american towns.com/md/baltimore/organization/cromwell-valley-csa).

Continue on the road, walking under the stone archway of the beautiful 1935 Sherwood House (now the park office) and through the parking lot. Just before you cross over a bridge, turn left into the woods on the Sherwood Farm Trail.

This area is a riot of mature hardwoods with a thriving understory. Just after entering the woods, head left onto the green-blazed Wellington Woods Trail. At just over 1.1 miles, you'll come to a grassy area on your left, but continue heading right into the woods. You'll immediately come to a Y-intersection, where you can continue straight for a shortcut; instead, go left uphill, following the green-blazed trail. At just under 1.5 miles, a trail intersects from the right—this takes you back to the Sherwood House, so keep left.

You'll soon reach a sign reading RADIO TOWER TRAIL, LEAVES PARK PROPERTY, and WELLINGTON WOODS TRAIL to the left; head left, and at 1.8 miles you'll reach an open area with several trail options. Take the trail on your right that leads into the woods (rather than the trail over the stream or the one to the left). Soon after, an open area with residential houses appears on your left; continue on the trail back into the woods.

At 2.1 miles you'll reach a junction with a red-blazed trail to your right and a yellow-blazed trail straight ahead. Go right, following the red-blazed trail. Abundant white-tailed deer live in the park, along with beautiful and elusive red foxes. Other animal residents include beavers, opossums, raccoons, woodchucks, and muskrats. CVP

# Cromwell Valley Park

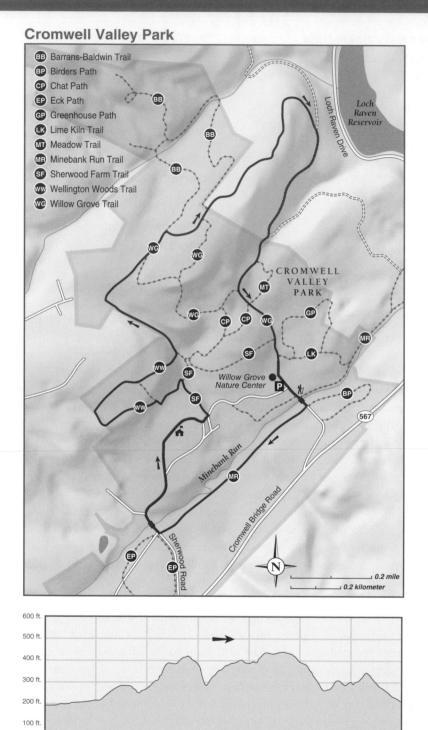

BB Barrans-Baldwin Trail
BP Birders Path
CP Chat Path
EP Eck Path
GP Greenhouse Path
LK Lime Kiln Trail
MT Meadow Trail
MR Minebank Run Trail
SF Sherwood Farm Trail
WW Wellington Woods Trail
WG Willow Grove Trail

CROMWELL VALLEY PARK

Loch Raven Reservoir

Loch Raven Drive

Willow Grove Nature Center

Minebank Run

Sherwood Road

Cromwell Bridge Road

567

N

0.2 mile
0.2 kilometer

also hosts many reptiles and amphibians, including frogs, toads, turtles, skinks, and salamanders, as well as more than a dozen different snakes. A word of warning: The northern copperhead lives in the park; in the unlikely event you see one (look for the telltale diamond-shaped head), give it a wide berth.

As you continue on the trail, you'll notice large chunks of Cockeysville marble, remnants of the marble that was heated to produce lime in large kilns in the early 1700s. A couple of the kilns still exist and can be seen near the parking area.

At 2.25 miles the trail intersects with the Barrans-Baldwin Trail; continue straight along this green-blazed trail, and at the next sign, head down a hill and into the woods. Here, the path becomes a little difficult to distinguish, especially in the fall, but follow the gap in the trees and you should find your way. You'll reach a Y-intersection at 2.7 miles; head right and begin walking downhill.

At this point, our trail briefly leaves CVP and enters Loch Raven Reservoir. You'll hear and then begin to see the edge of Loch Raven Reservoir through the woods. At 2.8 miles you'll reach the bottom of the hill and come to a T-intersection. Head left here to further explore some other trails within the Loch Raven water shed. However, to return to CVP and continue our hike, take a right. Stay straight on this well-groomed path, ignoring the paths to your left and right. At 3.1 miles at a Y-intersection, head right up the hill and soon reach an open field with vegetation in the middle. Turn right here, and at 3.3 miles you'll reach a picnic table and a sign pointing out the various routes. Go left toward the Willow Grove Nature Center. Continue straight, heading into the woods, and follow the crushed stone path to the parking area where you began. (You'll pass the white Lime Kiln Trail, a 0.2-mile trail that runs past the lime kilns, if you want to see them.)

## NEARBY/RELATED ACTIVITIES

Take I-695 to Exit 27B to visit **Hampton National Historic Site** (410-823-1309, nps.gov /hamp). Once the largest mansion in the United States and the northernmost slave-holding plantation in the country, it still boasts extensive gardens.

• • • • • • • • • • • • • • • • • • • • • • • •

**GPS TRAILHEAD COORDINATES** N39° 24.981'    W76° 32.773'

**DIRECTIONS** Take I-95 N 11 miles to I-695 W and drive 6 miles to Exit 29A (Cromwell Bridge Road). Turn left at the first light onto Cromwell Bridge Road and go about 1 mile. Pass the first entrance (Sherwood Farm), and in 0.5 mile turn left at the park entry road (2175 Cromwell Bridge Road). Cross the bridge and park in the gravel parking lot on the left. To begin the trail, backtrack across the bridge on foot and follow signs for Sherwood Farm.

# GUNPOWDER FALLS STATE PARK (HEREFORD AREA): Gunpowder North–South Circuit

Prettyboy Dam releases water from the reservoir into Gunpowder Falls.

**CIRCLE GUNPOWDER FALLS** at some of its prettiest and most scenic sections.

## DESCRIPTION

The wrought iron Masemore Road Bridge was built in 1898. A wooden pole sits just to the left of the bridge, pointing out the white-blazed Gunpowder South Trail. Follow this trail upstream along Gunpowder Falls over mossy rocks and fallen tree trunks for 500 feet to the blue-blazed Highland Trail on the left. Head uphill on the Highland Trail through mountain laurel and along a ridged groove. At 0.3 mile the Highland Trail heads right and narrows as it leads deeper into the woods. When you reach Bush Cabin Run, cross over it to the right. You'll cross a power line cut at 0.5 mile, and once you're back in the woods, the trail widens significantly and leads through stands of pine and cedar.

You'll reach the diminutive Falls Road and a small parking area at 1 mile. Cross the parking area and get back on the trail, which leads downhill; you'll see the horseshoe curve of Gunpowder Falls straight ahead. At 1.2 miles the trail splits; head left and walk alongside the river to reach Prettyboy Dam. The path to the dam is a treat—narrow and winding through and over exposed roots, moss, mountain laurel, mica schist columns, trees with bulbous knots, and hemlocks.

**DISTANCE & CONFIGURATION:** 13.2-mile loop

**DIFFICULTY:** Moderate–strenuous depending on length

**SCENERY:** Gunpowder River, Prettyboy Dam, varied flora, rock formations

**EXPOSURE:** Shady

**TRAFFIC:** Moderate

**TRAIL SURFACE:** Packed dirt, rock

**HIKING TIME:** 6–7 hours

**DRIVING DISTANCE:** 36 miles

**ELEVATION GAIN:** 350' at trailhead, 600' at high point

**ACCESS:** Sunrise–sunset; no fees or permits required

**WHEELCHAIR ACCESS:** No

**MAPS:** USGS *Hereford;* dnr.maryland.gov /publiclands/Documents/GFSP_HerefordMap.pdf

**FACILITIES:** Restrooms at the south side of Bunker Hill Rd.

**CONTACT:** 800-830-3974, dnr.maryland.gov /publiclands/Pages/central/gunpowderhereford .aspx

**LOCATION:** Masemore Rd., Parkton

**COMMENTS:** Several bridges and parking areas make it possible to vary the length of this hike. The hike described below begins at the Masemore Rd. parking area, west of Bunker Hill. Mountain bikes are prohibited on all trails.

You will reach the dam at 1.7 miles; if it's a summer day and you're lucky enough to catch the dam with one of the valves open, enjoy the cooling spray. The dam was built from 1924 to 1933 and was apparently named for a local farmer's horse that drowned in a nearby stream.

Turn around and head back; you'll come to the trail junction again at 2.2 miles. Turn left and you'll soon reach river level and see lots of little ripples; the rocky river has a series of little bends. The trunks of many of the trees along the riverbank bear telltale beaver gnaw scars. By 2.5 miles, the trail turns into a jumble of rocks, which requires a bit of scrambling.

You'll reach Falls Road again at 2.9 miles; cross the steel bridge and pick up the Gunpowder North Trail. Both the river and trail level out a bit here, making a relatively easy stroll along the riverbanks in the grass. Summer blooms in this area include woodland sunflowers, aster, and goldenrod. You'll come to a little bog at 3.3 miles and pass through a stand of pines before reaching Masemore Road again at 3.5 miles. Your car is just on the other side of the road, but if you want to continue hiking, stay along the river; the trail will take you through more stands of oak and tulip poplar. Soon the river becomes quite shallow and you can see a multitude of pretty, light-colored stones in the water. A little farther, the trail runs beneath a limestone rock base some 30 feet high.

You'll reach Bunker Hill Road at 4.7 miles; you can't cross here because the old bridge washed out, leaving only two stone abutments. Continue along the river, where the trees crowd the riverbanks a bit more, providing some wonderful canopy. Not surprisingly, opportunities for supreme birding abound: thrushes, vireos, warblers, and woodpeckers populate the forests, while blue herons and kingfishers can be found along the river. Red-tail and red-shouldered hawks circle above in the clearings, while Carolina chickadees, indigo buntings, peewees, and phoebes inhabit the trees and shrubs.

## Gunpowder Falls State Park (Hereford Area): Gunpowder North–South Circuit

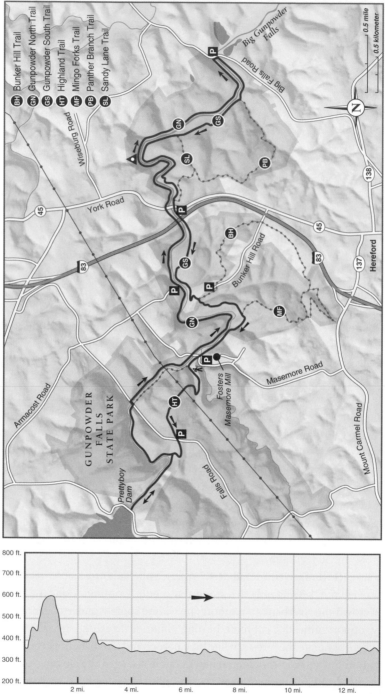

Unfortunately, the only unpleasant stretch of this entire hike comes soon. You'll hear it first and then pass under I-83. But you'll quickly leave this area behind. Reach York Road at 5.9 miles and see a parking area across the bridge on the right. Cross York Road and pick up the trail at the break in the guardrail; you'll see a series of white rocks leading toward the river, and blue blazes will quickly follow.

The path is initially uphill and down, but it quickly settles down to water level. The trail begins to feel more isolated here, and the river finally completely overtakes the faint echoes of the traffic on I-83.

At 6.8 miles you'll pass Raven Rock Falls on the left. It's not a high vertical waterfall but rather a riffle of rock that ends at the trail. Cross a little stream immediately beyond the falls; the trail soon heads up a little higher on the hill among big rocks, moss, ferns, and more mountain laurel. The trail goes a bit deeper into the woods and reaches a junction at 7.3 miles, right after another stream. Go straight uphill, crossing several deer paths and following the blue blazes.

Coming back down the hill, the trail levels out at 7.7 miles and reaches a big river curve at 8 miles. This is a great spot to take in the topography of the area, marked by midsize hills rolling gently to the water; it's typical piedmont Maryland. You'll soon come to a gravel park road; head right, passing a marshy bog. The gravel road ends at Big Falls Road Bridge at 8.3 miles. Cross the bridge and pick up the white-blazed Gunpowder South Trail on the other side. This section is one of the many trout catch-and-return areas.

Now walking upstream, the trail on the south side of the river really hugs the edge of the water and is much more narrow than the other side. At 9.2 miles the trail splits; the Panther Branch Trail, named for a panther that once lived in a cave visible from the trail, goes to the left and loops into the woods, eventually rejoining the Gunpowder South Trail. If you take Panther Branch Trail, look for the remains of two old mills, built in the mid-1700s and destroyed by accidental explosions in 1874. The entire length of the Panther Branch Trail covers 2.2 miles, and taking it will give you 0.5 mile less of total hike than if you remained on the Gunpowder South Trail.

Taking either option will bring you to the pink-blazed Sandy Lane Trail (0.3 mile in length), which connects Panther Branch Trail and Gunpowder South Trail. Back on the Gunpowder South Trail, you'll soon see Raven Rock Falls across the river.

At the next trail junction at 9.8 miles, turn right toward the river; going the other way takes you into the woods over the hill. The trail along the river gets very narrow, becoming at some points just an eroded knife-edge hanging over the water. You should not have trouble keeping your footing if it isn't snowy or icy, but be very careful nonetheless. If you have any fears of slipping and falling, take the wooded option.

Beyond this narrow section, the trail widens and joins the other end of the Panther Branch Trail. Cross the Panther Branch (the waterway) and come to York Road just ahead. This section of the trail back to Bunker Hill changes only when it runs away from the river and through the forest, where wildflowers and ubiquitous rocks reappear. For the next 3 miles you will follow the same route as before toward the turnaround, just on the other side of the river. Hug the river and bypass the two trails heading to your left. The south side between York and Masemore Roads hosts many more pines than the north side; despite that, the two sides of the river in this stretch generally differ little, and both are beautiful. You will reach Masemore Road and your car at 13.2 miles.

## NEARBY/RELATED ACTIVITIES

Just west are several hikes at **Prettyboy Reservoir** (pages 162–173), and to the south you'll find **Oregon Ridge Park** (page 135). After your hike, you may want to enjoy a beer at **Inverness Brewing** (16200 Markoe Road, Monkton; 443-829-2142; inverness brewing.com), the first Baltimore County Farm Brewery.

• • • • • • • • • • • • • • • • • • • • • • • •

**GPS TRAILHEAD COORDINATES** N39° 36.674'  W76° 40.977'

**DIRECTIONS** Take I-95 N 11 miles to I-695 W. Take I-695 10 miles west to Exit 24 (I-83 N). After 12.5 miles take Exit 27 (Mount Carmel Road). Go west 0.6 mile and take the first right onto Masemore Road. Follow Masemore Road as it winds past Fosters Masemore Mill (built in 1797); look for the parking area on the right at the bottom of the hill. Walk toward the bridge and pick up the trail there.

Baltimore's drinking water flows from the Prettyboy Reservoir, just behind Pretty-boy Dam pictured here, down Gunpowder Falls and into Loch Raven Reservoir.

Lake Roland Dam was originally constructed between 1858 and 1861 to help create the first municipal water supply for Baltimore.

**FOLLOW AN OLD** railbed along the Jones Falls to Lake Roland and back.

## DESCRIPTION

Climb over the guardrail and head right on the red-blazed trail, which runs along the railbed of the now-defunct Baltimore and Susquehanna Railroad. You will parallel the Jones Falls downriver on the right, and on the left you'll see rock outcrops with clinging tree roots. Oak and maple trees dominate this section, offering wonderful, colorful foliage in autumn and abundant shade on hot days. At 0.6 mile you'll begin heading east, away from the Jones Falls.

At 0.75 mile you'll come to a post indicating the red trail straight ahead and the blue trail toward the left (0.8 mile). The blue trail ends at L'Hirondelle Club, so continue straight on the red trail going east. Soon after, you'll walk over a wooden bridge crossing a stream and continue straight on the wide path. The trail runs through tall, mature oaks. You'll see lots of trails cut by mountain bikers on either side of you, as well as the green trail to your right at about 0.9 mile. Ignore these and continue straight; you'll have no problem recognizing the main red-blazed trail—it's wide and well trod.

At just under a mile, you'll come to a trail junction with red-blazed trails going in either direction. They parallel and rejoin each other at 1.25 miles. I took the main route to the right. At various points along the trail you may stumble upon art

**DISTANCE & CONFIGURATION:** 7.2-mile out-and-back

**DIFFICULTY:** Moderate

**SCENERY:** Jones Falls, Lake Roland, upland forest

**EXPOSURE:** Mostly shade

**TRAFFIC:** Light–moderate on the trail; moderate–heavy at the lake

**TRAIL SURFACE:** Packed dirt, short stretch of asphalt

**HIKING TIME:** 2.5 hours

**DRIVING DISTANCE:** 19 miles

**ELEVATION GAIN:** 245' at trailhead, with no significant rise

**ACCESS:** Sunrise–sunset; you can reach the park from the Falls Rd. Light Rail stop and walk

east on Copper Hill Rd. to Lake Roland; no fees or permits required

**WHEELCHAIR ACCESS:** No

**MAPS:** USGS *Cockeysville*

**FACILITIES:** Pavilions, restrooms, and dog park at the lake; nature center is open Tuesday–Sunday, 9 a.m.–5 p.m.

**CONTACT:** 410-887-4156, lakeroland.org

**LOCATION:** Falls Rd. (just after Old Court Rd.), Baltimore

**COMMENTS:** This trail used to offer a shortcut walking along the light rail tracks to cross Lake Roland on your return trip. Now, you'll need to retrace your steps back around Lake Roland due to park rules.

installations as part of Lake Roland's Art on the Trail initiative. When I hiked, there was a metal raptor in the tree where the red trails rejoined.

At this same trail junction you'll also intersect with the yellow trail, but for now, stay on the red-blazed trail. You'll see the entrance to the yellow trail on your left at 1.45 miles and will take that on your return.

At just under 1.5 miles you'll begin to see Lake Roland through the trees on your left. At 1.6 miles you'll see some wooden steps heading left down to the water—you can go sit at the lake's edge and watch the birds, turtles, and snakes.

Back on the trail, you'll soon see the defunct railroad tracks, now covered with plants, and follow them for a while. You can either stay on this wide path or take the smaller one that parallels it about 10 feet to the left, closer to the water. Either way, the two trails connect at 2 miles.

At this point, you'll come to the light rail tracks. Of course, use caution when crossing, even though this section sits in the middle of a long straightaway, making it impossible for a train to surprise you.

Once you cross the tracks, head uphill on the steps. At the top of the hill, you'll see a pavilion and picnic tables. Now you're on a paved asphalt path; turn left and follow the paved path around the water. (The gravel path that leads closer to the water dead-ends at Paw Point Dog Park.) Although this is a nice spot to sit water-side and contemplate the lake, I recommend you keep moving—your chances for solitude here are next to none. So circle around on the asphalt path—you'll have the opportunity for good views and solitude on the other side of the lake. Pass a playground on your right and portable bathrooms on your left at 2.4 miles, and then take the asphalt path on your left, where you'll be able to see Lake Roland Dam. At 2.5

## Lake Roland

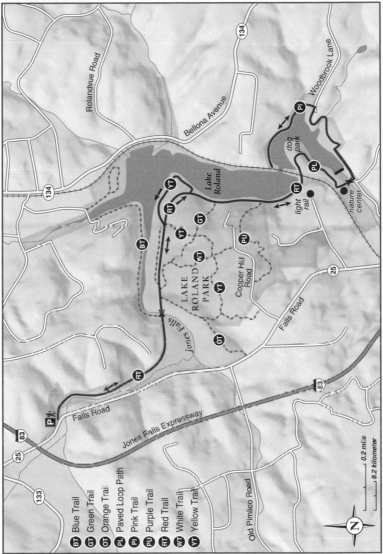

miles you'll reach the Lake Roland Nature Center (directly in front of you) and take the pedestrian bridge on your left to cross Lake Roland.

Once across, take the road to the left; you'll see a lovely spot to sit next to the marble building that reads LAKE ROLAND 1861, a reminder of the lake's prior use as a city reservoir. At 2.75 miles you'll come to a parking lot and a little picnic area with grills to your left. Walk straight to the edge of the parking lot past the portable bathrooms and take the dirt path with pink blazes that runs next to the lake. This portion of the trail is quite uneven with roots and some overgrowth. At 2.8 miles you'll come to a little parking area and continue left, going northeast. As the path turns right, you'll have a glorious view of the lake. At 3 miles the trail cuts down to the left, closer to the lake, and you'll have spectacular views in all seasons—spring blooms, summer green, fall foliage, and winter barrenness.

At 3.1 miles an Eagle Scout Project allows you to cross over a stream using a wooden footpath. The raised wooden footpaths on portions of this trail traverse muddy areas. Follow the trail to a rock grotto at 3.35 miles, a great lookout point over the lake. Continue on and reach the light rail tracks at 3.6 miles.

You'll see an area to walk on the left of the tracks that used to allow you to link back to the red trail (where you'd turn right to continue retracing your steps). However, the bridge is no longer open to pedestrian traffic according to signage. There is a plan to work with the state to provide a safe crossing for individuals over the trestle bridge; however, please follow all park signage. As of press time, this means backtracking along your original path to reach this portion of light rail on the other side of Lake Roland.

On your return trip, we recommend veering right on the yellow trail for a change of scenery. The yellow trail links back to the red trail. Once it does, continue back to reach your car at 7.2 miles.

## NEARBY/RELATED ACTIVITIES

You might be interested in visiting two nearby sites that have great historical significance. You can walk from the trailhead to **Rockland Historic District,** listed on the National Register of Historic Places, at the corner of Falls Road (north of the trailhead), Ruxton Road (to the east), and Old Court Road (to the west). The buildings in Rockland, Baltimore County's first permanent settlement dating back to 1706, remain and have been lovingly maintained, while the mill now houses businesses and shops. From Rockland, you will have a short drive to the **Colored Methodist Protestant St. Johns' Chapel of Baltimore County.** Built for free blacks in 1833, it has held services continually since 1886. To get there, head north on Falls Road and take the first right onto Ruxton Road; when it ends at a stop sign, turn right onto Bellona Avenue, and you will see the church 0.3 mile ahead on the right.

• • • • • • • • • • • • • • • • • • • • • • • • •

**GPS TRAILHEAD COORDINATES**  N39° 23.777'   W76° 39.796'

**DIRECTIONS**  Take I-95 S 3 miles to Exit 49B (I-695). Take I-695 W 13.5 miles to Exit 23 (Falls Road). Follow Falls Road to the first light at Joppa Road and make a left back onto Falls Road going south. Cross Old Court Road and go another 0.3 mile. Park on the left shoulder where the road sweeps to the right. The trail starts just beyond the guardrail.

The serpentine barren midway through the hike provides a surprising change in scenery after a mostly wooded trail and is home to several rare plant species.      *Photo by Heather Consla*

**FOLLOW AN OLD** railbed along the Jones Falls to an upland forest containing rare serpentine landscape.

## DESCRIPTION

The first 0.75 mile of this hike follows the same route as the previous hike in this book: Lake Roland. For a more specific description of the beginning of this hike, see that hike profile. For now, climb the guardrail and follow the red trail 0.75 mile to the steel bridge spanning the Jones Falls.

Cross the bridge and look for two path offshoots—both to the right, one leading downhill and one leading uphill; pass both of these and take the next path you see to the right, which is blazed orange and easy to spot. This trail is very rocky and rooty, and, depending on the recent weather, may be quite wet. At just over 0.8 mile, the trail suddenly opens up, and you'll be in an entirely new landscape in an area that's part of Bare Hills. You'll see prairie grass and smell the short, stubby pines as you walk over the rocky topsoil. The sharp rocks you see around you are serpentine, or serpentinite, a mineral that produces extremely nutrient-poor soil. According to the Maryland Geologic Society, serpentine landscapes are "stony, unfertile, and sparsely vegetated—hence the term 'serpentine barren'." Typically, a serpentine barren contains scrub oak, pine, cedar, grasses, and some unique and rare wildflowers. It also

**DISTANCE & CONFIGURATION:** 3.7-mile out-and-back with loop

**DIFFICULTY:** Easy–moderate

**SCENERY:** Jones Falls, serpentine ecosystem, upland forest

**EXPOSURE:** Mostly shade

**TRAFFIC:** Light–moderate

**TRAIL SURFACE:** Packed dirt, serpentinite

**HIKING TIME:** 2 hours

**DRIVING DISTANCE:** 19 miles

**ELEVATION GAIN:** 245' at trailhead, with no significant rise

**ACCESS:** Sunrise–sunset; no fees or permits required

**WHEELCHAIR ACCESS:** No

**MAPS:** USGS *Cockeysville*

**FACILITIES:** Pavilions, restrooms, and dog park at the lake; nature center is open Tuesday–Sunday, 9 a.m.–5 p.m.

**CONTACT:** 410-887-4156, lakeroland.org

**LOCATION:** Falls Rd. (just after Old Court Rd.), Baltimore

**COMMENTS:** Because of their differing natures, the two Lake Roland hikes described in this book are treated separately; however, because they share the same trailhead, you can easily combine them for one long hike. See the previous hike in this book for details.

produces chromium, or chromite, the raw ingredient for chrome. This extremely rare ecosystem exists in only a few places in Maryland. (For a heavy dose of serpentine, take the hike at Soldiers Delight Natural Environmental Area, described on pages 174–179. Between Bare Hills and Soldiers Delight, almost all the chrome in the world was mined and produced in the early to mid-19th century.)

The landscape here is a new world from the forest you just left. After turning uphill, follow the trail 500 feet to a clearing. Here, the trail splits; go left, following the white blazes. The foliage is dominated by short, stubby pines, crisscrossed by loads of deer trails. There are also many little trail offshoots. Take the main trail, which is recognizable as the widest. It's full of rocks and heads uphill. But do note all these little paths; they offer plenty of opportunities to explore, as they form a spiderweb of trails across the hillside. The hike described here simply follows the main trail, but feel free to veer off and explore.

This is a beautiful place and can be a real revelation to those living in the Baltimore area who have never seen a serpentine landscape before. With its many rocks and minimal vegetation, it looks little like the typical hardwood and piedmont forests of the region. At a little over 1 mile, you'll see the remnants of a pit mine to the left. Don't expect a massive open pit, but rather a filled depression about 3 feet by 3 feet across. There's a very pretty stream that you'll jump over soon after. Next, a path to the right eventually leads to a private road, so head left on the yellow trail.

After another couple hundred feet, where the trail opens onto another clearing, head right up the hill. In spring, this area is dotted with little white wildflowers. At 1.2 miles the foliage begins to change again, to the more recognizable forests of the area. At the next four-way junction, head straight, and you'll soon cross over another stream. Go uphill, and when you reach the next fork, head left into another open area labeled as SERPENTINE RESTORATION AREA on park maps. You'll now be on the

## Lake Roland: Serpentine–Bare Hills

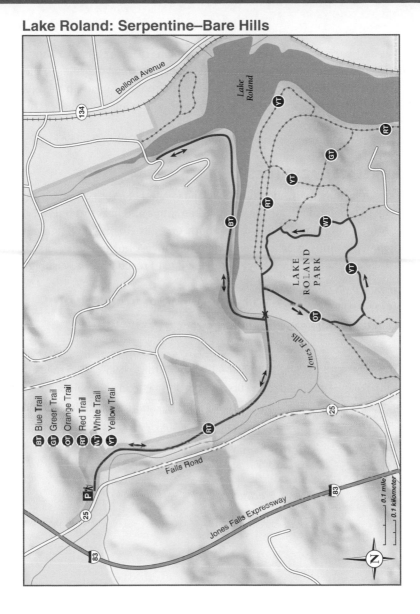

white trail, though blazes are sparse. Walk through this beautiful landscape, and then at 1.5 miles head back into the woods, crossing over another stream. Turn left on the green trail, which soon meets up with the main red trail. Turn left to head back to the bridge. (Another trail goes left uphill soon after, so if you want to do more exploring in the serpentine area, take it.)

This time, when you cross the bridge, head immediately downhill to the right on the blue trail. This little trail follows the Moores Branch of the Jones Falls for a

1-mile out-and-back, toward where Roland Run enters Lake Roland. Along the way, look for the foundations and existing brick structures of some old ruins to the left, 0.1 mile from the steel bridge. You'll have to leave the trail and head up the hill; there's no established path. Do tread considerately—just up the hill from these structures is a private home.

You will reach the steel bridge on your return at 2.9 miles. Backtrack to your car.

## NEARBY/RELATED ACTIVITIES

See the previous hike in this book, **Lake Roland** (page 111), for two nearby historical sites. If you're hungry, look for the great coffee shops and bakeries lining Falls Road heading south. Continuing a few miles south on Falls Road, you'll come to **Mount Washington,** with shops, markets, and one of the nicest business districts anywhere around. Take a right over the Kelly Avenue Bridge to reach Mount Washington.

• • • • • • • • • • • • • • • • • • • • • • • • • •

**GPS TRAILHEAD COORDINATES** N39° 23.774'   W76° 39.794'

**DIRECTIONS** Take I-95 S 3 miles to Exit 49B (I-695). Take I-695 W 13.5 miles to Exit 23 (Falls Road). Follow Falls Road to the first light at Joppa Road and make a left back onto Falls Road going south. Cross Old Court Road and go another 0.3 mile. Park on the left shoulder where the road sweeps to the right. The trail starts just beyond the guardrail.

View of Loch Raven Reservoir    *Photo by Steven Sturm*

**FIND SOLITUDE AT** Deadman's Cove, which is inside the heavily visited Loch Raven watershed.

## DESCRIPTION

Loch Raven Reservoir offers many beautiful trail options, and this one is perfect for a quick, quiet hike with beautiful views and perhaps a picnic lunch at the reservoir. The trail initially runs along an old fire road. It's very wide and, though in the thick woods, also well exposed. At first you'll hear lots of traffic noise, but that quickly disappears. By 200 feet, as the trail heads down a little hill, the sounds of the woods take over. Tall oaks dominate, rising above thick underbrush.

At 0.2 mile you'll parallel a dry creekbed to the left. Though the trail is still very wide, it's now shaded due to the height of the trees. The grass is tall, so expect a few shin scrapes during summer. By 0.25 mile you'll see lots of pines, along with plentiful white oaks, hickories, and sycamores. These woods, like much of the Loch Raven watershed, provide a haven for white-tailed deer, and you're likely to scatter more than a few. Woodpeckers make their homes here, too, and the sound of their tree pounding echoes all along the trail. To the left, an interesting wall of trees fronts the creekbed; their uniformity suggests that they were planted here long ago. At just over 0.3 mile,

**DISTANCE & CONFIGURATION:** 1.3-mile out-and-back

**DIFFICULTY:** Easy

**SCENERY:** Loch Raven Reservoir, pine forest, hardwoods

**EXPOSURE:** Mostly shade

**TRAFFIC:** Light

**TRAIL SURFACE:** Packed dirt

**HIKING TIME:** 30 minutes

**DRIVING DISTANCE:** 21 miles

**ELEVATION GAIN:** 280' at trailhead, with no significant rise

**ACCESS:** Sunrise–sunset; no fees or permits required

**WHEELCHAIR ACCESS:** No

**MAPS:** USGS *Towson*

**FACILITIES:** None

**CONTACT:** 877-620-8367, dnr.maryland.gov /wildlife/Pages/publiclands/central/lochraven .aspx

**LOCATION:** Dulaney Valley Rd., Lutherville-Timonium

**COMMENTS:** Take great care crossing Dulaney Valley Rd. There's a bit of a blind curve from the south, and drivers tend to take it too quickly. Dogs are welcome on the trail but must be leashed.

head left and follow the tire tracks through towering pines and abundant honeysuckle. Soon after, you'll have your first glimpse of the water through the trees on the right.

At just over 0.5 mile, a vein of large rocks cuts across the path. When you see a particularly large rock at a trail split, head to the right. The trail gets lost a bit in the tall grass, but you'll have better and better views of the water, so it's easy to tell where you're going. You'll reach the water at just over 0.6 mile and enjoy clear, beautiful views across the reservoir. Loch Raven Reservoir is a popular spot for boating and fishing. If you'd like to try your luck, visit the Loch Raven Fishing Center, which is just across the reservoir. To reach it, continue on Dulaney Valley Road. There, you can gather supplies and rent a boat to fish for largemouth and smallmouth bass, yellow perch, and northern pike. A fishing license is required for those 16 and older. These can be purchased online or in person at a license agent (for a list of agents, visit dnr.maryland.gov). Though the reservoir may have some visitors, more than likely you'll have the shore all to yourself. The water here is clear, and you'll probably see many fish swimming around at your feet. It's the perfect spot for a picnic, with plenty of space to spread out a blanket and enjoy the beautiful vistas.

At this point, though there's a trail along the water indicated on trail maps, it's quite overgrown and doesn't make for a fun trip. Instead, I recommend you turn around and follow the original trail back to your car.

## NEARBY/RELATED ACTIVITIES

If you're here Thursday–Saturday, head to York Road to check out the **Pennsylvania Dutch Market** (padutchmarketcockeysville.com), which has a wonderful assortment of food and gift options and is open year-round.

If you'd like to do a longer hike, head just a few miles south on Dulaney Valley Road to check out **Loch Raven Reservoir: Glen Ellen–Seminary Road** (page 123).

## Loch Raven Reservoir: Deadman's Cove Trail

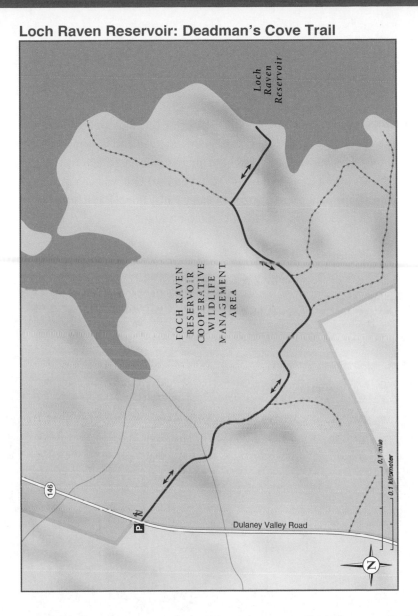

**Hampton National Historic Site** (410-823-1309, nps.gov/hamp), a stately home completed in 1790 and once the largest mansion in the United States, is also within easy driving distance. Built with a fortune amassed during the Revolutionary War, the site boasts extensive gardens on what was once the northernmost slave-holding plantation in the country. Head south on Dulaney Valley Road from Seminary Avenue; go three blocks and turn left onto Hampton Estate Lane. You will see the mansion and grounds entrance on the right.

• • • • • • • • • • • • • • • • • • • • • • • • •

**GPS TRAILHEAD COORDINATES** N39° 27.321'   W76° 35.534'

**DIRECTIONS**  Take I-95 N 11 miles to I-695 W. Drive 7.5 miles on I-695 W to Exit 27 and go north on Dulaney Valley Road. Cross Timonium Road and look for the signs for the entrance to Stella Maris Hospice. Roughly a quarter mile past Stella Maris is the parking area on the left (if you come to the light at Old Bosley Road, you've passed it). The trail starts opposite the parking area across Dulaney Valley Road; it is marked by an orange cable and a sign reading WOODS ROAD CLOSED TO BIKES.

Enjoy a brief trek through the woods on your way to peaceful Loch Raven Reservoir.   *Photo by Steven Sturm*

Loch Raven Reservoir supplies Baltimore with its drinking water, and also provides a welcome habitat for more than 200 species of birds.   *Photo by Steven Sturm*

**FOLLOW THE NATURAL** contours of the southeastern edge of Loch Raven Reservoir before ascending the hills above to come back through upland forest.

## DESCRIPTION

At the trailhead, a bulletin board explains which trails are open to mountain bikes and which aren't. Be aware: This is largely ignored. According to the sign, bikes are allowed only on the Glen Ellen Trail that begins to the right of where you stand. Even though you are heading left at 200 feet on the narrower dirt path, expect cyclists.

You'll immediately enter thick woods, full of oak and tulip poplar. The first view of the reservoir comes at 0.3 mile as you begin to parallel a feeder stream to the left. It gets very marshy as the water expands into the main body of the reservoir. The trail is flat and level as it winds through the woods, and the water before you gets wider and wider. Before you momentarily wind away from the reservoir at 0.5 mile, expect to scatter frogs, turtles, and an occasional water snake from the thick underbrush that crowds the edges of the trail.

Hundreds of offshoots lead in both directions from the trail; these singletrack bike paths lead to some nice scenery, but they cause severe erosion. Besides, staying on the main path yields some fantastic views.

**DISTANCE & CONFIGURATION:** 7 miles, 2 loops

**DIFFICULTY:** Moderate

**SCENERY:** Loch Raven Reservoir, upland forest

**EXPOSURE:** Shady

**TRAFFIC:** Light–moderate (mostly bicycle)

**TRAIL SURFACE:** Packed dirt

**HIKING TIME:** 3–3.5 hours

**DRIVING DISTANCE:** 23 miles

**ELEVATION GAIN:** 262' at trailhead, 430' at high point

**ACCESS:** Sunrise–sunset; no fees or permits required. The MTA runs buses along Dulaney Valley Rd. and crosses Seminary Ave.; for a schedule, call 410-539-5000 or 866-RIDE-MTA or visit mta.maryland.gov.

**WHEELCHAIR ACCESS:** No

**MAPS:** USGS *Towson*; stationary trail map at trailhead

**FACILITIES:** None

**CONTACT:** 877-620-8367, dnr.maryland.gov /wildlife/Pages/publiclands/central/lochraven .aspx

**LOCATION:** Dulaney Valley Rd. and East Seminary Ave., Lutherville-Timonium

**COMMENTS:** The majority of the trail traffic is cyclists, but they tend to be considerate and usually alert you to their approach.

Cross over a small stream at 0.7 mile and then head slightly to the right into a grove of pine trees. This is part of the Glen Ellen Trail, and it is accordingly wide—only a thin strip made by tire tracks cuts a path in the middle. After another tenth of a mile, you'll come to a T-intersection. Turn right, keeping the water on your left, and stay right as the trail heads slightly uphill.

At 0.9 mile the trail runs to the water's edge. Shaded by mature pines, this nice spot stays cool even on a hot day. For the next 0.5 mile, the trail runs along the edge of the reservoir, following its natural contours. At 1.4 miles the trail moves away from the reservoir and rejoins the Glen Ellen Trail; this is the edge of the watershed property, and you'll see a few private homes to the right as you head left.

Immediately cross over a swiftly moving stream filled with big concrete slabs and head uphill. At the junction at 1.5 miles, turn left; at 1.7 miles take the narrow foot trail to the left. You'll parallel a very small creek to your left. The reservoir soon comes back into view through the woods. This trail ends at the water's edge and affords some magnificent views of the reservoir. Head back and take a left at the first opportunity (200 feet from the water's edge). For the next 2 miles, the trail literally is the reservoir edge.

Along this section, you'll pass through nice pine groves and over small creeks (where fish and frogs abound) and riparian buffers where lily pads and other aquatic plants grow. At a Y-intersection, head left. Expect to see many white-tailed deer leaping about. At 2.8 miles and then again at 3 miles, you'll see the remains of two dog burial sites. Another small rock pile with a cross on top sits just beyond. One couldn't wish for a nicer final resting place.

At 3.6 miles the trail heads abruptly uphill over a clear stream. Rocks and ferns dominate the banks, and trees dangle their roots over the water. As you go uphill, the ecosystem changes drastically. Alongside the mica-flecked trail, the pines fall away and are replaced by oaks, sycamores, maples, and beeches. When you reach the top of the hill at 3.8 miles, turn right on the Glen Ellen Trail to begin your return.

# Loch Raven Reservoir: Glen Ellen–Seminary Road

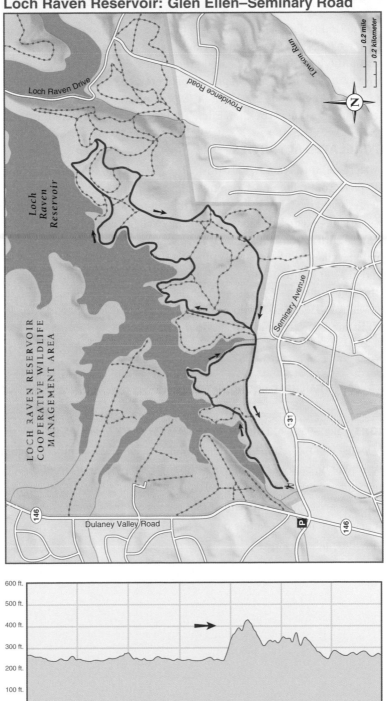

Here the trail is very wide and rocky, full of exposed roots, with lots of fallen, decaying tree trunks and ferns on both sides. At 4.6 miles a few private homes begin to appear on the left. You'll see cleared areas that delineate the edge of the watershed property and the beginning of private property, an occasional stand of bamboo, and some cuts in the woods on the right. More and more backyards appear as you descend the final section of the Glen Ellen Trail and return to the trailhead at 7 miles.

## NEARBY/RELATED ACTIVITIES

The **Fire Museum of Maryland** (1301 York Road, 410-321-7500, firemuseummd.org) houses 40 pieces of firefighting apparatus dating from 1822. The museum, which also has the largest working telegraph system in the United States, is open year-around on Saturdays, 10 a.m.–4 p.m. Head south on Dulaney Valley Road and turn right onto Seminary Avenue. Turn left onto York Road, and The Fire Museum is 0.75 mile on the left.

**Hampton National Historic Site** (410-823-1309, nps.gov/hamp), a stately home completed in 1790, is also within easy driving distance. Built with a fortune amassed during the Revolutionary War, the site boasts extensive gardens. Head south on Dulaney Valley Road from Seminary Avenue; go three blocks and turn left onto Hampton Estate Lane. The entrance is on the right.

• • • • • • • • • • • • • • • • • • • • • • • •

**GPS TRAILHEAD COORDINATES** N39° 25.521'   W76° 35.658'

**DIRECTIONS** Take I-95 N 11 miles to I-695 W. Then go 7.5 miles on I-695 W to Exit 27 (Dulaney Valley Road). Go north five blocks and turn left onto Seminary Avenue (after Meadowcroft Lane); park immediately on the right shoulder in front of the Church of Latter-Day Saints. Carefully cross Dulaney Valley Road and pick up the dirt path paralleling Seminary Avenue; follow the path until it comes out to Seminary Avenue and then quickly ducks back into the woods on the left. Two orange posts strung with a steel cable mark the trailhead.

This hike features beautiful vistas of Loch Raven Reservoir.

**FOLLOW THIS POPULAR** route to Merryman Point, where the reservoir spreads out in several directions.

## DESCRIPTION

From the parking area, you'll see two primary trailheads on your right and left and an overgrown trail in the middle. The one on the right leads straight down to the reservoir but peters out with no clear maintained path on which to continue. The one in the middle—this hike's original trailhead—is closed and quite overgrown. To begin your hike to Merryman Point, take the wide, well-maintained fire road on your left heading west—don't worry, you won't stay on it for long. At just under 0.25 mile, you'll see a trail split off to your right; this is the yellow trail, though you won't see any blazes for quite awhile. Take this narrow dirt path surrounded by ferns, and 0.1 mile later you'll cross over a footbridge. Note that mountain bikers also frequent the yellow trail. Oak, beech, sycamore, and tulip poplar trees populate the hillside, and spicebush abounds as well.

At just over 1 mile, you'll rejoin the fire road briefly. Turn right, and then make another immediate right to jump back on the yellow trail, which will lead you closer to the reservoir. At 1.3 miles the trail widens a bit, and you'll see your first yellow

**DISTANCE & CONFIGURATION:** 7.6-mile out-and-back

**DIFFICULTY:** Moderate–strenuous

**SCENERY:** Loch Raven Reservoir, upland forest

**EXPOSURE:** Shady

**TRAFFIC:** Moderate

**TRAIL SURFACE:** Packed dirt, crushed rock

**HIKING TIME:** 3.5 hours

**DRIVING DISTANCE:** 26 miles

**ELEVATION GAIN:** 280' at trailhead, 455' at high point

**ACCESS:** Sunrise–sunset; no fees or permits required

**WHEELCHAIR ACCESS:** No

**MAPS:** USGS *Towson*

**FACILITIES:** None

**CONTACT:** 877-620-8367, dnr.maryland.gov /wildlife/Pages/publiclands/central/lochraven .aspx

**LOCATION:** Dulaney Valley Rd. (just after Old Bosley Rd.), Cockeysville

**COMMENTS:** Parking at the Dulaney Valley parking area can be limited in the early morning when anglers and hikers share the few spots available.

blaze. At 1.5 miles head downhill. At the T-intersection at the bottom of the hill, turn left (north) onto Merryman's Mill Trail.

The reservoir soon comes into view on your right. At 1.7 miles you'll cross over a little stream and see a yellow blaze. You'll begin walking along a narrow ridge, with beautiful views of the water, though in summer you'll have quite a few tulip poplars and oaks to gaze through. At just under 1.9 miles, still heading north, you'll cross over a bridge and soon come to a three-way intersection, with the original fire road going left and right. Turn right, walking northeast.

This wide, more level, crushed rock trail heads downhill and crosses a beautiful little stream at 2.3 miles. Just on the other side of the stream, you'll see a trail to your right. This trail parallels the trail you'll take just ahead and is an option if you don't mind a little bushwhacking, depending on the level of maintenance at the time. To continue on our path, bypass this trail and take the next right, heading east. The reservoir and Dulaney Valley Bridge will come into view.

At 2.6 miles you'll reach another junction. The main fire road branches left and seems the obvious choice to follow, but head right (northeast) to go toward Merryman Point. In 0.2 mile you'll come to another intersection; you'll be turning left to continue the trail, but first go straight to take in a beautiful view of Loch Raven Reservoir.

Return to the intersection when you're ready and turn right (northeast). You'll continue to skirt through the woods along the edge of the reservoir, and in many places, a mere foot or two separates you from the water. Soon, you'll come to a clearing with beautiful views of the reservoir—perfect for a picnic. When you're ready, continue straight, walking along the water's edge. At just over 3 miles, you'll arrive at a Y-intersection and veer left (west). The trail is a little overgrown in summer, but you'll see a discernible path. At 3.2 miles you'll see a trail leading back to the fire road on your left, but continue straight; when the trail splits again at 3.6 miles, head left.

At just under 3.7 miles, you'll reach a power line cut. Continue straight, and in 0.1 mile you'll come to a carpet of pine needles. Here you can see wide expanses of

## Loch Raven Reservoir: Merryman Point

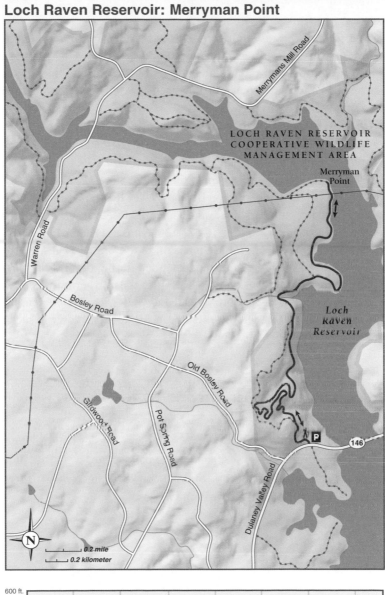

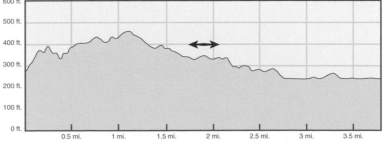

the reservoir to both the east and west. This is Merryman Point, which gives the trail its name. At this point, I recommend retracing your steps back to the starting point. The trail continues on and eventually pops out at Warren Road, but the scenery doesn't change much and some portions aren't as well marked or maintained.

## NEARBY/RELATED ACTIVITIES

The **Fire Museum of Maryland** (1301 York Road, 410-321-7500, firemuseummd.org) houses 40 pieces of firefighting apparatus dating from 1822. The museum, which also has the largest working telegraph system in the United States, is open year-around on Saturdays, 10 a.m.–4 p.m. Head south on Dulaney Valley Road and turn right onto Seminary Avenue. Turn left onto York Road, and The Fire Museum is 0.75 mile on the left.

**Hampton National Historic Site** (410-823-1309, nps.gov/hamp), a stately home completed in 1790 and once the largest mansion in the United States, is also within easy driving distance. Built with a fortune amassed during the Revolutionary War, the site boasts extensive gardens on what was once the northernmost slave-holding plantation in the country. Head south on Dulaney Valley Road from Seminary Avenue; go three blocks and turn left onto Hampton Estate Lane. You will see the mansion and grounds entrance on the right.

• • • • • • • • • • • • • • • • • • • • • • • •

**GPS TRAILHEAD COORDINATES** N39° 27.764'   W76° 35.183'

**DIRECTIONS** Take I-95 N 11 miles to I-695 W. Then go 7.5 miles on I-695 W to Exit 27 (Dulaney Valley Road) and go north 3.5 miles. The parking area is on the left just after Old Bosley Road and just before the bridge over Loch Raven Reservoir. The trail begins just beyond the parking area at the edge of the woods.

The steel Loch Raven Reservoir bridge was built in 1923. You'll hear cars traversing it at points along your hike. *Photo by Evan Balkan*

**THIS RELATIVELY UNVISITED**—and beautiful—section of Loch Raven Reservoir does its best impression of Gunpowder Falls State Park's Wildlands.

## DESCRIPTION

You'll find a number of trail choices all along this hike. Wide and prominent trails parallel each other along the hills. Generally, there are three options: high, middle, and water level. This hike stays fairly level and takes the middle road (a fire road), keeping the reservoir a few hundred feet to the right below. To start the hike, cross a small feeder stream to get to the fire road.

The scenery is immediately beautiful: sloping hills to the left, studded with mature beech trees, and an abundance of wading birds as the reservoir widens on the right. With lots of rock, moss, and ferns, the area looks a bit more like the wild sections of Gunpowder Falls State Park than typical Loch Raven scenery. You might, however, be a bit startled by a low growling noise in the distance; this is the sound of cars going over the steel bridge on Warren Road. Despite the noise, the bridge's graceful span over the reservoir is a lovely sight.

Follow the contours of the reservoir, as well as its feeder streams, making a wide leftward curve around the first one at 0.4 mile. Cross over the little valley stream flowing through a massive metal tube. Just beyond the stream, you'll arrive at a three-way

**DISTANCE & CONFIGURATION:** 4.8-mile out-and-back

**DIFFICULTY:** Moderate

**SCENERY:** Upland forest, rock outcrops, Loch Raven Reservoir

**EXPOSURE:** Shady

**TRAFFIC:** Light

**TRAIL SURFACE:** Packed dirt

**HIKING TIME:** 1.5 hours

**DRIVING DISTANCE:** 27 miles

**ELEVATION GAIN:** 238' at trailhead, 450' at high point

**ACCESS:** Sunrise–sunset; no fees or permits required

**WHEELCHAIR ACCESS:** No

**MAPS:** USGS *Towson* and *Cockeysville*

**FACILITIES:** None

**CONTACT:** 877-620-8367, dnr.maryland.gov /wildlife/Pages/publiclands/central/lochraven .aspx

**LOCATION:** Warren Rd. (just after Bosley Rd.), Cockeysville

**COMMENTS:** Some fantastic trails offer up spectacular beauty in the extreme western sections of Loch Raven Reservoir. They are tantalizingly close to the hike described here, but unfortunately are blocked off from this hike by the wide arm of Western Run as it flows into Loch Raven Reservoir. See Nearby/Related Activities on page 134 for instructions on reaching them.

intersection where you can go left uphill, straight ahead, or right down to the water. Take the middle path (the left one eventually comes out in the same place you're headed once you round the ridge). But if you want to head to the water, this is a good opportunity to do so. In that case, hug the feeder stream all the way to the reservoir. Just beware: the trail eventually ends, and you'll either have to backtrack or make your way uphill through the forest, neither of which is such a terrible prospect, of course.

Back on the fire road, you'll have yet another opportunity to head down to the water at the next trail junction. The same deal applies as before—the trail eventually peters out at the water's edge. Continuing straight, you'll come to another trail junction and veer left. The trail heads up and down gradually among moss- and lichen-covered rocks and boulders. Towering poplars and pretty little rock outcrops line the way. These outcrops rarely give you a clear view of the reservoir, but they tend to be wild and beautiful nonetheless.

Continuing on, the landscape becomes even rockier, and ferns and pines flank the trail. Head straight uphill into a pristine forest with mountain laurel, azalea, and lots of birdsong. Follow the trail around another feeder stream, and then, at 1.8 miles, come to the carcass of an abandoned car. The trail continues past it but soon heads out of the reservoir property, so instead turn around and you'll see a trail heading into the woods on your left; take that, heading downhill. Because you're now off the fire road, the trail narrows, as it's not as well used. (When we hiked this section, there was a huge downed tree we had to navigate around, and there's no telling how quickly it may be removed.) At 2.4 miles you'll come to a feeder stream covered by some old railroad ties. Beyond them, the trail dies. This is where Western Run—to the right—cuts you off from the beautiful trails just to the north. Instead of attempting a difficult crossing of Western Run and a serious bushwhack if it's summertime,

## Loch Raven Reservoir: Northwest Area Trails

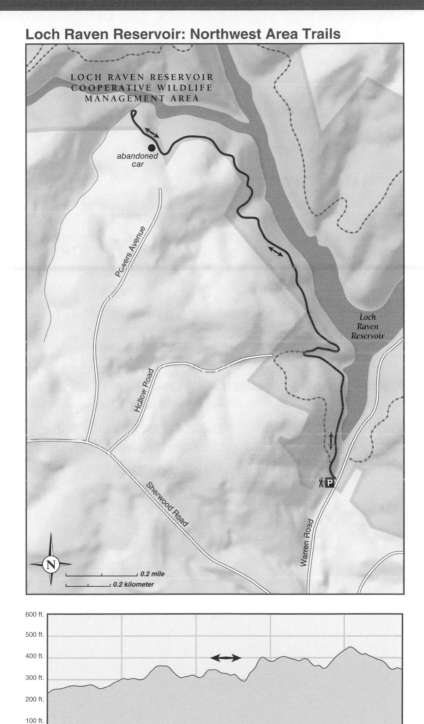

LOCH RAVEN RESERVOIR
COOPERATIVE WILDLIFE
MANAGEMENT AREA

*abandoned car*

Powers Avenue

Hollow Road

*Loch Raven Reservoir*

Sherwood Road

Warren Road

N

0.2 mile
0.2 kilometer

600 ft.
500 ft.
400 ft.
300 ft.
200 ft.
100 ft.
0 ft.

0.5 mi.      1 mi.      1.5 mi.      2 mi.

133

simply backtrack to your car and make the short drive to those other trails—see Nearby/Related Activities below.

To get back to your car, turn around and go left almost immediately. Parallel the stream on the left, and then head precipitously uphill, making a little loop here. More pristine beeches abound. You'll reach the portion where you just were in 0.1 mile; take a left here to backtrack.

## NEARBY/RELATED ACTIVITIES

To reach the western trails described previously by car, take Warren Road west back to York Road and turn right. Turn right onto Ashland Road. When Ashland swings to the left and becomes Paper Mill Road, take a right (at Ashland Presbyterian Church) to stay on Ashland. Keep on Ashland until it ends at the Ashland North Central Railroad (NCR) Trail parking area. Follow the NCR for 0.25 mile to a rightward cut through an easy and prominent path. This section offers roughly 3 miles of relatively easy but rewarding trails covering the beautiful section of Loch Raven Reservoir south of Paper Mill Road.

• • • • • • • • • • • • • • • • • • • • • • • • • •

**GPS TRAILHEAD COORDINATES** N39° 28.866'    W76° 36.911'

**DIRECTIONS** Take I-95 N 11 miles to I-695 W. Stay on I-695 for 9.5 miles, and then take I-83 N 4 miles to Exit 18 (Warren Road). Go east 1.7 miles to the gravel turnoff area on the right. On foot, cross the road and the trailhead is just on the other side, past the orange cable.

This pond surrounded by towering hemlocks at Oregon Ridge Park is the perfect spot for a break.
*Photo by Evan Balkan*

**HIKE UP AND DOWN** hills in one of the Baltimore area's most popular parks, well known for its annual Fourth of July celebration, cross-country skiing trails, swimming beach, restaurant, and theater.

## DESCRIPTION

Because you're starting from the nature center, it makes sense to stop in for a moment or two. Inside, you'll find live animals—turtles, snakes, a bee colony, and amphibians, as well as stuffed owls, foxes, elk, European starlings, and woodpeckers.

If you're facing the entrance of the nature center, head toward the long wooden bridge to the left to start your hike; pick up a brochure and follow the self-guided nature trail before you cross the bridge. From the bridge, look out over the valley below to see what's left of the iron ore pit from the mid-1800s. This mined pit yielded primarily goethite, one of the main ingredients in the manufacture of pig iron. Now you can see American chestnut trees growing here; a plague wiped out more than 95% of these trees east of the Mississippi River, making them rare today.

Head right after the wooden bridge onto the red-blazed Loggers Trail. You'll understand how it got its name when you see a cleared section along the slope of the hill above the nature center.

**DISTANCE & CONFIGURATION:** 4.75-mile loop

**DIFFICULTY:** Moderate

**SCENERY:** Upland forest, Baisman Run, historical structures

**EXPOSURE:** Shady

**TRAFFIC:** Moderate

**TRAIL SURFACE:** Packed dirt

**HIKING TIME:** 2 hours

**DRIVING DISTANCE:** 28 miles

**ELEVATION GAIN:** 400' at trailhead, 625' at high point

**ACCESS:** March–October, sunrise–sunset; November–February, 8 a.m.–5 p.m.; no fees or permits required

**WHEELCHAIR ACCESS:** The paved Marble Quarry Loop begins to the right of the nature center.

**MAPS:** USGS *Cockeysville;* trail maps available at nature center and online at oregonridgenature center.org/trailmap.html

**FACILITIES:** Restrooms in nature center and lodge, swimming beach, playgrounds, restaurant, theater

**CONTACT:** 410-887-1818, baltimorecountymd.gov /Agencies/recreation/countyparks/mostpopular /oregonridgelodge/index.html and oregonridgenaturecenter.org

**LOCATION:** 13555 Beaver Dam Rd., Cockeysville

**COMMENTS:** The nature center is open Sunday– Tuesday, 9 a.m.–5 p.m. No bikes are allowed on the trails. Dogs must be leashed.

After 900 feet the trail splits at the tan-blazed Ridge Trail, which takes a higher elevation than the Loggers Trail; the two link after 0.3 mile. For a more interesting trek, where coyotes have been seen, turn right, following the Loggers Trail. At 0.3 mile you'll begin to parallel a stream on the right that cuts through the center of the valley; hills rise on either side of you. At 0.6 mile the trail heads uphill and soon becomes rather precipitous. It's very rocky and rooty, which makes it tough to hike in ice and snow. At a T-intersection at 0.8 mile, turn right and head toward the red blazes (the Ridge Trail is to the left). Over the last 0.5 mile you've gained more than 200 feet of elevation.

At 0.9 mile you'll come to and pass through the first of four gas line cuts. When you enter the woods on the other side, at 1 mile, turn right onto the Shortcut Trail, as the Loggers Trail begins to loop back to the nature center.

The Shortcut Trail makes a gradual descent through a grove of ferns before it links with the yellow-blazed Ivy Hill Trail at 1.2 miles. Turn right onto the Ivy Hill Trail. Come to another gas line cut at 1.4 miles, and after 100 feet, you'll be back in the woods.

At 1.6 miles low-lying bushes and pines make an appearance. Many hawks inhabit this area. The trail descends, heads left, and becomes rocky again. Many of the rocks shine with quartz and feldspar. Heavy rains may wash out this section a bit.

Suddenly, you will hear the sound of running water as Baisman Run appears on the right. A wooden bridge goes over the run, but stay on the trail—you'll cross the run several times over the next 0.5 mile.

Come to a stationary map kiosk at 1.75 miles and head left up the railroad ties to the pond. After the pond, you'll soon see a sign for the S. James Campbell Trail, which also has yellow blazes. Despite the two names, this and the Ivy Hill Trail are actually the same, so if you stay on yellow-blazed paths, you'll be fine. At 1.9 miles cross the quick-moving but shallow Baisman Run on a series of rocks.

# Oregon Ridge Park

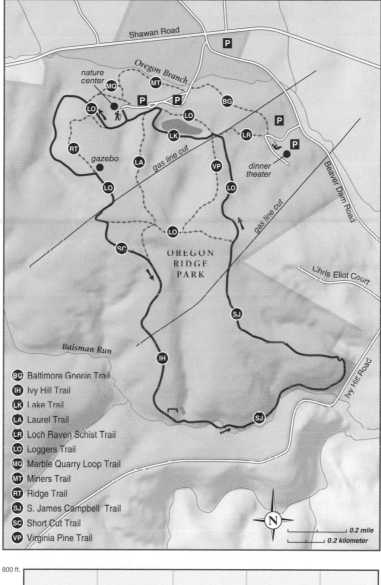

Shawan Road

nature center

Oregon Branch

gazebo

gas line cut

OREGON
RIDGE
PARK

dinner theater

gas line cut

Baisman Run

Beaver Dam Road

Chris Eliot Court

Ivy Hill Road

**BG** Baltimore Gneiss Trail
**IH** Ivy Hill Trail
**LK** Lake Trail
**LA** Laurel Trail
**LR** Loch Raven Schist Trail
**LO** Loggers Trail
**MQ** Marble Quarry Loop Trail
**MT** Miners Trail
**RT** Ridge Trail
**SJ** S. James Campbell Trail
**SC** Short Cut Trail
**VP** Virginia Pine Trail

N

0.2 mile
0.2 kilometer

800 ft.
700 ft.
600 ft.
500 ft.
400 ft.
300 ft.
200 ft.

1 mi.    2 mi.    3 mi.    4 mi.

137

When you see a trail straight ahead up the hill, take a left; a sign points you again to the S. James Campbell Trail. Cross Baisman Run again; there are fewer rocks here, so you may get a bit wet. The trail gets tighter and woodsier, but it soon opens up again as you walk beside Baisman Run, heading downstream. Cross the stream again at 2.1 miles with the aid of several large rocks, then cross yet again about 70 feet later.

At 2.3 miles the trail heads uphill to the left as Baisman Run turns right. Ivy Hill Road appears through the woods to the right. You're skirting the park boundary here, but you won't see or hear much traffic, and you'll soon head away from the road again as you go uphill. It's very steep here; you'll gain more than 200 feet of elevation quickly. Go through another gas line cut, and at 3 miles turn right to follow the Loggers Trail once again. Go downhill into a section that is thickly wooded, much more so than the top of the hill on Ivy Hill Trail.

At 4.2 miles you'll reach the final gas line cut and make a left, walking west uphill for 100 feet. You have two choices to return to the trailhead. The first is the more direct Loggers Trail, which you'll see first. This descends steeply toward the lake and allows you to skirt the lake on the right, walking through the recreation area. If it's swimming season (April–October), you'll hear people playing in the water.

For a more interesting return trip, just a few steps farther up the gas line cut, turn left on the orange-blazed Lake Trail. Follow it as it winds around the lake and crosses a wooden bridge. At 4.5 miles head up a log staircase and reach the parking lot at 4.75 miles. Turn left to return to the trailhead.

Before you leave, check out the re-created Oregon Furnace Town, just downhill to the right of the nature center entrance. The Tenant House Museum features historical exhibits on woodsman's tools and clothing worn by the men who mined the pits here in the 1800s. Approximately 225 people lived here, mostly Irish and German immigrants and emancipated slaves.

## NEARBY/RELATED ACTIVITIES

Check out the **Pennsylvania Dutch Market** (open Thursday–Saturday, 11121 York Road, padutchmarketcockeysville.com). To get there, turn right onto Shawan Road and then make another right onto York Road.

• • • • • • • • • • • • • • • • • • • • • • • •

**GPS TRAILHEAD COORDINATES** N39° 29.596'   W76° 41.495'

**DIRECTIONS** Take I-95 N 11 miles to I-695 W. Stay on I-695 W 9.5 miles, and then take I-83 N 5.5 miles to Exit 20. Follow Shawan Road west to Beaver Dam Road. Turn left and follow signs to the park entrance. Once inside the park, head right at the split in the road to go to the nature center; park in the nature center parking area. The trail starts at the end of the long wooden bridge to the left of the nature center.

Little Falls pours over rocks. *Photo by Evan Balkan*

**CHOOSE WHAT LENGTH** hike you want to take, and go—well-spaced turnaround points and parking areas make this the perfect trail for anything from a quick walk to an all-day trek.

## DESCRIPTION

This popular rail-trail is a treasure. Area residents know it as the NCR (Northern Central Railroad) Trail, but its official name is the Torrey C. Brown Rail Trail, in honor of Maryland's third Department of Natural Resources secretary and the driving force behind development of the former railway, which was initially dedicated in 1984. It's one of several hikes in this book that make up a portion of the East Coast Greenway, a 3,000-mile-long system of trails connecting Maine to Florida. European settlers came here as early as the 1600s and by the mid-1800s established a rail line bisecting the stream valley and linking Baltimore with the northern industrial states.

The trail actually begins 0.4 mile to the south, at the Ashland parking area; however, the Paper Mill parking area is much larger, and the first 0.4 mile, from Ashland to Paper Mill, really only serves as a preview of what's to come. That said, if you do begin at Ashland, you'll pass some paths that lead to the edge of Loch Raven Reservoir on the right, affording some spectacular views. However, Paper Mill is your much better bet to find parking.

**DISTANCE & CONFIGURATION:** 19.2-mile point-to-point

**DIFFICULTY:** Easy–strenuous

**SCENERY:** Gunpowder River, Little Falls and Bee Tree Run, forest, riparian buffers, historical structures

**EXPOSURE:** More shade than sun in summer, reverse in winter

**TRAFFIC:** Moderate–heavy near parking areas

**TRAIL SURFACE:** Crushed rock

**HIKING TIME:** 7.5 hours for entire trail one-way

**DRIVING DISTANCE:** 28 miles

**ELEVATION GAIN:** 280' at trailhead, 800' at high point

**ACCESS:** Sunrise–sunset; no fees or permits required

**WHEELCHAIR ACCESS:** ADA accessible, but the trail is crushed rock, so it may be difficult.

**MAPS:** USGS *Hereford, Phoenix,* and *New Freedom;* map of the Maryland section of the trail online at ncrtrailsnails.com/ncr_trail.html

**FACILITIES:** Most parking areas have restrooms; some have water fountains.

**CONTACT:** 410-592-2897, dnr.maryland.gov /publiclands/Pages/central/tcb.aspx

**LOCATION:** 1300 Paper Mill Rd., Cockeysville

**COMMENTS:** Plentiful parking areas along the route make choosing shorter or longer lengths easy. If you're hiking the full length, leave a shuttle car at the end so you'll only be taking the trail one-way.

Heading north from Paper Mill, you'll pass the remains of a lime kiln at 0.5 mile. There's a beautiful overlook soon after, with the Gunpowder River flowing underneath. The trail is wide but well shaded because of the mature-tree canopy. While you'll certainly see walkers and hikers, and even people pushing strollers, the majority of the trail traffic consists of bicyclists.

You'll reach the Phoenix parking area at 1.5 miles. After another mile, you'll see where the trail was blasted through the limestone. Fortunately, enough time has passed that these rock walls are no longer naked and exposed: straggly roots of clinging trees that perch atop the rocks have taken hold, and wildflowers pepper the area, lending splashes of white, yellow, and purple in summer. At 2.6 miles be on the lookout for a natural-rock amphitheater to the right, a bit off the trail; it's a stunning spot.

You'll reach the Sparks parking area at 3.2 miles. The Sparks Bank Nature Center, located in the old bank building visible from the trail, is open on summer weekends 10 a.m.–5 p.m. At 5.2 miles there's a nice rural scene with a bridge over the river and a barn to the left. This section is particularly beautiful, and, because it's between parking areas, it tends to not be busy either.

Cross Corbett Road (not a parking area) at 5.7 miles. Soon, there's another pretty overlook, at just under 6 miles. The Monkton parking area arrives at 6.5 miles. It's a popular spot, often serving as a meet-up place for tubing and hiking trips. Here you'll find telephones, restrooms, rest areas, a café, an art gallery, and other shops. Monkton dates to the 1730s. The restored 1898 Monkton Train Station serves as a museum, gift shop, and ranger station; it's open Wednesday–Sunday 9 a.m.–4 p.m. in summer.

At 7 miles you'll pass a beautiful old collapsed stone building, part of the mid-19th-century settlement of Pleasant Valley. This is a popular put-in spot for

## Torrey C. Brown Rail Trail

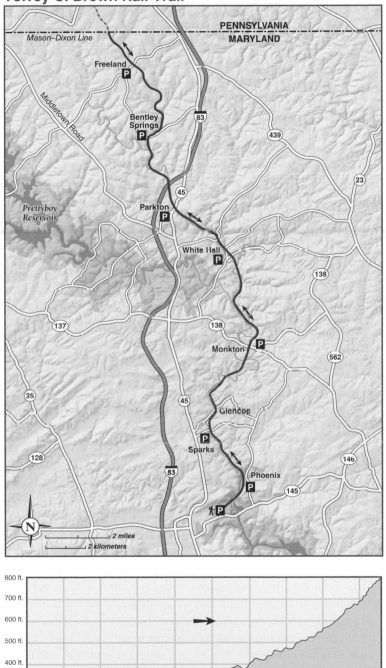

tubing. There's a railroad abutment over the river at 8.3 miles. Cross the lily-studded Little Falls twice; this is yet another beautiful stretch of the trail. Pass some electrical-light signals from the 1930s and arrive at the White Hall parking area at 10.6 miles, roughly halfway up the trail.

As you head north from the White Hall parking area, the narrow Little Falls to the left dominates the scenery. Cross Graystone Road at 11 miles. Soon after, cross a wooden bridge over Little Falls. At 11.4 miles you'll cross the water again and have great views of Little Falls pouring over the rocks below. As you parallel the falls on the left, heading upstream, thick woods and ferns along the hillsides surround you. Come to a put-and-take trout-fishing area and bench at 11.8 miles. Soon after, at 12 miles, you'll find a little overlook area that provides a great view of the water spilling over the rocks.

After crossing a bridge at 12.7 miles, you'll come to the Parkton parking area, which has a small general store on the left and an old train depot on the right. You'll soon see I-83 ahead; it gets a bit loud for a moment, but you'll soon leave the highway behind and regain serenity after you walk under the I-83 ramp.

Cross Walker Road at 14.2 miles; the next parking area is Bentley Springs, a little more than a mile away. Enjoy the shaded stretch of trail beyond Walker Road; first you'll cross water and then the trail opens up, with a farmhouse up the hill on the right. Cross water again at 14.6 miles and come to a shaded bench just beyond. Mountain laurel abounds here, making this a truly lovely spot when the flowers are in bloom.

You'll reach Bentley Road at 15.1 miles; cross Bee Tree Run, and you'll see the Bentley Springs parking area just ahead, with restrooms and a public telephone. At 15.4 miles the trail gets very boggy, and you'll pass a nice marsh on the left where you're likely to see great blue herons, kingfishers, and mallards. Other prominent fauna along the trail includes beavers, monarch butterflies, white-tailed deer, flying squirrels, red foxes, raccoons, black snakes, and Eastern box turtles.

At 16.3 miles cross Bee Tree Road. Soon after, you'll cross what's left of an old railroad bridge. Watch out for occasional piles of horse manure—this section of the trail is used by equestrians from the nearby camp in Bee Tree Reserve.

The trail soon opens up in an area dominated by wildflowers and then plunges back into the woods; in fact, for the next mile, you'll see no sign of humanity aside from the trail and the folks you pass along it. Bee Tree Run, when it comes into view, is narrow and pretty tame in this section; a smattering of ferns winds up the hill on the left.

You'll reach the Freeland parking area, with a restroom, at 17.9 miles. The Pennsylvania state line is less than 2 miles away. As you walk away from Freeland, you'll see an open marshy area on the right. Soon you'll cross into Oakland, where there's a beautiful old barn to the left. As the trail opens up again, you'll get a good sense of the rural nature of the immediate area. At 19.1 miles the trail begins to resemble the section at White Hall, with blasted rock and clinging tree roots.

At 19.2 miles you'll reach the Mason–Dixon Line, created between 1763 and 1767 to settle a dispute between the Maryland and Pennsylvania colonies. Stones marking the line carry William Penn's seal on the north and Lord Baltimore's on the south. Here you'll find benches and a rest area—a perfect place to relax, eat your lunch, and enjoy that particular thrill one gets from walking from one state into another.

If you're feeling incredibly ambitious, you can keep going. The York County (Pennsylvania) park system picks up where the Torrey C. Brown leaves off, following the railbed another 20 miles north into York.

## NEARBY/RELATED ACTIVITIES

For activities near the southern portion of the trail, see the hike profiles for **Loch Raven Reservoir: Northwest Area Trails** (page 131) and **Oregon Ridge Park** (page 135).

• • • • • • • • • • • • • • • • • • • • • • • • • •

**GPS TRAILHEAD COORDINATES** N39° 30.108'   W76° 38.022'

**DIRECTIONS** See maps for directions to individual parking areas. For the Paper Mill parking area (where this hike begins), take I-95 N 11 miles to I-695 W. Stay on I-695 for 9.5 miles, and then take I-83 N 5.5 miles to Exit 20 and go east on Shawan Road. Turn right onto York Road. Go 0.3 mile and turn left onto Ashland/Paper Mill Road. The parking area is 1 mile on the left.

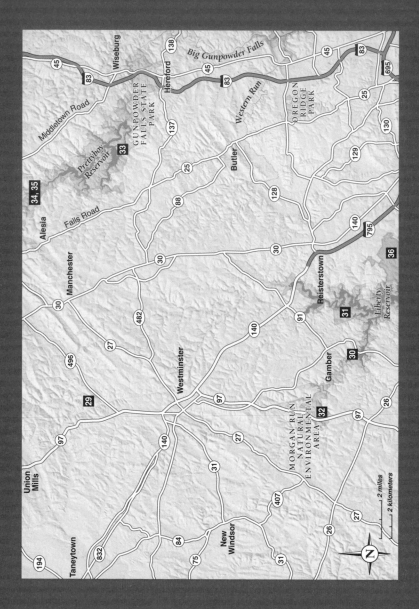

# NORTHWESTERN SUBURBS

Lake Hashawha provides ample opportunities for birding and fishing.

**START AT BEAR BRANCH** Nature Center and stroll through 10 different examples of environmentally friendly land usages.

## DESCRIPTION

Enter the trailhead and follow the sign to the pavilion. Follow the crushed rock trail down to the bottom of the hill and into an open area. You'll come to the pavilion on your left and see a trail continuing into the woods in front of you, but head right (southwest) through the open field. A gravel road heads right, but veer left and you'll see a sign pointing to the white-blazed Vista Trail. At the three-way intersection, with a pond to your right, take a left up the hill, following the white blazes.

You'll be on a wide dirt path surrounded mostly by short oaks and dogwoods. At the top of the hill, you'll come to a bench, and then at 0.4 mile and again at 0.5 mile, trails head left back to the pavilion area. Stay straight on the wide, well-maintained trail, heading uphill into a pine grove; the surrounding farmland lies beyond the pines. You'll pass another bench; soon the trail turns grassy and veers left as you emerge at a raptor pen at about 0.6 mile. A number of birds are here either because of injuries or because they have imprinted on humans.

The Vista Trail continues past the birdcages on your left, but instead take the gravel road toward the asphalt road, heading west. Turn right on the asphalt road; in about

**DISTANCE & CONFIGURATION:** 2.5-mile loop with short spur

**DIFFICULTY:** Moderate

**SCENERY:** Wildflower meadows, Bear Branch, raptors

**EXPOSURE:** More sun than shade

**TRAFFIC:** Moderate

**TRAIL SURFACE:** Dirt, rock, asphalt

**HIKING TIME:** 1–1.5 hours

**DRIVING DISTANCE:** 40 miles

**ELEVATION GAIN:** 710' at trailhead, 600' at low point

**ACCESS:** Sunrise–sunset on trails; no fees or permits required. Bear Branch Nature Center

open Wednesday–Saturday 11 a.m.–5 p.m. and Sunday noon–5 p.m.

**WHEELCHAIR ACCESS:** At Bear Branch Nature Center

**MAPS:** USGS *Manchester;* trail maps also available in Bear Branch Nature Center or online at ccgovernment.carr.org/ccg/mapserver4/gis /webpage/trails.html

**FACILITIES:** Water, restrooms, and playground at Bear Branch Nature Center

**CONTACT:** 410-386-3580, ccgovernment.carr.org /ccg/recpark/hashawha

**LOCATION:** 300 John Owings Rd., Westminster

**COMMENTS:** The Hashawha Residential Camp is closed to the public; please respect the no-entry areas, which designate the private rental area.

100 feet, you'll see yellow (Wilderness Trail) and green (Stream Trail) arrows pointing to the right. Straight ahead lies the restricted area of the Residential Hashawha Camp, a camp for Carroll County sixth-graders. Turn right to follow the trail signs and pass the cornfields, heading back into the woods. At 1.1 miles, just as the restored Martin Log Cabin comes into view, the Wilderness Trail heads right. Trails going north here head toward Saw Mill Road and are part of the Union Mills trail network.

Continue straight on the Stream Trail, passing the Martin Cabin and paralleling a wildflower meadow on the right. Another trail junction leads you to the Wilderness Trail on your right, but head left, following the green arrow, and walk through another wildflower meadow.

At 1.4 miles the trail veers left through an open field. You might need to step carefully, as it can become a bit soggy after heavy rains. When you cross the pasture, you'll come to a three-way intersection; follow the green arrow to the left to continue along the Stream Trail, paralleled by Bear Branch on your right.

At 1.6 miles you'll see a seating area to your right for nature demonstrations; this is a nice spot to walk down and take a closer look at Bear Branch. At 1.8 miles an old maple in a beautiful open area shades a picnic table by the creek. Head left here, going uphill with the stream on your right (the boardwalk straight ahead provides an alternative route that reconnects shortly). At 1.9 miles the trail opens up into a wildflower area. Veer right here, walking downhill, and you'll see Lake Hashawha. This lake is a restored wetland area, so be on the lookout for great blue herons, red-winged blackbirds, and belted kingfishers. Fishing is allowed with a Maryland fishing license, and docks allow easy access to the water; bluegills and green sunfish are common catches.

Continue walking with the lake to your left. When you reach the corner of the lake, a green marker points to your right, but make a left, keeping the lake on your

## Hashawha Environmental Appreciation Area at Bear Branch Nature Center

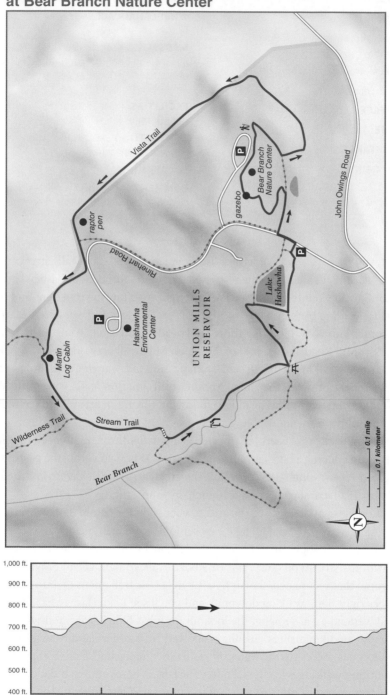

left. You'll pass through a grove of pines, and then come out onto a pavilion at 2 miles. Continue straight along the sidewalk, and when you reach the parking lot, head left up to Rinehart Road. Turn left, walking along the shoulder, and in just a few moments you'll see a sign welcoming you to Hashawha on your right. Turn right, taking care as you cross the road, and you'll see a marker for the white-blazed Vista Trail. At 2.1 miles you'll pass a gate, a park sign, and a bench. Continue around the gate on the wide, grassy trail.

At 2.2 miles be on the lookout for a trail junction. The most obvious trail continues straight (and to the nature center). To the right, a grassy trail leads to some birdhouses, but you should head left on the grassy trail leading uphill. Veer left when the trail splits, and go right 0.1 mile later to reach a paved trail with a bench. Turn left on the paved trail, which ends at a gazebo, where you can view examples of land usage that maintain the 10 healthy environments in the Hashawha Environmental Appreciation Area (HEAA): wildlife habitat, field strip cropping, grass waterway, contour strip cropping, grass diversion, lined outlet (rip-rap), pond, woodland, field border, and nontidal wetland. Continue past the gazebo, now walking on grass, and you'll come to the back of the nature center, which has exhibits on hundreds of butterflies, as well as live box turtles, and stuffed minks, deer, raccoons, and beavers.

## NEARBY/RELATED ACTIVITIES

HEAA sits within the Union Mills environmental area, which contains approximately 8 miles of hiking trails that aren't always as well maintained as those in Hashawha.

For sustenance after a hike at Hashawha, head south on MD 97 into downtown **Westminster.** Full of restaurants, antiques shops, and museums, Westminster is also surrounded by several beautiful vineyards: **Galloping Goose, Serpent Ridge,** and **Old Westminster Winery.** The **Maryland Wine Festival** takes place each September at the **Carroll County Farm Museum** grounds; for information, visit marylandwine.com. For the museum, check out ccgovernment.carr.org/ccg/farmmus.

• • • • • • • • • • • • • • • • • • • • • • • • • •

**GPS TRAILHEAD COORDINATES** N39° 38.824'    W76° 59.172'

**DIRECTIONS** Take I-95 south 3 miles to Exit 49B (I-695). Drive west 10 miles on I-695 to Exit 19 (I-795 W) and continue until I-795 ends at MD 140 (Baltimore Boulevard). Continue on MD 140 N for 12 miles to Westminster, and turn right onto MD 97 N, which becomes Littlestown Pike. Go 2.8 miles and then turn right onto John Owings Road. After 1 mile you'll see a WELCOME TO HASHAWHA AND BEAR BRANCH NATURE CENTER sign on the left; turn here and then take a right at the sign for the nature center. The trail begins to the left of the nature center, past the playground by the treeline. You'll see a sign for the Vista Trail and Pavilions.

View of Liberty Reservoir through the trees

**THIS HIKE WILL** give you a taste of Loch Raven Reservoir, but with fewer people.

## DESCRIPTION

You may not think that starting a hike on a fire road with busy MD 32 just above you is very pleasant, but you'll quickly move away from civilization. About 900 feet down the fire road (which can sometimes be completely overgrown with grass), you'll see another fire road heading downhill on your left. Take the road downhill, and at 0.25 mile you'll reach the reservoir and see a thick forest of white pines on the right.

The trail more or less follows the contours of the reservoir. As you walk along, notice the edge of the reservoir as you parallel it; heavy rainfall raises the water level and submerges the trunks of the trees, giving the area a look reminiscent of a cypress swamp. Ravens and red-winged blackbirds frequent this area.

The trails at Liberty Reservoir run uphill, away from the water a bit. This is because these trails have remained primarily fire roads, as opposed to singletrack for bikes. Because the fire roads run about 100 feet or so above the water, you will have many good views of the reservoir spreading out in several directions.

By 0.7 mile once again the trail runs through the pine forest and will continue to do so for a while. Cross a stream over a wooden bridge at 1.3 miles. Look for a bog and milkweed swaying in the breeze at 1.8 miles. Here you'll head up a steep

**DISTANCE & CONFIGURATION:** 7.2-mile loop

**DIFFICULTY:** Moderate

**SCENERY:** Liberty Reservoir, Morgan Run, Little Morgan Run, white pine plantations

**EXPOSURE:** Shady

**TRAFFIC:** Light

**TRAIL SURFACE:** Packed dirt

**HIKING TIME:** 2.5 hours

**DRIVING DISTANCE:** 30 miles

**ELEVATION GAIN:** 475' at trailhead, 560' at high point

**ACCESS:** Sunrise–sunset; no fees or permits required

**WHEELCHAIR ACCESS:** No

**MAPS:** USGS *Finksburg*

**FACILITIES:** None

**CONTACT:** 410-795-6151, dnr.maryland.gov /fisheries/Pages/hotspots/liberty.aspx

**LOCATION:** Sykesville Rd., Sykesville

**COMMENTS:** This hike includes a difficult river crossing at Little Morgan Run; expect wet feet in all but the lowest water levels.

hill, away from the reservoir, and arrive at a power line cut at the top of the hill at 2 miles. Walk toward the first tower you see, but before you reach it, head left down the middle of the open field. It's completely overgrown with only a slightly discernible path, but keep to the middle, and the trail will naturally veer left into the valley, where you'll hit the woods again at 2.6 miles.

You'll cross a stream and soon come to Morgan Run, a wide river with small rapids coursing over rocks. The trail is hard to distinguish here, but hug Morgan Run as you walk upstream. Eventually, you'll need to climb an embankment to continue along the trail until you reach London Bridge Road, a small rural road. Cross the bridge and immediately head back down the other side, walking downstream. At times, the trail is a bit eroded, so take care as you walk along these rocks. The narrow trail winds through an area forested mostly with oak trees. This section bears little resemblance to the previous 2 miles, highlighting the varied nature of this hike.

At a grouping of fir trees, you'll pass a marsh on the left; if you're walking in late spring or summer, the chorus of frogs will be almost deafening. Green blazes appear as you head away from the run; at just over 3 miles, you'll reach a junction, where you can go straight on the orange-blazed trail or right on the green-blazed trail. Head right, and you'll soon come to Poole Road, marked by a set of orange cables. Go left about 150 feet and reach a large parking area. On the left side, if you're facing the parking area, a green-blazed trail is marked by an orange cable. Take this trail back into the woods and through a white pine plantation. Once you enter the woods, you'll see a junction with a blue-blazed trail to your right and a green-blazed trail to your left; head left. Again, at just over 3.5 miles, you'll reach another junction and continue on the green-blazed trail.

Soon after, civilization comes into view, and you'll see a few houses on the right. Over the next 0.5 mile or so, you'll pass a bunch of trails leading off to the left—these all dead-end at the reservoir, so remain on the green-blazed trail. When you reach the end of a residential road to the right and a set of orange posts straight ahead, follow the orange posts, continuing straight alongside the narrow paved road

## Liberty Reservoir: Liberty West–Morgan Run

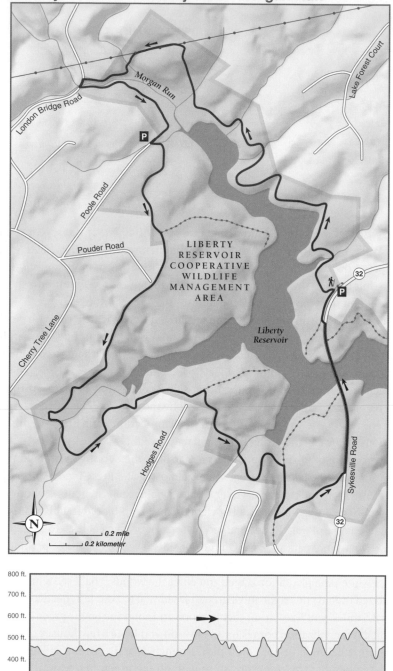

to the right. Though it's a bit disappointing to be passing backyards, if you look only left, it's all pines as far as you can see—and you'll probably hear the hammering of a woodpecker or two. Keep an eye out for red foxes as well. You'll soon see green blazes again along this portion of the trail. Bypass another trail to the left and head up a steep hill at 4.2 miles. At the top of the hill, you'll reach a Y-intersection and veer left, following the pink-blazed trail now.

The pink-blazed trail will take you to a stream valley and across a little stream. Immediately after, you'll come to Little Morgan Run. You might have difficulty crossing here without getting wet. If the water level is low, however, you should be able to cross relatively easily and stay dry.

On the other side of Little Morgan Run, the trail parallels a twisty little stream that empties into a marsh and then bleeds into the edge of the reservoir. At the junction at just under 5.6 miles, take a left on the pink-blazed trail to stay in the woods.

At just over 5.6 miles, you'll come to a three-way trail intersection; head right to continue on the pink-blazed trail and you'll soon reach another junction, where you turn right again. When you reach the top of the fire road, go left uphill (take care not to miss this hard left, or you'll be walking toward a neighborhood). You'll start to hear the traffic on MD 32 again. Take the narrow footpath through the woods and soon arrive at MD 32; walk carefully along the shoulder of the highway, taking extra care when you cross the Liberty Reservoir Bridge, as the shoulder narrows considerably. You'll find your car on the right on the other side of the bridge.

## NEARBY/RELATED ACTIVITIES

To the south, check out the **Hugg-Thomas Wildlife Management Area of Patapsco Valley State Park;** it is open to hikers on Sundays, mid-February–August (open to hunters only the rest of the year). Take MD 32 south to the first right over the Patapsco River and turn left onto Main Street and then right onto Forsythe Road. Also consider visiting **Morgan Run Natural Environmental Area** to the west (page 158) and **Piney Run Park** (page 211).

• • • • • • • • • • • • • • • • • • • • • • • • •

**GPS TRAILHEAD COORDINATES** N39° 26.297'   W76° 56.267'

**DIRECTIONS** Take I-95 S 3 miles to Exit 49B (I-695 W). Stay on I-695 W for 5 miles, and then take I-70 for 11 miles to Exit 80 and head north on MD 32. Go 10 miles to Liberty Reservoir Bridge. Cross the bridge and immediately look for the gravel parking area to the right. Carefully walk across MD 32 (it can be a bit treacherous) and head for the guardrail down the road to the right. The trail starts on the fire road at the bottom of the hill.

# 31 LIBERTY RESERVOIR:
## Middle Run Trail

One of the many stream crossings you'll make across Middle Run

**DESPITE THIS HIKE'S LOCATION** at Liberty Reservoir, it rarely offers views of the water itself. Nevertheless, it's arguably the prettiest and most diverse hike in the Liberty Reservoir watershed.

## DESCRIPTION

The wide, pine needle–covered trail heads left (south). Pine dominates the landscape, evidenced by the smell and innumerable needles underfoot. At just under 0.25 mile, you'll come to a four-way junction; turn right, moving away from the pines and into a forest of oak, poplar, mountain laurel, and redbud, filled with birdsong.

On the left at 0.4 mile, you'll pass a great rock outcrop rippling down the hill like a dinosaur's spine. When the trees are bare, the tip of the ridge offers a great view of the river valley. Mountain laurel lines both sides of the trail. Down the hill on the left, you'll see the edge of the reservoir, with a marshy buffer area between the reservoir's end and the trail. At 0.8 mile a rock outcrop appears on the right, along with a trail junction. Middle Run flows on the left, where you'll end up in a few miles.

Turn right at the junction to head gradually uphill, passing through a pine and spruce forest that supports a plentiful white-tailed deer population, at 1 mile. At 1.7 miles you'll see a power line cut straight ahead; turn left (turning right leads to another parking area at Deer Park Road, north of where you parked).

**DISTANCE & CONFIGURATION:** 3.75-mile out-and-back with loop

**DIFFICULTY:** Moderate

**SCENERY:** Middle Run, pine plantations, mixed hardwoods

**EXPOSURE:** Mostly shade

**TRAFFIC:** Light

**TRAIL SURFACE:** Packed dirt

**HIKING TIME:** 1.5 hours–2 hours

**DRIVING DISTANCE:** 25 miles

**ELEVATION GAIN:** 580' at trailhead, 425' at low point

**ACCESS:** Sunrise–sunset; no fees or permits required

**WHEELCHAIR ACCESS:** No

**MAPS:** USGS *Finksburg*

**FACILITIES:** None

**CONTACT:** 410-795-6151, dnr.maryland.gov /fisheries/Pages/hotspots/liberty.aspx

**LOCATION:** Deer Park Rd., Finksburg

**COMMENTS:** This hike requires crossing Middle Run four times, so consider wearing sturdy hiking sandals that dry quickly. Although the water is never too wide nor too deep, expect wet feet and legs, perhaps up to your knees.

The wide trail is shared with a little stream, making this portion of the route quite muddy. At 1.9 miles Middle Run appears. This decent-size crossing requires removing your shoes; take time to look in both directions, upstream and down, while you're crossing. The beautiful, meandering stream runs clean and clear. On the other side, continue straight ahead, moving gradually uphill through more pines. The pine plantation ends abruptly and gives way to oak and poplar, with a few flowering dogwoods here and there.

The trail splits again at 2.1 miles; this time go left. Mountain laurel dominates this section of the trip, and if you're lucky to catch it during spring bloom, you're in for a treat of white clustered flowers. You'll cross Middle Run a second time at 2.3 miles; again needing to ford the river. If you remove your shoes, don't lace them back up too tightly when you reach the other side—you'll be crossing the water again in 0.1 mile.

After you cross Middle Run the third time—this time a bit wider and deeper—you'll see blue blazes on some of the trees, but they promptly disappear. At 2.8 miles, after a little stream crossing (that doesn't require you to remove your shoes, finally!), you'll see a steep trail going straight up to the right, but you should continue on your current path to the left (southeast).

At 3 miles the main trail continues straight ahead, and a cut to the left leads back to the water; follow the cut and cross Middle Run for the fourth and final time. If you've somehow managed to make it this far without removing your shoes, you'll have to do it before crossing here, where the stream is wide. Be extra cautious walking over the rocks, which can be quite slick. Once across, turn right and backtrack. This time, when you reach the dragon's back rock outcrop, you may want to take the trail down to your right to enjoy views of the reservoir. Return to the parking area, remembering to take a left at the four-way crossing at 3.6 miles, before reaching the parking area at 3.75 miles.

## Liberty Reservoir: Middle Run Trail

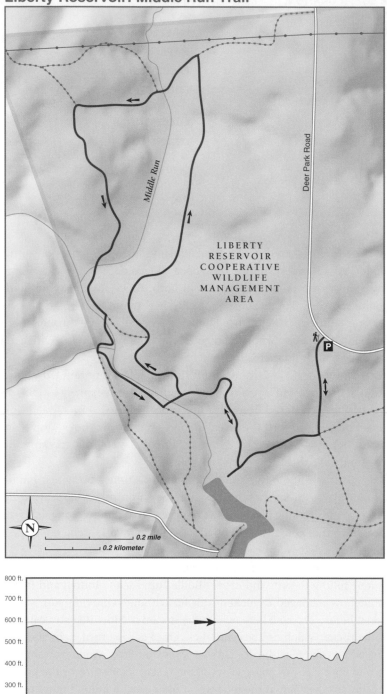

## NEARBY ACTIVITIES

If you're looking for more hiking, **Morgan Run Natural Environmental Area** is nearby to the west (page 158). From Liberty Reservoir, continue on Deer Park Road and turn left onto Gamber Road. Turn right onto Nicodemus Road, and then turn left onto MD 97 south. Look for Morgan Run on the left. If you're interested in antiques or a meal in a cozy restaurant, go to historic **Reisterstown,** which dates back to the mid-18th century; backtrack toward I-795, take a left onto Ivy Mill Road, and then turn right onto Westminster Pike, which turns into Main Street.

• • • • • • • • • • • • • • • • • • • • • • • •

**GPS TRAILHEAD COORDINATES** N39° 26.926'    W76° 53.803'

**DIRECTIONS** Take I-95 S 3 miles to Exit 49B (I-695 W). Stay on I-695 W for 10 miles to Exit 19 (I-795 W). Take Exit 7 (Franklin Boulevard), but head west to Nicodemus Road, just before you get to Franklin Boulevard. Nicodemus Road turns into Deer Park Road after Ivy Mill Road. Cross Liberty Reservoir Bridge and continue 1 mile to the big turn to the right; look for the gravel parking area on the left. At the parking area, two different trails lead down; both quickly link up to the same main wider trail, so you can take either one.

This Eastern American toad blends with its surroundings.

A field full of wildflowers borders this grassy trail.

**MORGAN RUN NATURAL** Environmental Area includes approximately 2,000 acres of natural land. The entire area has been blissfully left alone, with well-maintained trails but no unnecessary "improvements," making it a perfect place to get away from it all.

## DESCRIPTION

Numerous trails at Morgan Run, many of which are connector trails, provide various configurations for hiking. To make the longest hike, keep heading left whenever you come to intersecting trails. The map on the park's website can help you make better sense of the trails that head out in many directions.

The first thing you'll notice at Morgan Run is birds: songbirds flit about the tall trees, regenerating fields, and birdhouses; within the woods, woodpeckers and owls make their incessant noises; hawks and turkey vultures wheel above; and startlingly massive wild turkeys waddle over the trails.

At the first trail junction, head left into the woods; be on the alert for manure, evidence of the trail's equestrian traffic. Also be alert for ticks, which lurk in the tall grasses in the treeline buffer, and take extra time looking for and removing ticks from your clothing and body at the end of the hike.

**DISTANCE & CONFIGURATION:** 5.7 miles, 2 loops

**DIFFICULTY:** Easy–moderate

**SCENERY:** Mixed hardwoods, regenerating fields, stream valleys

**EXPOSURE:** Half shade and half sun

**TRAFFIC:** Light

**TRAIL SURFACE:** Packed dirt, grass

**HIKING TIME:** 2 hours

**DRIVING DISTANCE:** 34 miles

**ELEVATION GAIN:** 775' at trailhead, 620' at low point

**ACCESS:** Sunrise–sunset; no fees or permits required

**WHEELCHAIR ACCESS:** No

**MAPS:** USGS *Finksburg* and *Winfield;* also available online at dnr.maryland.gov/publiclands /Pages/central/morganrun.aspx

**FACILITIES:** None

**CONTACT:** 410-461-5005, dnr.maryland.gov /publiclands/Pages/central/morganrun.aspx

**LOCATION:**
Benrose Lane, Westminster

**COMMENTS:** Trails are typically mowed regularly, but if the weather has been rainy, it may be overgrown; a sign at the trailhead recommends waiting at least a day to hike after rain events. Regardless, waterproof boots will help in the muddy areas.

After 0.25 mile you'll be able to hear the traffic on MD 97 on the left, but a thick buffer of poplar, oak, maple, sassafras, ash, and dogwood prevents you from seeing it. Unfortunately, the trail continues toward MD 97, coming as close as 10 feet before heading away at a branch of Morgan Run, which at this point is not much more than a trickle. An overgrown foot trail heads toward the water, but go right instead on the obvious wide trail that leads uphill. As you head away from MD 97, the sounds of civilization fade away and isolation returns.

Look for some old stone foundations on the right at 0.6 mile. At 0.8 mile emerge into an opening where you have several options; again, head left. Deer favor this habitat. Clumps of isolated vegetation pock the land. Unfortunately, autumn olive, an invasive species, has found a home; in spring, you'll smell a pleasant scent reminiscent of lilac from its white flowers.

Some old abandoned silos sit on the left at 1.3 miles. Continue around the silos and swing back into the woods at 1.4 miles. When you emerge at the next clearing, head right to stay away from MD 97 (going straight will lead you to the same place but add 0.1 mile to the hike). Just before you reenter the woods, turn around for a great view of a wooded valley—a farm on the right is the only indication that people live in this area.

When you reemerge in the open field, turn left. Swing around where the hill levels a bit, and take a left back into the woods. You'll see oak, maple, and dogwood trees on your left, and pines on your right. Take another left after another 900 feet. You'll quickly come to a path on the right; pass it and take the next right instead. The path becomes a well-worn groove in the grass, merges with the more obvious trail, and links to the other end of a loop you skipped earlier. (Again, this can get confusing with the profusion of paths, so bring a map.) You'll come to another wide path immediately after; turn left, but notice the path to the right at 2.5 miles—you'll take it on the way back.

## Morgan Run Natural Environmental Area

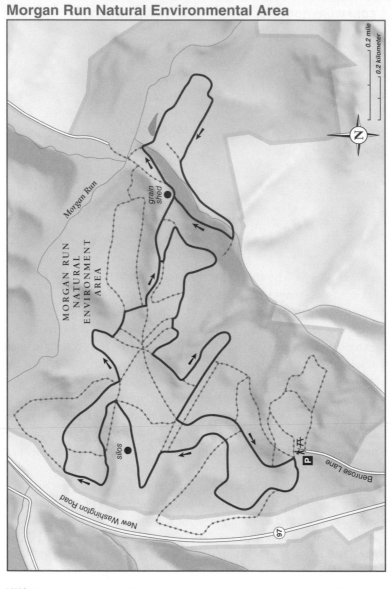

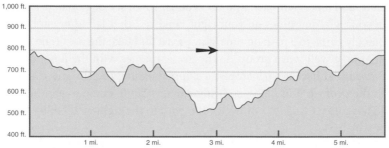

At 2.6 miles you'll see an old decrepit shed and a newer one closer to the trail. Swing around to the left to continue the hike, and you'll see a corn bin just ahead. Cross a branch of Morgan Run on some logs; once across, you can head right to go back to the parking area or straight to extend the hike. Be sure to look left to see a beautiful pond in a grove of towering beech trees.

Ultimately, you'll take a right, and you have three chances to do so: a path at 3 miles, one just beyond that, and then a third path that takes you to the farthest edge of the property. I recommend taking the third path because it leads you through thick forest with no sign of humanity, even though the park boundary means you'll see nearby suburban backyards. Reenter the woods at 3.3 miles, and take a left at 3.4 miles to head deeper into the woods. Parallel a branch of Morgan Run as you walk upstream and cross it at 3.6 miles. It soon joins the wider Morgan Run, which operates as a catch-and-release trout stream; cross the water again. After this crossing, you might have some trouble spotting the trail; look for it about 10 feet to the right of where you cross.

Go uphill and turn right onto the wider path that runs along a hillside covered with ferns and honeysuckle. You'll gradually rise above the stream valley on the right and emerge from the woods at 3.8 miles at the shed you passed earlier. Turn left and backtrack a bit before heading left again, at the path you noted earlier at 2.5 miles. At a little over 4 miles, turn left at a T-intersection. You'll begin passing paths to the right at about 4.5 miles; all head back to the parking area, but pass them to extend the hike.

For some variation, turn right at the connector trail at 5.1 miles (otherwise you'll continue to the parking area along the treeline, adding 0.5 mile to the hike), and then turn left at the central field trail. It will lead you straight to the parking area, affording some nice views of the entire area on the way.

## NEARBY/RELATED ACTIVITIES

Nearby 300-acre **Piney Lake** is often lauded as one of the best fisheries in the state. Head back to MD 26 and turn left. Then turn right onto White Rock Road and follow the signs. For a description of Piney Run Park's hiking trails, see pages 211–215.

• • • • • • • • • • • • • • • • • • • • • • • • • • •

**GPS TRAILHEAD COORDINATES** N39° 27.951'   W77° 00.063'

**DIRECTIONS** Take I-95 S 3 miles to Exit 49B (I-695 W). Stay on I-695 W for 5 miles, and then take I-70 W to Exit 76. Take MD 97 N to Westminster. After you cross MD 26, turn right onto Bartholow Road and then make an immediate left onto Jim Bowers Road and an even more immediate left onto Benrose Lane. Continue straight to the gravel parking area at the end of the road. The trail begins at the far left end of the parking area straight beyond the picnic tables. In about 200 feet you will be able to discern the trail's worn path.

Prettyboy Reservoir contains about 19 million gallons of water and is one of Baltimore's water supplies.
*Photo by Steven Sturm*

**ENJOY A SOLITARY** stroll through a pine forest on an old fire road. The beginning portion of the loop will tease you with water views, and the return loop will lead you to the water's edge.

## DESCRIPTION

Beginning at the trailhead, you'll enter the forest on a very wide path, cut by Roosevelt's Civilian Conservation Corps (CCC), the Depression-era jobs program that put 30,000 Marylanders to work. The dirt-and-gravel trail here has two clearly discernible tire tracks with higher grass in the middle. Deep woods flank the trail, but the width of the path gives you open walking space.

You'll pass through areas with tall pines and dense underbrush on either side of the trail. Even though you've just left the road, you probably won't hear any traffic at all; this section of Baltimore County is still very rural. At 0.2 mile the woods open up a bit, exposing the trail even more. You'll begin to see side trails on the left and right, but stay straight for now; you'll take one of the side trails on the return trip. At 0.3 mile an interesting phenomenon occurs that's easy to miss. On the right, the forest is almost entirely pine, but on the left, oaks, hickories, and maples dominate with very few pines at all.

Though it almost defeats the purpose of a hike to keep your eyes on the ground, if you're hiking the CCC Trail in summer, you may want to keep an eye out for little frogs

**DISTANCE & CONFIGURATION:** 3.8-mile out-and-back with a loop and spur

**DIFFICULTY:** Easy

**SCENERY:** Pine forest, Prettyboy Reservoir

**EXPOSURE:** Mostly shade

**TRAFFIC:** Light

**TRAIL SURFACE:** Packed dirt, gravel

**HIKING TIME:** 1.5 hours

**DRIVING DISTANCE:** 40 miles

**ELEVATION GAIN:** 580' at trailhead, 680' at high point

**ACCESS:** Sunrise–sunset; no fees or permits required

**WHEELCHAIR ACCESS:** No

**MAPS:** USGS *Hereford* and *New Freedom*

**FACILITIES:** None

**CONTACT:** 410-887-5683, baltimorecountymd .gov/agencies/environment/watersheds/pbmain .html

**LOCATION:** Traceys Store Rd., Parkton

**COMMENTS:** The trailhead is easy to miss, so pay attention to the directions below; the difficulty in finding the trail and the rural nature of the area almost guarantee solitude.

congregating in the grooves of the path. Tread carefully—they are especially prominent in areas where the trail is exposed, such as the section between 0.4 and 0.6 mile.

Beyond this point, oaks and hickories overtake the previously dominant pines, and while this results in something of a barren view in winter, the payoff comes in autumn when the trees explode in vibrant colors. You'll begin to see the beautiful and calm Prettyboy Reservoir through the woods on the left, even though the water is pretty far away and it can be difficult to get a good view.

By 0.8 mile the trail remains wide and the loop begins; you can go in either direction because you'll come back to this same spot regardless. We went straight and were followed the entire way by an owl, who remained just out of sight but continued to alert us to his presence with hoots. The grass grows much higher here on the path, signaling a lack of use. At 1.13 miles the trail splits. Here, you can head down to the reservoir or go left to continue along the loop. Go left, continuing on the loop, and you'll complete it by rejoining the main trail at 1.8 miles. Begin heading back from where you came, and in 0.5 mile, just past some trees overhanging the trail, take the wide trail to the right.

The scenery is essentially the same as the trail you've been on, but this time you'll reach the water's edge after 0.6 mile. You'll see a little loop with an island of trees in the middle. Look to the left of the loop to locate a small rocky path that will lead you down to the water. Reach the water at 2.9 miles, and you'll find a nice rock ledge where you can rest and have a picnic. When you've had your fill, head back and turn right on the main trail to return to your car.

## NEARBY/RELATED ACTIVITIES

Sample Maryland wines and tour the facility where they're made at **Basignani Winery** (15722 Falls Road in Sparks, 410-472-0703, basignani.com). To get there, take Exit 20B off I-83. Other local wineries include **Galloping Goose Vineyards** (4326 Maple Grove

# Prettyboy Reservoir: CCC Trail

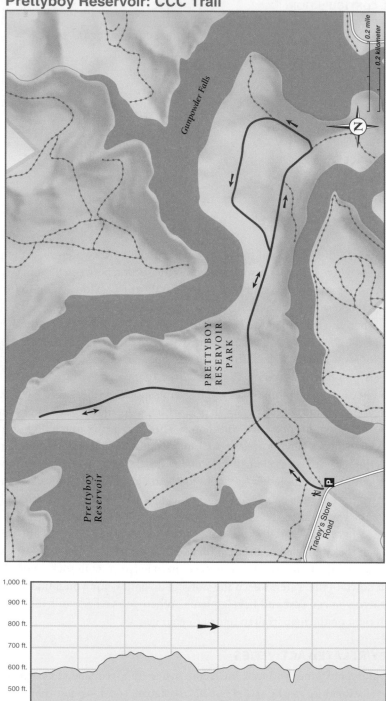

Road, Hampstead) and **Royal Rabbit Vineyards** (1090 Jordan Sawmill Road, Parkton). If you'd prefer to do more hiking, opportunities abound at **Prettyboy Reservoir** (pages 162–173).

• • • • • • • • • • • • • • • • • • • • • • • • • •

**GPS TRAILHEAD COORDINATES** N39° 37.196'   W76° 44.119'

**DIRECTIONS** Take I-95 N 11 miles to I-695 W. Drive 10 miles on I-695 W to Exit 24 (I-83). Take I-83 N 13 miles to Exit 27 (Mt. Carmel Road). Go west 3.6 miles and turn right onto Prettyboy Dam Road. Go 1 mile and turn left onto Tracey's Store Road. Go 1.1 miles to where the road turns sharply to the left; you'll see a small parking area on the right where the road bends. Wooden posts strung with an orange cable mark the trailhead.

Ferns blanket an embankment at Prettyboy Reservoir.          *Photo by Steven Sturm*

Gunpowder Falls provides a soothing soundtrack along the last portion of this hike.

**FEEL THE TEMPERATURE** drop as you descend from wooded hills to the swift Gunpowder Falls, scrambling through an untamed and isolated section along the way. Despite its location in the Prettyboy Reservoir watershed, this hike doesn't afford views of the reservoir itself; rather, it circles where Gunpowder Falls begins to enter the northwestern edge of Prettyboy.

## DESCRIPTION

Entering the woods, you'll quickly be in thick vegetation of oaks, pines, black walnuts, chestnuts, flowering dogwoods, maples, and poplars above, with several varieties of ferns, raspberry bushes, and honeysuckle below. Cardinals, jays, thrushes, woodpeckers, warblers, and vireos avail themselves of this great habitat.

The trail is a wide fire road, which is good because of the profusion of trailside poison ivy. Pass a path to the right at 0.4 mile, as well as several more paths leading right soon after. These lead to Gunpowder Falls, where you're headed on a more scenic route. The fire road narrows a bit to a foot trail for about 0.2 mile and then widens again along the edge of the watershed boundary—to the left, over a buffer of trees, is a farm field. Mountain laurel and blackberry soon appear; if it's summer, and you didn't fill up on the raspberries earlier, the blackberries are a special treat.

**DISTANCE & CONFIGURATION:** 3.9-mile loop

**DIFFICULTY:** Easy with short moderate–strenuous section

**SCENERY:**
Gunpowder Falls, hemlock groves

**EXPOSURE:** Mostly shade

**TRAFFIC:** Light

**TRAIL SURFACE:** Packed dirt

**HIKING TIME:** 1.5 hours

**DRIVING DISTANCE:** 45 miles

**ELEVATION GAIN:** 710' at trailhead, 560' at low point

**ACCESS:** Sunrise–sunset; no fees or permits required

**WHEELCHAIR ACCESS:** No

**MAPS:** USGS *Lineboro*

**FACILITIES:** None

**CONTACT:** 410-887-5683, baltimorecountymd.gov/agencies/environment/watersheds/pbmain.html

**LOCATION:** Gunpowder Rd. (right after Hoffmanville Rd.), Manchester

**COMMENTS:** I strongly recommend wearing long pants because the trail is overgrown with thorns in certain portions.

You'll come to a Y-intersection at 1.22 miles and continue left uphill. The trail narrows and becomes increasingly rocky as you leave Baltimore County and enter Carroll County. At 1.6 miles you'll reach another trail junction where you head straight and begin to descend a rocky hill. At nearly 2 miles, you'll reach a third trail junction. Heading left takes you to Grave Run Road and the entrance to River Valley Ranch, a resort and Christian youth camp founded in 1952 by two Irish immigrants. Instead, turn right to continue on the trail; as it loops around, you'll hear Gunpowder Falls below you to the left. The river is narrow and twisty, carving banks out of the meadow. Similarly, the trail you're now on is also twisty and narrow. Unlike the fire road coming in, this trail is spotted with manure from the horses at the nearby ranch, so watch your step. To the right, moss-covered rock outcrops dot the hillside. If you look through the trees to the left toward the ranch, you might catch a glimpse of the resident bison.

Below you and about 200 feet to the left, the river widens considerably and provides a nice loud accompaniment. Continue to descend, soon reaching the river and joining a wide fire road filled with the aroma of hay-scented fern. A jumble of moss-covered rocks and fallen trees gives the area an Appalachian feel.

At 2.4 miles you'll reach a barely visible trail junction. The fire road heads right up the hill, and a little foot trail goes left toward the river. Take the foot trail, but prepare yourself first by pulling up your socks: a lot of vegetation crowds the trail, including poison ivy and thorny rose. The reward for braving the overgrown vegetation is utter isolation, which comes almost immediately. A massive rock in the river provides a great place to stop and have a picnic.

Soon the trail becomes completely overgrown, but you can still discern it through the thorns and underbrush. Make your way along the hillside through the brush, passing big rocks and wildflowers, mostly wild geranium and jewelweed, or "touch-me-not," the name derived from the popping noise that comes when you

167

# Prettyboy Reservoir: Gunpowder Falls

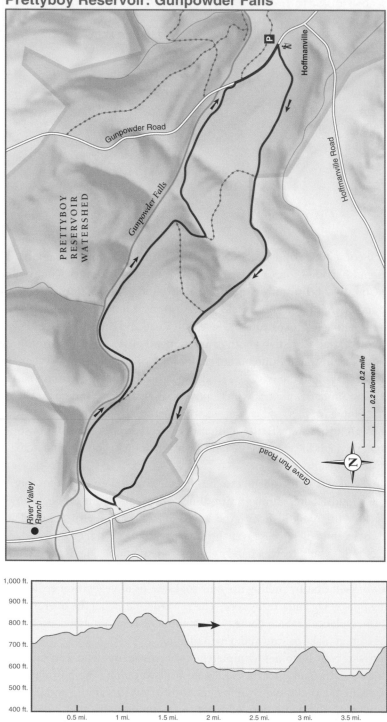

touch the plant's mature seed pods. The river alternates between roiling over rocks and then settling into deep, flat pools. It's very cool in the river valley, with an obvious temperature drop after coming off the hill.

Leave the river valley and ascend the hill. To the left, you'll see big beautiful hemlocks shading the river. At 3.4 miles, at the junction at the top of the hill, continue straight, crossing over a stream on a natural bridge and then hitting another intersection. Turn left, heading back down in the direction of the river. Soon Gunpowder Falls comes back into view past the hemlocks. Descend once again to river level, where things open up. At 3.7 miles you'll reach Gunpowder Road, cross it, and walk along the shoulder to the right.

Before you go too far, look to the left. Over the bridge is another parking area. If you want to add a quick but memorable hike through a hemlock gorge to a spectacular swimming spot, head there for the Hemlock Trail (pages 170–173). Otherwise, continue up Gunpowder Road and reach your car at 3.9 miles.

## NEARBY/RELATED ACTIVITIES

Sample Maryland wines and tour the facility where they're made at **Basignani Winery** (15722 Falls Road in Sparks, 410-472-0703, basignani.com). To get there take Exit 20B off I-83.

• • • • • • • • • • • • • • • • • • • • • • • • •

**GPS TRAILHEAD COORDINATES** N39° 41.199'   W76° 46.665'

**DIRECTIONS** Take I-95 N 11 miles to I-695 W. Drive 10 miles on I-695 W to Exit 24 (I 83). Take I-83 N 16 miles to Exit 31 (Middletown Road). Go west 4.6 miles to Beckleysville Road and turn left. At 0.2 mile the road bears left. Stay straight. The road becomes Cotter Road. Cotter turns into Clipper Mill Road at 1.9 miles at a stop sign. Go straight and cross Prettyboy Reservoir on a white bridge. Go 0.4 mile and turn right onto Gunpowder Road. After 0.5 mile pass the Hoffman Cemetery and park immediately after on the right side of the road. Walk across the road and find the trailhead leading into the woods beyond an orange cable.

Gunpowder Falls shimmers in the sunlight.

**GET A TASTE** of Appalachia within a grove of centuries-old hemlocks. After a hike that can be strenuous at times, cool off with a refreshing dip in the icy Gunpowder Falls.

## DESCRIPTION

At some points along the first half of the trail, there seems to be no trail at all, but passage is guaranteed by the open forest floor. The trail is packed dirt and can be very close and narrow, especially in summer. Pull up your socks or wear pants if you don't want poison ivy. The river to the right is swift and loud, and occasionally you'll see it through the thick underbrush. Over the river, as well as up the hill to your left, you'll see tall trees, but this part of the path is pretty exposed.

At 0.1 mile the trail opens up a bit, and you'll begin to see some beautiful rock formations on the hill to the left. The trail becomes rocky, and moss abounds. The well-defined path heads right to the river at 0.2 mile but then strays from the river soon after, going uphill at 0.25 mile. Just ahead, three different paths diverge; take the lower route on the right, and you'll come to an old stationary trail sign (with no map) at the bottom of the hill. Immediately after, cross over a large stream. This can prove challenging, but if you walk upstream a bit, some well-placed rocks make crossing a little easier. You'll emerge into a hemlock forest where these beautiful old

**DISTANCE & CONFIGURATION:** 2.1-mile loop

**DIFFICULTY:** Strenuous

**SCENERY:** Hemlocks, Gunpowder Falls, swimming hole, rock outcrops

**EXPOSURE:** Mostly shade

**TRAFFIC:** Light

**TRAIL SURFACE:** Packed dirt

**HIKING TIME:** 1 hour (longer if you decide to swim)

**DRIVING DISTANCE:** 45 miles

**ELEVATION GAIN:** 570' at trailhead, 705' at high point

**ACCESS:** Sunrise–sunset; no fees or permits required

**WHEELCHAIR ACCESS:** No

**MAPS:** USGS *Lineboro*

**FACILITIES:** None

**CONTACT:** 410-887-5683, baltimorecountymd .gov/agencies/environment/watersheds /pbmain.html

**LOCATION:** Gunpowder Rd. (soon after Hoffmanville Rd.), Manchester

**COMMENTS:** This trail is only for those up for a difficult adventure. I suggest bringing a hiking partner, just in case.

trees completely dominate the landscape. It's a beautiful spot, but now things begin to get a bit tricky.

The trail becomes very hard to follow. Because of the nature of these thick trees, they crowd out sunlight and little to no underbrush grows. This creates wide alleys between the trees that can look very much like a trail. Due to the trail's inexplicable underuse, you can find yourself at a loss as to exactly where to go. That said, as long as you keep the river within view on your right, you'll be fine.

When it seems that you should head to the water, the path gets swallowed up by an eroded bank or a stand of vegetation. Then you decide to head uphill, clambering over the rocks and through the hemlocks. Depending on how you decide to navigate this route, the hike can become strenuous very quickly. The going was very difficult at times, and it's easy to lose your footing. Every now and then, you'll find a nice level middle ground between hill and river. Here, pine needles carpet the soft soil. In this middle ground, you'll have the swift, clean river to your right and lots of rock outcrops covered in moss to the left, all the while traversing the many hemlocks around you. All this zigzagging will take you to the hike's turnaround point all the same.

You'll pass a deep swimming area and beach surrounded by big rocks. It's the perfect destination on a hot summer day. *Beware:* because of the swiftness of the river, the water is downright icy and is only for the brave or numb. Continue on, and at 1 mile you'll reach a grassy area where the trail is slightly distinguishable. When you come to a large stream, take the trail toward your left to begin your return trip. Head uphill and reach the top at just over 1.25 miles. You'll be thankful to now have a wide, pine needle–covered path to enjoy after all of the earlier exertion. Begin heading downhill at 1.6 miles, and in 0.1 mile the stream you forded earlier will come into view on your left. At just over 1.75 miles, you'll reach the same large stream but at a different crossing point. This time, you might not be able to avoid getting your feet wet, but the water is moving a little more slowly than downstream, so it should be a bit easier.

# Prettyboy Reservoir: Hemlock Trail

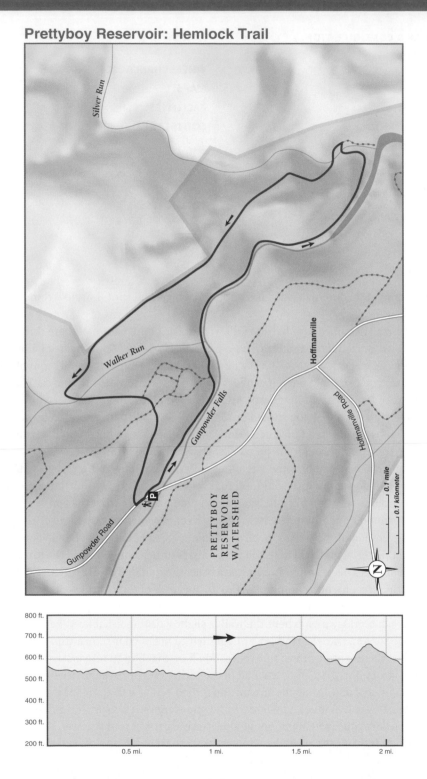

Begin heading uphill after you cross, and at just under 2 miles, you'll reach a fenced-in graveyard and a trail leading to the right. This is the Hoffman family cemetery. The Hoffmans owned a paper mill used for making the first paper currency in the United States. Many of the headstones date to the 1700s. Pass the graveyard and stay on the main trail. At 2.1 miles the trail ends at the street, about 100 feet from where you entered.

## NEARBY/RELATED ACTIVITIES

Sample Maryland wines and tour the facility where they're made at **Basignani Winery** (15722 Falls Road in Sparks, 410-472-0703, basignani.com). To get there take Exit 20B off I-83.

• • • • • • • • • • • • • • • • • • • • • • • • • •

**GPS TRAILHEAD COORDINATES**  N39° 41.401'   W76° 46.860'

**DIRECTIONS**  Take I-95 N 11 miles to I-695 W. Drive 10 miles on I-695 W to Exit 24 (I-83). Take I-83 N 16 miles to Exit 31 (Middletown Road). Go west 4.6 miles to Beckleysville Road and take a left. At 0.2 mile the road bears left. Stay straight. The road becomes Cotter Road. Cotter turns into Clipper Mill Road at 1.9 miles at a stop sign. Go straight and cross Prettyboy Reservoir on a white bridge. Go 0.4 mile and turn right onto Gunpowder Road. After 0.7 mile you'll come to a bridge. Park on the shoulder on the left as soon as you cross the bridge. Once you've parked, you'll see a guardrail on the other side of the road 100 feet or so from the bridge. There's a sign telling you not to swim, wade, camp, etc. The trail begins just behind that sign. (*Note:* there's another, wider path about 100 feet to the left. You'll be returning on this trail.)

Mining was big business in this area in the 1800s, so you'll come across abandoned mines along the trail.

**TAKE A QUICK** trip to a look-alike Midwest prairie, where the serpentine landscape provides a rare environment. Then head to the other side of Soldiers Delight, which is more typical of the Mid-Atlantic.

## DESCRIPTION

Many mistakenly assume that the Soldiers Delight Serpentine Trail is thus named because of its shape. In fact, the name refers to a type of soil. Serpentine, or serpentinite, is a mineral that produces extremely nutrient-poor soil, making plant growth a difficult prospect. Exceptions include the serpentine grasslands found in Soldiers Delight. Many of these grasses are not only atypical in Maryland, but rare all over the planet.

Before European settlement, much of Baltimore County was covered by serpentine grassland, cultivated by American Indian fire hunting. Natives used to set extensive fires to drive deer toward the open areas; the fires also had the effect of creating the grasslands that fed the deer. According to the Maryland Department of Natural Resources, even though what serpentine grassland remains in Maryland amounts to less than 5% of the original, it harbors no fewer than 39 rare and endangered plant species. Those found in Soldiers Delight include papillose nut rush, serpentine aster, whorled milkweed, grooved flax, and fringed gentian. Soldiers Delight

**DISTANCE & CONFIGURATION:** 5.4 miles, 2 intersecting loops

**DIFFICULTY:** Moderate

**SCENERY:** Rare prairie, Chimney Branch, abandoned mines

**EXPOSURE:** Half and half

**TRAFFIC:** Moderate

**TRAIL SURFACE:** Packed dirt, serpentine rock

**HIKING TIME:** 2.5 hours

**DRIVING DISTANCE:** 23 miles

**ELEVATION GAIN:** 708' at trailhead, 500' at low point

**ACCESS:** Sunrise–sunset; no fees or permits required. Visitor center is open Saturdays

11 a.m.–3 p.m. and Sunday–Friday depending on staff availability (call ahead to check).

**WHEELCHAIR ACCESS:** No

**MAPS:** USGS *Reisterstown;* trail maps at bulletin board outside visitor center and online at dnr.maryland.gov/publiclands/Documents/SoldiersDelight_map.pdf

**FACILITIES:** Restrooms, water, vending machines in visitor center

**CONTACT:** 410-922-3044, dnr.maryland.gov/publiclands/pages/central/soldiersdelight.aspx and soldiersdelight.org

**LOCATION:** 5100 Deer Park Rd., Owings Mills

**COMMENTS:** Wear sturdy hiking boots or trail shoes—serpentine rock is very sharp.

remains the largest serpentine area in the eastern United States and is among the most species-rich in the world.

Begin the hike by heading left on the white-blazed Serpentine Trail. Very soon you'll see the Red Dog Lodge, an old defunct hunting lodge built in 1912, in front of you. At the same time, a sign points right for the Serpentine Trail. Go right, continuing on the white-blazed trail. At just under 0.2 mile, emerge onto an open area created by a power line cut, and continue straight on the trail that leads back into the woods. Inevitably, along the way, you're bound to hear a sudden shuffle and then see the bounding hops of white-tailed deer, which are abundant in Soldiers Delight.

You'll pass through several empty fields with serpentine covering the trail and lots of grass. Leave the pastures and come to a narrow, rocky path surrounded on both sides by prickly bushes. You may find the trail here a bit damp, depending on the weather conditions.

At just under 0.75 mile, the trail veers right (north). Go through another clearing and enter a pine forest at 0.85 mile, a welcome spot of shade on a hot day. Jump over a small creek before coming to another cleared area. And then, at just under 1 mile, cross over the larger Chimney Branch.

The trail here is entirely loose rocks; this is the serpentinite. As the trail takes you back into a pine forest at the top of the hill, turn around. The view before you is astounding: prairie sweeping in all directions. The prairie is dotted here and there with the stubs of culled pines. This is no act of arson, but rather an ongoing attempt to restore the grasslands, free of the invasive and non-native pines. Head back into the woods and, at 1.5 miles, come to another section of the power line cut that you crossed earlier.

After the power line cut, things are still pretty stubbly, but some small, drought-resistant trees offer shade, mostly blackjack oak, post oak, and Virginia pine. The trail becomes packed dirt—what we're typically used to in Maryland. Approach

## Soldiers Delight Natural Environmental Area

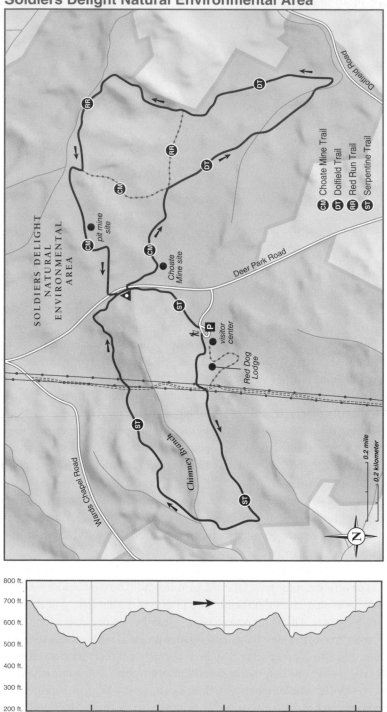

Deer Park Road and come to an overlook on Deer Park at 1.9 miles. A historical marker here tells you that chrome was first discovered in Baltimore County in 1808. Chromite mines existed at Soldiers Delight from 1828 to 1850, and they produced almost all of the world's chromium.

Across Deer Park Road, you'll see two signs for the Choate Mine Trail—one on the left and one toward the right. Take the trail on your right, crossing at the crosswalk; you'll return on the trail to your left.

Begin on the rocky red-blazed trail. Initially, the landscape looks much as it does in the serpentine section. But, as there is far less serpentine grassland on this side of Soldiers Delight, many mature Virginia pines line both sides of the trail, with wildflowers to the right. At 2 miles veer left to see the remains of the abandoned Choate Mine on your right, sitting within a wooden fenced area. The mine was part of the big operation that thrived in the area in the early to mid-1800s, digging for chromite, talc, asbestos, magnesite, and soapstone, among other minerals.

Moving on, the trail becomes very rocky; often the entire trail itself is one large slab of rock, spreading across the landscape. At just under 2.4 miles, the trail opens up at an intersection. You can head left to make a quick loop of the red Choate Mine Trail (1 mile total) or diagonally left to take the orange Red Run Trail (2 miles). However, turn right on the yellow Dolfield Trail, heading southeast, to make the complete 3-mile circuit.

At 2.8 miles into the hike, you'll come to Red Run Stream and what looks like the end of the trail. Head left, where you'll see the trail continue, and then cross the stream where it's narrow, following the path up into a clearing. At 3 miles come to and cross Red Run Stream; go right when you reach the other side of the stream. The trail may be a bit wet for a little while, depending on weather conditions. At 3.2 miles the trail veers left (northeast). Cross through another open serpentine area before plunging back into the woods. The trees are still mostly conifers but much taller than elsewhere. The soil also supports oak, beech, sycamore, and maple trees. Amazingly (and testament to the varied nature of Soldiers Delight), there's even enough moisture in this section to allow ferns and mosses.

At 3.5 miles cross Sherwood Road, a narrow lane that leads to a private home, and pick up the trail on the other side. Soon after you'll see a yellow-blazed tree, and the path continues, veering left (west) away from the townhomes in front of you. Unfortunately, the trail skirts the edge of the park boundary, and lots of backyards appear to the right among the mixed hardwoods.

At 3.6 miles you'll intersect with the orange-blazed Red Run Trail. For the full loop, head straight. At 3.9 miles you'll reach another junction where a path heads right and steeply uphill and the orange-blazed Red Run Trail continues, veering slightly to the left. Stay on the Red Run Trail, which begins to parallel Red Run Stream on your right.

Chimney Branch and the Serpentine Barrens

At 4.2 miles you'll cross a muddy stream and head uphill to emerge into a serpentine barren, with its attendant cut pines. Walk across the field and over a stream, and then you'll see a post marked with red. Turn right to get on the red-blazed Choate Mine Trail. A tree marked with red will confirm you're heading in the right direction. At 4.5 miles a red wooden post and a fenced area to the right mark a pit mine. It's closed off but still quite dangerous. Peer into the hole, but don't climb the fence. You'll reach the road at 4.9 miles, cross it, and head left looking for the small sign that reads TRAIL TO VISITOR CENTER. Follow the trail into the woods, with the road on your left, to make your way back to the visitor center.

## NEARBY/RELATED ACTIVITIES

Just down the road from Soldiers Delight is the family-friendly **Northwest Regional Park** (410-887-1163, baltimorecountymd.gov/agencies/recreation/programdivision/regionalparks/northwestrlgpark.html), home to a playground, paved paths, and wheelchair-accessible gardening plots. From the Deer Park Overlook, head back toward MD 26 on Deer Park Road. The park entrance is approximately 3 miles on the left, just before Lyons Mill Road.

• • • • • • • • • • • • • • • • • • • • • • • • • •

**GPS TRAILHEAD COORDINATES** N39° 24.638'   W76° 50.296'

**DIRECTIONS** Take I-95 S 3 miles to Exit 49B (I-695 W). Take I-695 W to Exit 18 (MD 26). Go west 4.5 miles and turn right onto Deer Park Road. The park entrance is 1.9 miles on the left. Park in front of the visitor center. Facing the visitor center, you'll see the trailhead to your right (turn left on the trail).

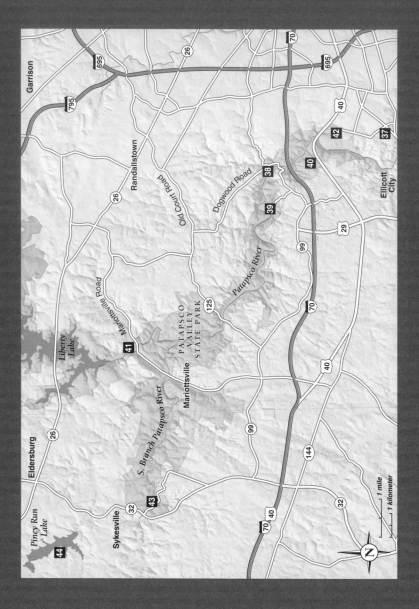

# WESTERN SUBURBS

A sign marks the entrance to the Trolly Line #9 Trail.

**TAKE IN HISTORICAL SITES** with a big dose of nature. Along the way, enjoy a good meal and shopping in Ellicott City.

## DESCRIPTION

The Trolly Line #9 Trail follows the route of the old trolley line built by the Columbia and Maryland Railway in the 1890s to establish rail service between Baltimore and Ellicott City. The #9 Trolly ran until 1955. Several artifacts from the old line can still be spotted along the trail.

Begin at the terminus of Edmondson Avenue and take the paved trail heading west toward Ellicott City. The route first runs through the town of Oella; named for the first woman to spin cotton in America, it was home to cotton mill workers for generations. The first residents built their homes of stone a few years before the War of 1812, while those who settled here in the years leading up to the Civil War used brick. Oella bustled until 1972, when Hurricane Agnes swept through the Patapsco Valley and destroyed much of the town. A nice wooded buffer flanks the trail, with the Cooper Branch of the Patapsco River running on the left.

Quickly cross Oella Avenue at 0.8 mile. On your right you'll see The Breadery, a great stop for fresh bread and coffee. Just after crossing Oella Avenue, a permanent wooden trail kiosk notifies you that Benjamin Banneker Historical Park and

**DISTANCE & CONFIGURATION:** 3.9-mile out-and-back

**DIFFICULTY:** Easy

**SCENERY:** Historic sites, Cooper Branch, abundant birdlife

**EXPOSURE:** Slightly more sun than shade

**TRAFFIC:** Moderate

**TRAIL SURFACE:** Asphalt on Trolly Line #9 Trail, packed dirt at Banneker

**HIKING TIME:** 1.5 hours

**DRIVING DISTANCE:** 12 miles

**ELEVATION GAIN:** 385' at trailhead, 133' at low point

**ACCESS:** Sunrise–sunset; no fees or permits required

**WHEELCHAIR ACCESS:** Yes, on Trolly Line #9 Trail

**MAPS:** USGS *Ellicott City;* Banneker property trail maps available inside the museum (open Tuesday–Saturday, 10 a.m.–4 p.m. and some Sundays in summer—call to confirm)

**FACILITIES:** Restrooms, phone, and water at museum

**CONTACT:** 443-326-5474, catonsvillerailstotrails .com/9-trolley-trail, baltimorecountymd.gov /agencies/recreation/countyparks/mostpopular /banneker

**LOCATION:** End of Edmondson Ave. near Chalfonte Dr., Catonsville

**COMMENTS:** You can easily explore the trails around the Banneker property and the Trolly Line #9 Trail separately, but combining them allows for a number of possible configurations.

Museum is just up the hill to your left. Head left up the hill, following the yellow trail to make your way to the Benjamin Banneker Park and Museum. White-tailed deer abound in this area, so be on the lookout. You'll see a sign directing you to the Molly Bannaky House, a circa-1850 stone farmhouse that has been fully restored and now houses a library and meeting room. To continue to the Banneker Museum, follow the ample signage. There are several paths here, so you may find yourself on one other than those described here, but you'll find your way to the museum with little trouble in any case, reaching it at roughly 1.1 miles.

A wildlife-habitat checklist, available inside the museum, alerts you to look for spicebush plants, tulip poplars, Christmas ferns, Eastern bluebirds, yellow-bellied sapsuckers, warblers, Baltimore orioles, goldfinches, cedar waxwings, blue jays, red-shouldered hawks, box turtles, and owls. The museum also has a "Birds of the Banneker Historical Park Birding Checklist" for more experienced bird-watchers. This brochure lists 60 birds, including four different finches, five sparrows, three owls, and four woodpeckers.

Benjamin Banneker, the foremost African American man of science in the early years of the United States, lived his entire life on the land where the museum now sits. Open since 1998, the museum and park continue to grow and develop. The property also features a replica of a colonial cabin, a demonstration orchard, and 6 miles of trails over 142 acres. Banneker was born a free black in 1731 and lived until 1806. His life's accomplishments included constructing a wooden striking clock and a projection of a solar eclipse; helping survey the land for Washington, D.C.; publishing six almanacs; and exchanging antislavery correspondence with Thomas Jefferson. The museum does an excellent job of illuminating the life and contributions of this underappreciated figure in American history and is definitely worth a visit.

# Banneker Historical Park and Trolly Line #9 Trail

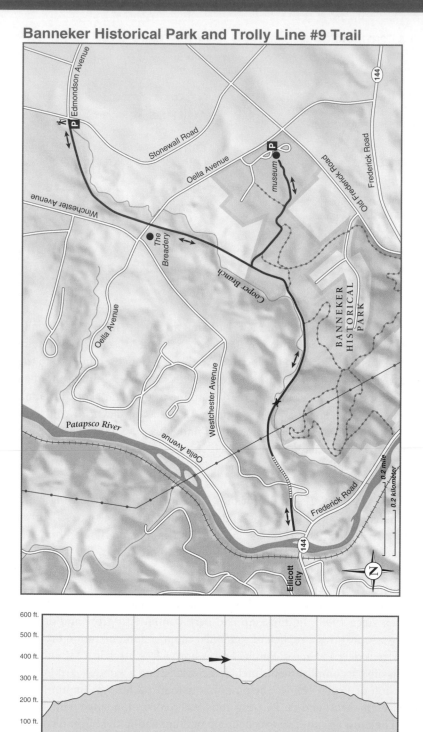

When you've finished your museum visit, retrace your steps down the yellow trail until you return to the paved Trolly Line #9 Trail; head left on it.

Back on the Trolly Line #9 Trail, you'll see Cooper Branch again to the right as you walk downstream. To the left sits a marshy area, surrounded and protected by a fence. The sound of water spilling over the big rocks in Cooper Branch provides a pleasing accompaniment. A big hill studded with beeches and Christmas ferns rises to the left. It's easy to see the natural contours of the valley and the ease with which the trolley ran through here. At first glance, it appears that no blasting was necessary in the construction of the line, and judging by the size of the nearby oaks, little of the surrounding area was disturbed.

Cross Cooper Branch on an old stone bridge, a relic from the trolley line; your path doesn't change because the water runs underneath the trail. The legacy of rock blasting soon becomes apparent as you see jagged rocks, covered in fern and moss, jutting toward the trail from the left. Walk under a power line cut, and be sure to look up for the hawks and turkey vultures that frequently glide above. I saw no fewer than two dozen of them circling around in the sky.

More jagged, moss-covered rocks, decorated here and there with sumac, crowd the trail until it turns into a long wooden boardwalk at 2.2 miles. In this area, look for the dangling cables tethered to the rocks; these used to support the trolley's electrical service. The boardwalk runs under the Westchester Avenue bridge. Although the bridge is a few hundred feet above your head and Westchester Avenue is only a narrow, two-lane road, you might feel a bit unnerved walking under this noisy steel bridge when cars go over. You can spot a stone column for the original bridge, ending below the current bridge.

You'll reach Ellicott City at just under 2.4 miles and see a sign that reads HISTORIC ELLICOTT CITY/BALTIMORE TROLLY LINE #9 TRAIL with a parking area just beyond. From this vantage point, it's easy to spot the remnants of the old train bridge over the Patapsco to the left. The trail soon ends; swing around and go down the wooden stairs lined with a row of Eastern red cedar. You'll see the brick trolley shop to the left, open and serving the public since the mid-1800s. Once down the stairs, you'll come to Ellicott Mills, established in 1772. The original rail line that ran from Baltimore, completed in May 1830, ended at this point. Railroading is prominent here, as Ellicott City boasts America's first railroad station. The same building now houses the B&O Railroad Station Museum (410-313-1945, howardcountymd.gov/Baltimore-Ohio-Station-at-Ellicott-City), which is open Wednesdays and Thursdays, 10 a.m.–2 p.m.; Fridays and Saturdays, 10 a.m.–7 p.m.; and Sundays, noon–5 p.m.

Because downtown and Main Street are right in front of you, why not take advantage and eat, shop, or browse? When you're ready to go back to your car, head back up the stairs to the trail and retrace your steps. This time, when you reach the Banneker property at 3.1 miles, pass by it and continue straight to Edmondson Avenue.

## NEARBY/RELATED ACTIVITIES

Assuming you've already spent significant time in the Banneker Museum and checked out Ellicott City's many attractions, you might want to experience the great hiking at nearby **Patapsco Valley State Park.** The Hollofield Area of the park (page 195), with its ball fields, camping, playgrounds, equestrian trails, picnic areas, and, of course, hiking trails, can be reached by taking MD 40 E/Baltimore National Pike. You'll come to the park entrance a couple of miles before you reach the river.

• • • • • • • • • • • • • • • • • • • • • • • • • •

**GPS TRAILHEAD COORDINATES**  N39° 16.125'    W76° 46.505'

**DIRECTIONS**  Take I-95 S 3 miles to Exit 49B (I-695 W). Take I-695 W to Exit 14 (Edmondson Avenue) and drive west on Edmondson until it ends at Stonewall and Chalfonte Roads. The trail begins at the end of Edmondson.

To drive directly to the Benjamin Banneker Historical Park and Museum: Take I-695 to Exit 13 and take Frederick Road toward Catonsville. Go 3 miles and turn right onto Oella Avenue; continue 0.5 mile to the Banneker Historical Park and Museum gates, on the left. Park in front of the museum; the trailhead is behind the museum.

# **38** PATAPSCO VALLEY STATE PARK:
## Alberton and Daniels Area

Daniels Dam was used to generate 400 horsepower for the nearby mills.

**STROLL ALONG THE** Patapsco River and visit numerous historical sites along the way.

## DESCRIPTION

A hike in this portion of Patapsco Valley State Park serves as the best reminder of the thriving nature of the area long before it was a park. Historical structures dot the entire walk.

From the parking area, walk straight beyond the metal gate on the asphalt. A private house sits to your right, and signs direct you to keep left. Follow the road on the left straight past the house, and at 0.1 mile you'll come to a stationary trail map that marks the beginning of the white-blazed trail. Alberton Road used to be a traffic through-road, heading toward the community of Daniels. It traverses a wide valley, loaded with birds. Thick forest flanks the abandoned road to the right, and the Patapsco River, full of rocks and running swiftly, is just on the left. Near the river, sycamores and box elders dominate, but the whole area—up the hills—is studded with beech, dogwood, oak, and tulip poplar trees. Understory growth includes mountain laurel, redbud, serviceberry, spicebush, and witch hazel.

Walk upstream and look for the CSX rail lines on the other side of the river. Also keep an eye out for belted kingfishers, great blue and little green herons, killdeer,

**DISTANCE & CONFIGURATION:** 3.5-mile out-and-back

**DIFFICULTY:** Easy

**SCENERY:** Historical ruins, Patapsco River, piedmont stream valley

**EXPOSURE:** Shady

**TRAFFIC:** Light–moderate

**TRAIL SURFACE:** Cracked asphalt, crushed rock, packed dirt

**HIKING TIME:** 1.5 hours

**DRIVING DISTANCE:** 13 miles

**ELEVATION GAIN:** 200' at trailhead, with no significant rise

**ACCESS:** 9 a.m.–sunset; no fees or permits required

**WHEELCHAIR ACCESS:** Yes, but may be difficult

**MAPS:** USGS *Ellicott City*; trail map available online at dnr.maryland.gov/publiclands /documents/patapsco_danielsmap.pdf

**FACILITIES:** None

**CONTACT:** 877-620-8367, dnr.maryland.gov /publiclands/pages/central/patapsco.aspx

**LOCATION:** Intersection of Dogwood Rd. and Hollofield Rd., Windsor Mill

and a variety of ducks. Even bald eagles have been known to make an appearance. Big rocks decorate the river, sometimes changing the water's course. Even more enormous rocks, invariably composed of erosion-resistant mica schist, litter the hillsides. The best example of these rocks comes at 0.6 mile, where a fantastic column towers over the road.

Look for a trail to your right at 1 mile. Follow it gradually uphill until you see a large wire basket of rocks on your right. Take the path by this basket, walking past a rusted-out car in the gully beneath you, to the ruins of Saint Stanislaus Kostka Catholic Church. Founded in 1879 (the stone structure you'll see was erected shortly thereafter), the church was in use until the town of Daniels was razed in the late 1960s. There's a graveyard behind the church; the large number of children buried there tells of the harsh realities of late-19th- and early-20th-century life.

When you've had your fill of poking around the church ruins, return to the Alberton Road trail and turn right, following along the river upstream. You'll soon see the remnants of the abandoned town of Daniels, founded in the 1830s as a cotton-milling community. This town was essentially owned by the C. R. Daniels Company, and its residents were mill workers. (This portion of the town, on the Baltimore County side, was actually known as Guilford, but it was, in fact, considered part of Daniels.)

Continuing along the river, keep an eye out for the best view of the abandoned Daniels Mill across the river. Also here is the still-active CSX bridge, as well as the ruins of the old pedestrian bridge.

Just beyond the bridges, to the right at 1.8 miles, are the ruins of the community's Pentecostal church. Dating only to 1940, this church pales in comparison to the older church at the hike's beginning. Just after is the Daniels Dam, used to generate power for the mill. Cut left a few hundred feet after the church; the path goes along the river, which brings you closer to the dam. Head up so you're above the dam and

## Patapsco Valley State Park: Alberton and Daniels Area

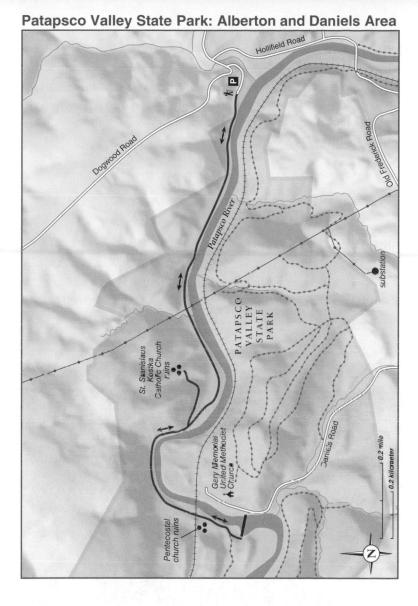

looking over it. Pocking the banks near the dam are numerous beaver lodges. The path circles around to the right and then rejoins the main wide trail. Head right to return to your car, reaching it at 3.5 miles. Continuing to the left eventually brings you to unmaintained portions of Patapsco Valley State Park in the Granite and Woodstock Areas.

## NEARBY/RELATED ACTIVITIES

If you'd like to explore the other side of the Patapsco, check out the Patapsco Valley State Park: Daniels Area Old Main Line Trail hike. Western Run Park is the home of the **Diamond Ridge Golf Course** (baltimoregolfing.com/course/diamond-ridge). To reach it, head back toward Hollofield Road and turn left on Ridge Road. The golf course will be on the right.

• • • • • • • • • • • • • • • • • • • • • • • • • •

**GPS TRAILHEAD COORDINATES**  N39° 18.919'   W76° 47.599'

**DIRECTIONS**  Take I-95 S 3 miles to Exit 49B (I-695 W). Take I-695 W 6 miles to Exit 17. Take Security Boulevard west past the Security Mall and follow signs to Johnnycake Road. Follow Johnnycake until it ends, and turn right onto Hollofield Road. Take a left onto Dogwood Road and then an immediate left into the parking area off Alberton Road.

Evidence of a beaver along the trail

A cave and wooden staircase greet you near the end of this hike.

**HIKE ALONG THE** Patapsco River in a popular spot for swimming, and then get a bird's-eye view of the river while hiking along the ridgeline.

## DESCRIPTION

Begin the trail just in front of the parking area, walking upstream along the Patapsco River. You'll immediately traverse a shallow stream, but you can do so without getting wet due to well-placed rocks. On the other side of the stream, the trail joins a wider gravel path along the river. This is the Old Main Line Trail, named after the railroad line on the opposite side of the river. This portion of railroad served as the Baltimore and Ohio Railroad's main line, stretching from Baltimore to just east of Harper's Ferry.

Walk along the river gorge, with towering oaks to your left and the river to your right. The trail is quite flat in this section, and you'll pass several rope swings on your right, which may be in use if you hike during summer, as swimming is allowed unless otherwise marked. This portion of the Patapsco also offers ample fishing opportunities. The river is home to smallmouth bass, rock bass, redbreast sunfish, hogsuckers, and white suckers. Additionally, rainbow and brown trout are stocked in this portion of the river in spring. A fishing license is required; for details visit eregulations.com/maryland/fishing. As you continue, you'll occasionally see the trail marked by little red tags mounted to trees with a hiker icon labeled PATAPSCO VALLEY NORTH.

**DISTANCE & CONFIGURATION:** 3.4-mile loop

**DIFFICULTY:** Easy on Old Main Line Trail; moderate if you return via singletrack and back side of Daniels

**SCENERY:** Patapsco River

**EXPOSURE:** Shaded

**TRAFFIC:** Moderate

**TRAIL SURFACE:** Dirt, sand, crushed rock

**HIKING TIME:** 1.5 hours

**DRIVING DISTANCE:** 16 miles

**ELEVATION GAIN:** 220' at trailhead, 470' at high point

**ACCESS:** 9 a.m.–sunset; no fees or permits required

**WHEELCHAIR ACCESS:** No

**MAPS:** dnr.maryland.gov/publiclands /documents/patapsco_danielsmap.pdf

**FACILITIES:** None

**CONTACT:** 410-461-5005, dnr.maryland.gov /publiclands/Pages/central/patapsco.aspx

**LOCATION:** Daniels Rd., Ellicott City

At just over 0.25 mile, the trail splits, with a narrower dirt and sand path leading you closer to the water on the right, while the wider Old Main Line Trail continues straight ahead. These trails parallel each other, so you can choose whichever you prefer. The path closer to the river offers some nice vantage points, but if you prefer surer footing, stick to the Old Main Line Trail.

At 0.5 mile the Old Main Line Trail intersects with a gravel path leading up to the left. Regardless of which trail you chose (the riverside dirt path or the Old Main Line), continue straight (northwest) along the river. These two paths continue to parallel each other upstream. Soon after this junction, you'll see a sandy beach area. Across the river, at just over 0.6 mile, is a beautiful stone bridge constructed for the train tracks. In 0.2 mile the narrow riverside path joins the Old Main Line Trail; continue on.

At just under a mile, a trail intersects from the left, leading uphill and following a feeder stream. While this trail links up with the path you'll eventually join, stay straight to follow the Old Main Line Trail along the Patapsco. This beautiful section of the river includes hills rising up on either side, making it feel quite secluded.

At 1.35 miles pass a rock wall covered with lichen and moss on your left; just after, a trail on your left heads southeast, following another feeder stream. Turn left on this trail and follow it deeper into the woods and away from the Patapsco River. Turn around briefly just after making that left and admire the old stone bridge that allows the Old Main Line Trail to traverse the feeder stream.

At just under 1.5 miles, you'll reach an intersection where one trail leads over a footbridge, while another heads left (northeast). Head left, going steeply uphill for a beautiful vantage point of the Patapsco River at the top. Watch your footing, as this portion of trail is quite narrow, but don't worry—the trail soon levels out. At 1.75 miles houses come into view in front of you, and a trail heads left, but you should continue straight (southeast). These trails are popular with mountain bikers. Continue as the trail loops around and begins heading toward the river and away from the houses.

At 1.9 miles the path heads gradually downhill and into a thicket of mountain laurel. In 0.1 mile you'll hear (and soon see) a feeder stream down in the valley on your

## Patapsco Valley State Park:
## Daniels Area Old Main Line Trail

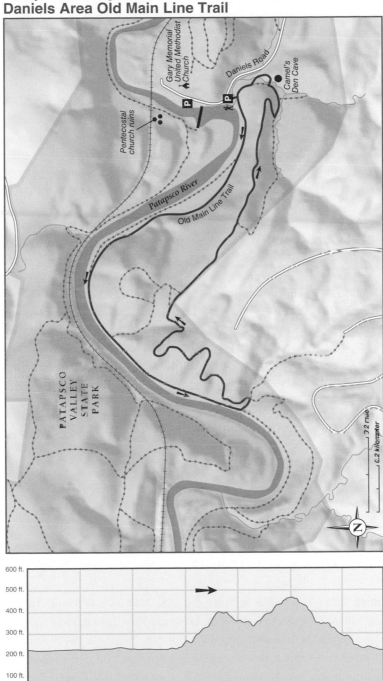

left. Continue as the trail makes a switchback and then leads you down to the stream at 2.1 miles. Cross over the stream, which is narrow and shallow enough that you won't get wet. Just after, at the junction, continue straight (southeast) and slightly uphill rather than veering left. Soon, another trail intersects from the left; bypass this one, too, and head straight, going uphill. At the junction at 2.5 miles, turn left (southeast) onto the Switchplate Trail, marked by actual switchplates nailed into trees. In winter, you'll have nearly 360-degree views of the surrounding hills and valley.

The trail becomes a bit of a rock scramble at this point as you walk along the ridge. You'll begin to hear a stream in the distance, and then, at 2.8 miles, depending on the foliage, it will come into view in the valley below. The trail begins to narrow here as you head downhill and to the right. At just under 3 miles, you'll reach the stream. Turn left, heading southeast with the stream on your right. Soon you'll pass an old structure on your left (now a pile of cinderblocks), and then see a trail leading to your right across the stream. Bypass that trail and stay straight on the Switchplate Trail.

A wooden staircase and a cave come into view on your right at just over 3 miles, across the stream. Here you have a choice. For an easier route, continue straight to avoid the stream crossing. You'll intersect with the Old Main Line Trail just ahead (and turn right to return to your car). To take a closer look at the cave and follow our route, turn right and cross the stream using the rocks to avoid getting wet. After checking out the cave, head up the stairs. Once at the top, turn left (you'll see another switchplate on a tree) and continue on the trail as it leads down to a gravel path. You'll see Daniels Road in front of you. Head left on the gravel path and cross over a stream. While it's fairly shallow at this point, you may still want to walk slightly upstream to jump along the rocks and avoid getting wet. At 3.3 miles you'll reach the Old Main Line Trail again and turn right, making it back to the parking lot at 3.4 miles.

## NEARBY/RELATED ACTIVITIES

At Patapsco Valley State Park: Alberton and Daniels Area (page 187), you can explore the other side of the Patapsco along a historic road.

• • • • • • • • • • • • • • • • • • • • • • • • • •

**GPS TRAILHEAD COORDINATES** N39° 18.822'    W76° 48.945'

**DIRECTIONS** Take I-95 S 3 miles to Exit 49B (I-695). Take I-695 W 5 miles to Exit 16 (I-70 W). Follow I-70 for 4.8 miles to Exit 87B for Columbia Pike. Take the first right in 0.1 mile onto Rogers Avenue. At the traffic circle in just under a mile, take the third exit onto Old Frederick Road. In 0.6 mile turn left onto Daniels Road and follow it a mile until you see a parking area on your left. Additional parking is just around the bend in front of Daniels Dam. The trail begins at the first parking area.

Enjoy sweeping views of the Patapsco River from the Hollofield lookout.

**TAKE IN ONE** of Patapsco Valley State Park's most popular areas, complete with one of the best bird's-eye views of the Patapsco River and a nice trek through the woods. A playground and bathrooms midway through the hike make this a convenient outing for families.

## DESCRIPTION

The orange-blazed Peaceful Pond Trail begins as a narrow dirt path, winding among pines, hollies, tall grasses, and short stubby trees. At 500 feet head left at the junction. After another 100 feet, split to the left again, where you'll find a bench. Unfortunately, *Peaceful Pond* is something of a misnomer with US 40 nearby, but it's pleasant nonetheless and home to many frogs, snakes, turtles, and herons.

Turn left at the pond and follow an unmarked trail around the pond, crossing over a small wooden bridge and making your way back to the original trail junction. This time, go left, past an area full of vines. At 0.4 mile, at the top of a steep hill, you'll reach the junction with the light blue Ole Ranger Trail. Turn left to follow the light-blue blazes.

The Ole Ranger Trail winds through tulip poplars, white pines, and multiflora rose. It soon visits an old radio-transmission tower, where in the 1940s women employed by the Maryland Forest Service kept a lookout for fires. Soon after the tower, the trail becomes a crushed-rock fire road. At the junction at 0.6 mile, go

**DISTANCE & CONFIGURATION:** 3.9-mile combination

**DIFFICULTY:** Moderate

**SCENERY:** Piedmont forest, Patapsco Valley overlook, pond, dam ruins

**EXPOSURE:** Mostly shade

**TRAFFIC:** Moderate, heavy at overlook and playgrounds

**TRAIL SURFACE:** Packed dirt, crushed rock, asphalt

**HIKING TIME:** 1.5 hours

**DRIVING DISTANCE:** 11 miles

**ELEVATION GAIN:** 450' at trailhead, 180' at low point

**ACCESS:** 10 a.m.–sunset. There is a $2/car fee on weekdays and $3/person fee on weekends if you enter the park at the overlook area.

**WHEELCHAIR ACCESS:** In small sections

**MAPS:** USGS *Ellicott City;* trail map available online at dnr.maryland.gov/publiclands /documents/patapsco_hollofieldpickallmap.pdf or purchase one at shopdnr.com/PVSP -Hollofield_Pickall.aspx

**FACILITIES:** Bathrooms, playgrounds, water, vending machines, campgrounds

**CONTACT:** 877-620-8367, dnr.maryland.gov /publiclands/pages/central/patapsco.aspx

**LOCATION:** 8020 Baltimore National Pike, Ellicott City

right to head deeper into the woods on the asphalt path (going left leads to Church Lane Road). Sloping, wooded hills flank the trail and rise above the Patapsco River gorge. Oak, hickory, and ash trees make up the canopy. On eye level, spicebush and witch hazel dominate, the perfect habitat for songbirds.

You'll reach a power line cut at 0.75 mile. While a paved road runs toward the transmission lines, the Ole Ranger Trail continues straight ahead as a packed-dirt foot trail. Soon after the power line cut, you'll see a trail split off to your left, but continue straight on the blue-blazed Ole Ranger Trail and cross a little stream at 1 mile. Notice the zigzag of the stream as it runs in a series of S-curves.

The trail becomes rocky and reaches another junction at 1.1 miles; turn left on the white gravel path. At 1.5 miles you'll reach another junction. Take note because you'll return on the trail to your right. For now, though, head straight. At 1.7 miles you'll reach Park Drive, a park road. Head left to go under US 40 (being careful of cars) and then go straight, passing the tollgate, and on to the overlook straight ahead through the parking lot. Described by park literature as "arguably the most breathtaking [vista] in the park," the overlook is a beautiful spot, with each season offering its own splendor.

To continue the hike, backtrack and turn right at the guard's gate. Walk through another parking lot, passing pavilions on your right and a playground on your left. At the end of the paved road, you'll see the sign for the white-blazed Union Dam Trail. It immediately crosses a picnic area and goes downhill toward the river on a twisty, rock-strewn path. Notice the CSX rail line below, heading into the hill you're walking on. When you reach the Patapsco River, turn left and walk alongside it. You'll reach the dam (or what's left of it after numerous floods) at 2.6 miles. When it was intact, the dam supplied water for the J. W. Dickey Textile Mills in nearby Oella.

# Patapsco Valley State Park: Hollofield Area

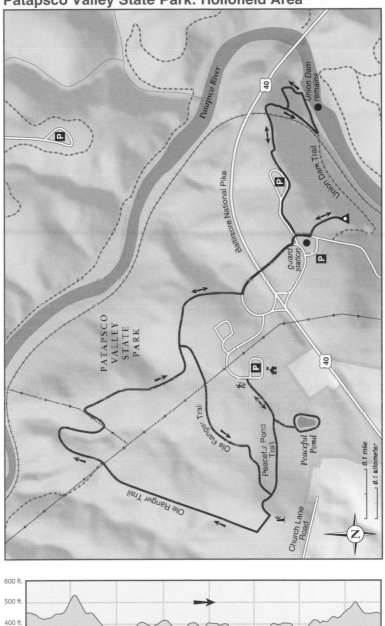

To return, make a left to head up the steep hill, following the white-blazed trail. You'll soon meet up with the same Union Dam Trail you took earlier. Turn right to head back up to the parking lot.

On the way back, return on the Ole Ranger Trail you took to the overlook. This time, at the junction head left at the sign reading TOWER 0.5 MILE at 3.3 miles. Go left at the orange arrow pointing to the pond, and backtrack to the headquarters, reaching it at 3.9 miles.

## NEARBY/RELATED ACTIVITIES

Just a bit farther west on US 40 is historic **Ellicott City** (ellicottcity.net), full of restaurants, antiques, museums, and shopping. In nearby Oella is the **Benjamin Banneker Historical Park and Museum** (410-887-1081; see page 182 for a hike there).

• • • • • • • • • • • • • • • • • • • • • • • •

**GPS TRAILHEAD COORDINATES** N39° 17.790'   W76° 47.474'

**DIRECTIONS** Take I-95 S 3 miles to Exit 49B (I-695 W). Take I-695 W to Exit 14 and go west on US 40/Baltimore National Pike toward Ellicott City. Drive 2 miles, crossing the Patapsco River, and turn right into the park. Take the first left toward the park headquarters. You'll pass the entrance to Peaceful Pond Trail to your right, on your drive in. With the headquarters to your back, walk down the hill and to the left until you see the brown Peaceful Pond Trail sign—the blazes are orange.

Liberty Dam is worth a quick out-and-back before heading over to the McKeldin Area for more hiking.

**WALK TO LIBERTY DAM** and then hike to the developed, popular McKeldin Area of Patapsco Valley State Park.

## DESCRIPTION

Starting at the trailhead, walk north on a rocky, packed dirt trail that parallels the North Branch of the Patapsco River. After about 300 feet, much of the rock spreads across the trail and into the water. Massive ferns and mountain laurel adorn both sides of the trail.

At 0.3 mile you'll encounter the first sign of the great contrasts this area offers: while much of this hike traverses upland forest, here you are in riverine wetland. A low-lying marsh and boggy area sits to the left, while the trail rises and crosses over a few feeder streams and brooks. You'll come to a trail junction where both directions parallel each other and soon link up. Head right to take the less overgrown of the two paths.

At 0.7 mile cross a stream in a pine forest. A path to the right goes to the top of Liberty Dam, but you should go straight and soon you'll come to the bottom of the dam, where the trail ends. Liberty Reservoir sits on the other side. When you've reached the dam at 0.8 mile, turn around and return to your car. You can either walk along Marri-ottsville Road to reach the McKeldin Area or drive and park (paying the entrance fee).

When you reach the McKeldin Area entrance, you'll see several trail options: the Switchback Trail, the Spring Glen Trail, and the Tall Poplar Trail. The white-blazed

**DISTANCE & CONFIGURATION:** 6.3-mile balloon

**DIFFICULTY:** Moderate–strenuous

**SCENERY:** Patapsco River, Liberty Dam, McKeldin Rapids

**EXPOSURE:** Shady

**TRAFFIC:** Light–moderate

**TRAIL SURFACE:** Dirt, asphalt

**HIKING TIME:** 2.5 hours

**DRIVING DISTANCE:** 22 miles

**ELEVATION GAIN:** 285' at trailhead, 495' at high point

**ACCESS:** 9 a.m.–sunset; no fees or permits required for primary trailhead; see Comments for more details

**WHEELCHAIR ACCESS:** No

**MAPS:** USGS *Sykesville* and *Finksburg;* trail map available online at dnr.maryland.gov/publiclands /documents/patapsco_mckeldinmap.pdf

**FACILITIES:** Restrooms, water, playground at maintained area; also youth camping, picnic facilities, and disc golf

**CONTACT:** 877-620-8367, dnr.maryland.gov /publiclands/pages/central/patapsco.aspx

**LOCATION:** Main trailhead: Marriottsville Rd., Marriottsville; official McKeldin entrance: 11676 Marriottsville Rd, Marriottsville

**COMMENTS:** To go directly to the official McKeldin entrance, follow the directions below but stay on Marriottsville Rd. for another 0.4 mile from the gravel road; the entrance will be on the left. On weekends and holidays April–October, there is a $3/person day-use fee; otherwise, it's $2/vehicle.

Switchback Trail crosses the entrance road and leads in both directions; turn right to take it west.

Though you bypassed the Tall Poplar Trail, the Switchback Trail also winds among tall poplars; taking the Switchback Trail simply yields a much longer hiking loop. At 2.9 miles the trail runs very close to Marriottsville Road, but fortunately it soon turns away toward the river. When you come to a bulletin board and trail junction, turn left; you'll pass the other side of the Tall Poplar Trail at 3.1 miles. At 3.2 miles, at a big bamboo grove where mallards congregate, the trail splits again; take the white-blazed trail uphill to the right for a great view of the river. You'll come to a paved park road at 3.4 miles and see a restroom on the right.

Cross the park road and pick up the white-blazed trail again; just 0.1 mile later, down the hill, follow the sign for the McKeldin Rapids Trail, which leads to a rapid on the Patapsco River that flows into a large, deep pool—it's a beautiful spot. Though swimming is prohibited due to strong undercurrents, fishing is very popular.

Turning left away from the rapids, you'll cross great rock formations. At one point, the trail itself is a huge rock slab. Be aware that these exposed rocks are favored spots for snakes, including copperheads, one of only two venomous snakes in Maryland. If you see a snake and it has an hourglass-shaped head, give it a wide berth.

At 3.8 miles you'll reconnect with the Switchback Trail. Go left at the junction and follow the river. Bypass the first left for the red-blazed Plantation Trail and take the second left onto the Plantation Trail as it heads gradually uphill into upland forest. (You could also continue to hug the river on the Switchback Trail. Both options will eventually take you to the same place, but taking the Plantation Trail varies the scenery.) The forest here is primarily oak, but you'll also see tulip poplar, beech,

## Patapsco Valley State Park: McKeldin Area

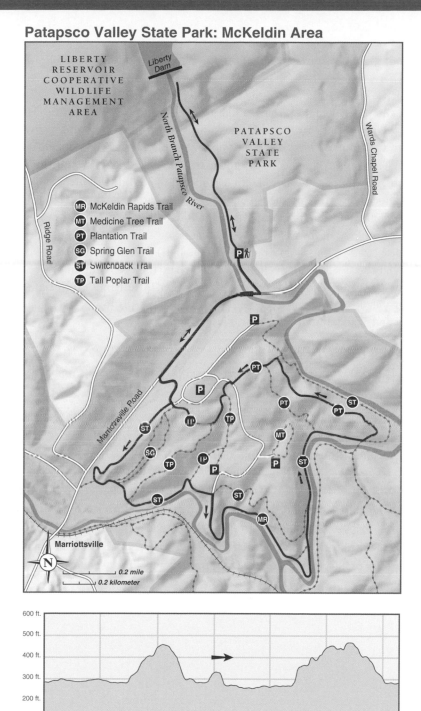

dogwood, maple, sassafras, redbud, and sycamore trees. Many wildflowers also abound here.

When you reach the top of the hill and a cleared area, you'll see the southern edge of the pine plantation; hawks like to congregate on this treeline. Head left toward the paved park roads, past a basketball court on the left and restrooms on the right. Cross the park road and pick up the purple-blazed Tall Poplar Trail at 4.8 miles. When you see a chalet-style shelter straight ahead and the trail goes in two directions, go right. At another junction at 4.9 miles, continue right.

You'll see holly trees on the left and the tollgate and contact station on the right; you'll reach the paved park entrance road at about 5 miles. (You've now completed the outermost loop of the McKeldin Area, but if you still want more, there's the 0.7-mile blue-blazed Spring Glen Trail loop to the left.) This time, follow the entrance road straight across Marriottsville Road and pick up the fire road; follow it downhill along the power line cut to where you were earlier. At 6.1 miles turn right toward Marriottsville Road and you'll see a river crossing in the shadow of the bridge. Cross the river and head left to reach your car just ahead.

## NEARBY/RELATED ACTIVITIES

You can enjoy more great hiking (as well as fishing) at nearby **Liberty Reservoir** (pages 150–157), just to the north.

• • • • • • • • • • • • • • • • • • • • • • • • •

**GPS TRAILHEAD COORDINATES** N39° 22.028'   W76° 53.129'

**DIRECTIONS**  Take I-95 S 3 miles to Exit 49B (I-695 W). Take I-695 W to Exit 18 and go west on Liberty Road toward Randallstown. Drive 4.5 miles and turn left onto Marriottsville Road. Go 3.9 miles and turn right onto a little gravel road just before the Patapsco River; go straight to the little parking area. The trail starts just beyond the parking area at the northern edge of the woods. (Don't take the trail leading directly down to the Patapsco; it peters out.)

The Patapsco River after a snowfall

**THIS PROTOTYPICAL PATAPSCO VALLEY** hike features river valleys and deep forest, with a sprinkling of historic structures.

## DESCRIPTION

Begin your trek on a wide, well-trod path. This is actually Rockhaven Avenue, a road once used for vehicle traffic but now in the process of being reclaimed by the forest floor. At 500 feet, you'll see a trail to your right, but continue straight—you'll eventually return on the trail to the right.

Just after, you'll see a red-blazed trail; take it to your right. At 0.3 mile, and then again at 0.4 mile, you'll see trails heading in either direction, but you should continue straight on the red-blazed trail. This path is fairly wild, full of broadleaf plants and surrounded by much undergrowth, such as dogwood, mountain laurel, witch hazel, redbud, serviceberry, and spicebush. Soaring trees such as oak, hickory, beech, and poplar make up the canopy.

At 0.8 mile you'll cross a stream on a wooden footbridge, and directly in front of you will be the beautiful Patapsco. You're now on the Mill Race Trail, a raised section of trail that follows the river for 1.1 miles. Occasionally, you'll see stones from the dam where the dirt has eroded.

**DISTANCE & CONFIGURATION:** 3-mile loop

**DIFFICULTY:** Moderate–strenuous

**SCENERY:** Piedmont forest,
Patapsco River

**EXPOSURE:** Mostly shade

**TRAFFIC:** Light–moderate

**TRAIL SURFACE:** Packed dirt

**HIKING TIME:** 1.5 hours

**DRIVING DISTANCE:** 10 miles

**ELEVATION GAIN:** 400' at trailhead,
180' at low point

**ACCESS:** 10 a.m.–sunset; no fees or
permits required.

**WHEELCHAIR ACCESS:** No

**MAPS:** USGS *Ellicott City;* trail map available
online at dnr.maryland.gov/publiclands
/documents/patapsco_hollofieldpickallmap.pdf
or purchase one at shopdnr.com/PVSP-
Hollofield_Pickall.aspx

**FACILITIES:** None

**CONTACT:** 877-620-8367, dnr.maryland.gov
/publiclands/pages/central/patapsco.aspx

**LOCATION:** St. Johnsbury Rd. and Rockhaven
Ave., Catonsville

Head right (north) on the Mill Race Trail, which runs along the top of an old retaining dam for a water-diversion channel created for a now-defunct mill downstream. It's a lovely section of trail, with the channel to the right, framed by sloping hills rising above. To the left is the Patapsco, full of rapids in this section. The combination is fantastic. This is also a great place to see the various river birds, such as great blue and little green herons, killdeer, and belted kingfishers, plus a multitude of geese and ducks making their nests among the sycamores and box elders.

At just under 2 miles, you'll reach the remains of Union Dam and see the US 40 bridge looming ahead. Union Dam, in use from 1808 to 1912, was originally constructed as a wooden dam. In 1912, a concrete dam was built to power the W. J. Dickey Textile Mills. It sustained heavy damage from Hurricane Agnes in 1972 and was finally removed in 2010 to restore the natural flow of the river. You may see hikers on the other side of the Patapsco, enjoying similar views from the Hollofield Area (see page 195).

Continue walking over the remains of the dam, and before you reach the US 40 bridge, take the unblazed trail heading steeply uphill to your right. You'll soon see a trail junction on your right, but remain straight, and you'll quickly come upon a red blaze. In another 0.1 mile, at the next junction, keep right. At 2.3 miles look for a very interesting hollowed-out tree on the right; it's large enough for you to squeeze in for a photo opportunity. Here you'll be winding through a forest of oak, pine, poplar, and dogwood trees.

At 2.5 miles a trail intersects on the left, but continue straight on the red-blazed trail, and in just 0.1 mile you'll return to Rockhaven Avenue. Turn left and follow the road-turned-trail back to the parking area, keeping an eye out for the incongruous 25 MPH speed-limit sign on your right.

## Patapsco Valley State Park: Mill Race Trail

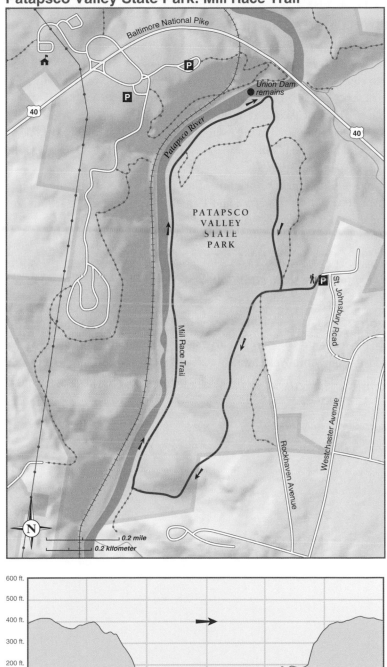

## NEARBY/RELATED ACTIVITIES

From the parking area, it's a quick-and-easy trip to the **Benjamin Banneker Historical Park and Museum** (see page 182 for a hike there). Follow St. Johnsbury Road 0.8 mile, then turn right onto Westchester Avenue. Go 0.7 mile and turn left onto Oella Avenue. Look for the park on the right, just before Frederick Road.

For more historical context on all of the sites you passed along the hike, visit the **Avalon Visitor Center,** located in the Avalon Area, where you can take a look at exhibits and photographs of the history of the area. It's open April 1–October 31, Saturdays and Sundays, 11 a.m.–3 p.m.

For more hiking, check out some other nearby hikes along the Patapsco: Hollofield Area (page 195), Alberton and Daniels Area (page 187), Hilton Area (page 234), and Orange Grove and Avalon Areas (page 238).

• • • • • • • • • • • • • • • • • • • • • • • •

**GPS TRAILHEAD COORDINATES**  N39° 17.232'   W76° 46.609'

**DIRECTIONS**  Take I-95 S 3 miles to Exit 49B (I-695 W). Take I-695 W to Exit 13 and follow Frederick Road toward Catonsville. Go 3 miles and turn right onto Oella Avenue. Go 0.7 mile and turn right onto Westchester Avenue. Go 0.8 mile and turn left onto St. Johnsbury Road. Park at the end of St. Johnsbury before it hits Rockhaven Avenue. The trail begins just across the street.

This less-traveled trail provides some quiet vantage points for contemplating the Patapsco.
*Photo by Steven Sturm*

**ENJOY A QUIETER** section of Patapsco Valley State Park, walking along the South Branch of the Patapsco River.

## DESCRIPTION

As you begin your hike with the Patapsco River on your left, you'll almost immediately cross a small stream. There will be quite a few stream crossings on this trek, but all are easily navigable without getting wet. Frequent paths on your left lead down to the Patapsco River if you'd like to get a closer view. But to continue along this hike, stay on the main path. While the trail is not blazed or otherwise marked, it's a nice, easily recognizable path, so you shouldn't have any trouble finding your way. Before you reach 0.5 mile, you'll cross three more small streams. At just over 0.5 mile, veer right as you begin hiking deeper into the woods through oaks, maples, and American beeches on a curvy trail leading away from the water.

At about 1 mile you'll begin to hear the river again, though you still won't be able to see it until 0.25 mile later when you emerge from the woods and once again begin paralleling it. At 1.3 miles you'll reach a Y-intersection. The right path takes you across a small stream and into the woods, and the left path takes you toward the river; head right. Just after another stream crossing, you'll reach another Y-intersection and head left to continue paralleling the Patapsco.

**DISTANCE & CONFIGURATION:** 10-mile out-and-back

**DIFFICULTY:** Moderate

**SCENERY:** Patapsco River, wildlife, railroading accoutrements

**EXPOSURE:** Mostly shade

**TRAFFIC:** Light

**TRAIL SURFACE:** Packed dirt

**HIKING TIME:** 3.5 hours

**DRIVING DISTANCE:** 25 miles

**ELEVATION GAIN:** 350' at trailhead, 460' at high point

**ACCESS:** Sunrise–sunset; no fees or permits required

**WHEELCHAIR ACCESS:** No

**MAPS:** Trail map available online at dnr.maryland .gov/publiclands/documents/patapsco _mckeldinmap.pdf

**FACILITIES:** None

**CONTACT:** 877-620-8367, dnr.maryland.gov /publiclands/pages/central/patapsco.aspx

**LOCATION:** River Rd., Sykesville

**COMMENTS:** I call this undeveloped section of PVSP Sykesville–Marriottsville because of its location between those two towns. If you wish to leave a car at one end to shorten this hike, there's ample parking off Marriottsville Rd. Take Marriottsville Rd. north 3.5 miles from I-70 and park in the gravel area on your left, just before you cross over the Patapsco River.

At just over 1.5 miles, you'll begin seeing the railroad tracks; 0.1 mile later, you'll reach a rock scramble directly next to the river. Here, you can dip your toes in the Patapsco and take a nice break. You'll cross a large stream at just under 2 miles and soon reach a 3-way junction; stay straight, paralleling the river. At 2.25 miles you'll see consecutive trails leading to the right, but stay straight. At 2.5 miles the trail splits again; this time, head uphill to the right. Cross over a bridge at just over 3 miles and you'll see a trail to your left, just before reaching Henryton Road. Head left into the woods on this trail, and stay right at the next trail junction.

Continue to keep right as Henryton Road comes into view and you pass several paths to your left. At 3.2 miles turn right to head up to the end of Henryton Road—another parking area is available here that people use to access the trails. The Henryton Bridge used to cross the Patapsco at this point, but it was washed out by Hurricane Agnes in 1972. This area was also once home to the Henryton Tuberculosis Sanatorium, built in 1922 to provide treatment to African Americans suffering from tuberculosis. It was converted to a state mental hospital when TB rates dropped but was eventually shut down in 1985 after institutionalizing such patients was no longer the norm. Once a well-visited site by urban explorers, it was demolished in 2013 and few remnants are left. The Henryton Tunnel, just on the other side of the Patapsco River, is still in operation by the CSX train tracks. Built in 1850, it's one of the oldest active railroad tunnels in existence.

Walk across the paved road and pick up the trail behind the Patapsco Valley State Park sign. Almost immediately you'll come to another junction; a path leads left to the river, but you should head straight. In another 50 feet, at the next junction, go left.

At just under 5 miles, you'll reach the train tracks and then Marriottsville Road. If you left a car here to shorten your hike, your car will be about 50 yards down the

# Patapsco Valley State Park (Undeveloped Area): Sykesville–Marriottsville

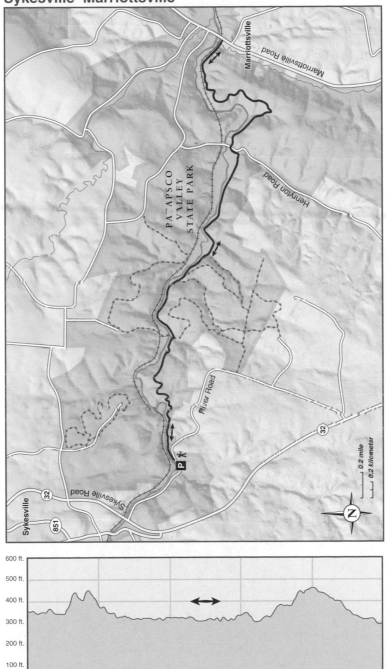

tracks (be careful, they're active!). Otherwise, turn around and retrace your steps to your car, reaching it at approximately 10 miles.

## NEARBY/RELATED ACTIVITIES

If you desire maintained trails, pavilions, ball fields, and picnic areas, as well as facilities, head to the McKeldin Area of PVSP (page 199).

• • • • • • • • • • • • • • • • • • • • • • • • • •

**GPS TRAILHEAD COORDINATES** N39° 21.424'   W76° 57.669'

**DIRECTIONS** Take I-95 S 3 miles to Exit 49B (I-695 W). Take I-695 W 5 miles to Exit 16 (I-70W). Follow I-70 for 11 miles to Exit 80 (MD 32) and head north toward Sykesville. In 3.7 miles follow the signs to Main Street Sykesville and Maryland History Aluminum Bridge, by taking a left onto West Friendship Road. Make your first right onto River Road and follow it 0.6 mile. Just after crossing over a white bridge, park in the gravel area on your left. To reach the trailhead, walk up River Road 0.1 mile, and you'll see the beginning of the trail on your left.

A stone chimney is all that remains of this dwelling.   *Photo by Steven Sturm*

A popular spot for fishing, Piney Lake is stocked with largemouth bass, tiger muskie, trout, and catfish.

**LEAVE THE BOATING** and fishing crowds behind as you explore the forests around popular Piney Lake.

## DESCRIPTION

Before you start your hike, stop in the nature center, which features live reptiles and knowledgeable naturalists. The nature center hosts an astounding 300 programs a year, ranging from presentations for toddlers to ones for senior citizens. Make sure you check out the outside hummingbird garden and aviary. The birds you might see include black vultures, turkey vultures, barred owls, great horned owls (the largest resident owl in Maryland), red-shouldered hawks, and red-tailed hawks.

Walk down toward the lake from behind the nature center and turn right to begin your hike. Pass the aviaries and follow a sign for the YAK SHACK, following the Lake Trail (it has blue blazes, but I didn't see any markings at this point). Piney Lake, which many believe to be the best fishery in the state, will be on your left. According to the Maryland Department of Natural Resources (DNR), fish species found in the lake include pumpkinseed sunfish, redbreast sunfish, brown bullhead, smallmouth bass, white sucker, spotfin shiner, bluntnose minnow, banded killifish, golden shiner, creek chub, and tessellated darter. These are in addition to the more

**DISTANCE & CONFIGURATION:** 3.2-mile loop

**DIFFICULTY:** Easy

**SCENERY:** Piney Run Lake, pine forests, mixed hardwoods

**EXPOSURE:** More shade than sun

**TRAFFIC:** Moderate on trails; heavy at boat ramp

**TRAIL SURFACE:** Packed dirt with small sections of asphalt

**HIKING TIME:** 1.5 hours

**DRIVING DISTANCE:** 29 miles

**ELEVATION GAIN:** 555' at trailhead, with no significant rise

**ACCESS:** March–November, daily, 7 a.m.–sunset; December–February, Monday–Friday, 8 a.m.–4 p.m. (closed weekends and holidays). The park charges a vehicle fee of $5 for Carroll County residents and $10 for nonresidents.

**WHEELCHAIR ACCESS:** No

**MAPS:** USGS *Finksburg;* some YOU ARE HERE maps along trails; trail map available online at ccgovernment.carr.org/ccg/recpark/pineyrun /hiking.aspx.

**FACILITIES:** Boat launch, pavilions, boat rental, restrooms and water at nature center; food at boat launch

**CONTACT:** 410-795-5165, pineyrunpark.org

**LOCATION:** 30 Martz Rd., Sykesville

**COMMENTS:** The nature center is open April–October, Wednesday–Saturday 11 a.m.–5 p.m and Sunday 12–5 p.m.; November–March, Monday–Friday 11 a.m.–4 p.m.

common largemouth bass, bluegill, yellow perch, channel catfish, black crappie, striped bass, and redear sunfish.

At 0.25 mile, following the contours of the lake, the Lake Trail leads you up to a well-trodden dirt path. Turn left and you'll see a trail sign with an orange blaze on it. You're now on the Inlet Trail and will soon come to an open field on the right buffered by pine trees and forsythia; an overwhelming scent of pine fills the air here, a sample of what's to come. At 0.5 mile, when the trail splits, veer left to continue on the orange-blazed Inlet Trail as it gradually rises above the lake through an oak and poplar forest with lots of moss and eventually enters a pine plantation.

When you reach a little clearing, head left, and when the trail splits at 0.9 mile, head left again following signs for the Shore Path. The Shore Path dead-ends to the left in just a few hundred feet. Take it for a nice view and an area of contemplation at the edge of the lake, where ducks, geese, and fish congregate.

Retrace your steps on the Shore Path, pass the path to the right that leads to Piney Path, and continue along the Inlet Trail to your left. You'll encounter a short exposed section before you plunge again into a pine forest with a very high canopy that offers blissful shade on a hot day. Despite the glorious smell and scenery, however, the high canopy blocks so much sunlight that ground-level growth is very limited and the forest floor is fairly barren.

Spruce, fir, and the occasional redbud trees stand along the edge of the woods before you reach a field. The trail then swings around to the right and reenters the canopy of pines; at 1.6 miles continue on the Inlet Trail to your left (heading right would connect you with the Piney Trail you passed earlier).

## Piney Run Park

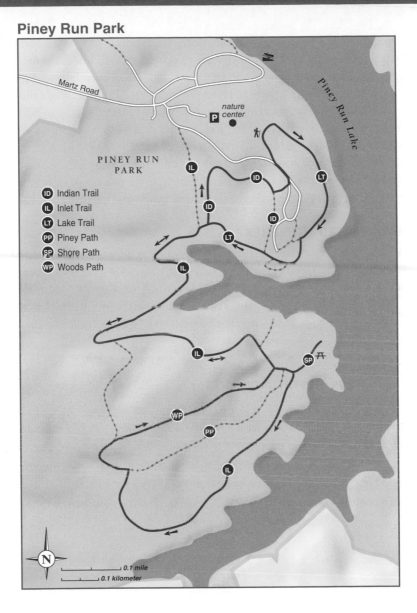

The trail splits again in 0.1 mile, with the Inlet Trail to your left, and the Woods Path straight ahead. This time, stay straight on the Woods Path, which parallels Inlet Trail. The forest on your left is entirely pines, while to the right it's mostly oaks. At 2 miles you'll reach a trail intersection where you were earlier. Turn left to retrace your steps on the Inlet Trail. This time when you reach a trail junction by the stream, turn right.

Continue on the Inlet Trail, but this time, at 2.5 miles, go straight and to your left (instead of heading right where you came in before) to follow signs for the red-blazed Indian Trail. When you come to a trail split at 2.6, turn left, and then take another left at just under 2.8 miles to leave the Indian Trail and head up to the paved road (don't follow the sign pointing you to the nature center).

Come to the paved park road at 2.8 miles and cross it to reach Pavilion 1. Walk behind it, and you'll see the blue-blazed Lake Trail on your right. This trail meanders back to the parking area and is dominated by red cedar. Cardinals, jays, ravens, and blackbirds flit about in the branches, while hawks circle overhead. Continue on the carpet of cedar needles until you reach the nature center and parking area at 3.2 miles.

## NEARBY/RELATED ACTIVITIES

You can find much more hiking at nearby **Morgan Run Natural Environmental Area** to the north (page 158), **Liberty Reservoir** to the east (pages 150–157), and **Patapsco Valley State Park's northern sections** to the south (pages 187–210).

If you're looking for a perfect antique for your home, visit the shops in **New Market,** Maryland's Antique Capital, just 10 miles down I-70 W in Frederick County.

• • • • • • • • • • • • • • • • • • • • • • • • • •

**GPS TRAILHEAD COORDINATES**  N39° 23.613'   W76° 59.049'

**DIRECTIONS** Take I-95 S 3 miles to Exit 49B (I-695 W). Take I-695 W 5 miles to I-70 W. Follow I-70 W to Exit 76 and take MD 97 N 4.5 miles. Turn right onto W. Obrecht Road and continue 0.8 mile. Turn right onto White Rock Road and go 0.7 mile. Turn right onto Martz Road and follow the signs to Piney Run Park. Take the first right to the parking area for the nature center; the trail starts 100 feet behind the nature center.

The sun pushes its way through the pine forest.

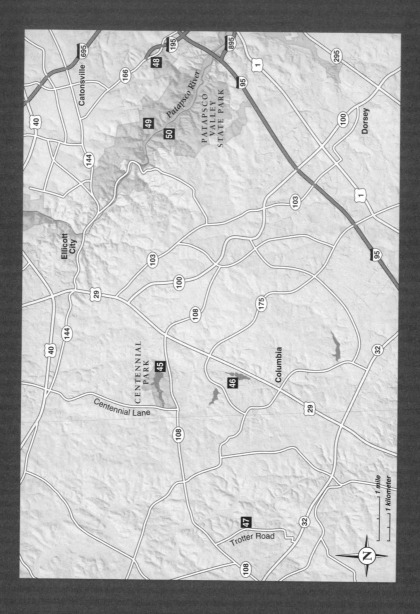

# SOUTHWESTERN SUBURBS

One of the many resting spots surrounding Centennial Lake

**STROLL AROUND MAN-MADE** 325-acre Centennial Lake, an oasis in the middle of Columbia, and enjoy the diversity of foliage in Centennial Arboretum.

## DESCRIPTION

Walk down the asphalt path and turn left at the lake. You'll be sharing the trail with many walkers, bicyclists, and people pushing strollers. It's obvious that Centennial Park is a recreational haven. Pass picnic pavilions on your left, and you'll reach the boat ramp at just over 0.2 mile. Passing the ramp on your right, you'll see just to the left a little wooden post marked TRAIL, denoting a trail heading into the woods. Take this packed dirt path as it winds through a stand of tall oaks. At 0.25 mile, still in the woods, take a left and enjoy all the flowering dogwood, white oak, beech, and tulip poplar trees here. You'll also pass a little seating area on your left. The trail ends at a parking area at just over 0.3 mile, where you can link back up with the asphalt lake loop. Before continuing your trip to the left around the lake, look to your right to see the Adventure Shack, which offers an array of activities, including kayaking, canoeing, and rock climbing, as well as creature comforts such as concessions and restrooms (seasonal hours may apply). Check out howardcountymd.gov/adventure shack for more details.

**DISTANCE & CONFIGURATION:** 2.5-mile loop

**DIFFICULTY:** Easy

**SCENERY:** Centennial Lake, wildlife management area, Centennial Arboretum

**EXPOSURE:** Mostly sunny

**TRAFFIC:** Moderate–heavy

**TRAIL SURFACE:** Asphalt, short section of packed dirt

**HIKING TIME:** 1 hour

**DRIVING DISTANCE:** 18 miles

**ELEVATION GAIN:** 350' at trailhead, with no significant rise

**ACCESS:** 7 a.m.–sunset; no fees or permits required

**WHEELCHAIR ACCESS:** Yes

**MAPS:** USGS *Savage;* park map available online at howardcountymd.gov/centennialpark

**FACILITIES:** Restrooms at pavilion at parking area; water fountain in front of tennis courts; other restrooms and water spread out at various parking areas around the lake; ball fields, playgrounds, pavilions

**CONTACT:** 410-313-7271 or 410-313-7256, howardcountymd.gov/centennialpark

**LOCATION:** 10000 Clarksville Pike, Ellicott City

Turn left to continue your walk around the lake. You'll pass a lakefront covered stage on the right. Here, on the South Lawn, the park hosts free summer concerts and shows movies into the fall. Bring your blanket, chairs, and a flashlight, The Adventure Shack serves concessions until the end of all movies. For more details, call 410-313-4700.

At just under 0.4 mile, you'll see a path on your left, but continue straight, following the main asphalt Lake Loop. It's now marshy wetlands—willows and cattails sway in the breeze for a few hundred feet before yielding once again to mixed hardwoods. Squirrels and chipmunks run across the path as butterflies flitter about. Soon you'll cross a wooden footbridge and veer right when the trail splits. The crowds thin out considerably in this section. Pass over another bridge, and when the trail splits again at 0.5 mile, continue straight. The path to your left leads to tennis, basketball, and volleyball courts, as well as restrooms and a playground.

Soon, you'll come to the first shady section of the Lake Loop, with mature trees forming a canopy. At 1.25 miles you'll reach a burgundy steel footbridge. On the other side is the Centennial Arboretum. Some of the trees you'll see here include black walnut, eastern red cedar, persimmon, redbud, scarlet oak, red maple, sassafras, bitternut hickory, black gum, beech, sweet cherry, black cherry, tulip tree, hornbeam (blue beech), staghorn sumac, post oak, dogwood, and black oak. Each is labeled and immaculately maintained.

When the trail splits at just under 1.5 miles, head right. You'll have a nice view of the entire lake on your right. At just under 1.9 miles, on your left, you'll see pavilion H, with a playground, tennis courts, and a parking lot (open only during warmer seasons). At 2 miles continue right to head back to the parking area where you began.

## NEARBY/RELATED ACTIVITIES

For restaurants and shopping, head to **Columbia Town Center** and **Lake Kittamaqundi** (page 222). To get there, go east on MD 108 to US 29 south and follow signs to Town Center.

## Centennial Park

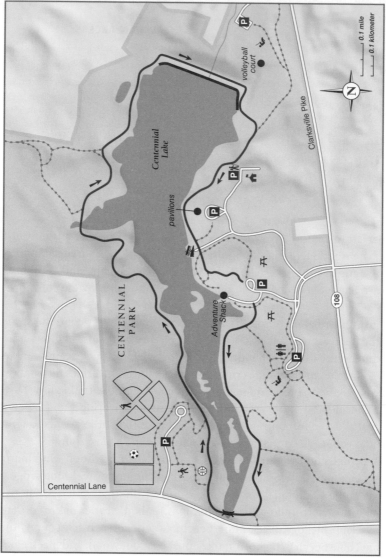

For more hiking opportunities, head to the **Middle Patuxent Environmental Area** (page 226), a 928-acre natural area that is home to 150 species of birds; more than 40 species of mammals; and numerous amphibians, reptiles, fish, butterflies, plants, and other wildlife. To reach the MPEA, continue west on MD 108, past Centennial Park, and turn left on Trotter Road between MD 108 on the north and MD 32 on the south, just east of Clarksville.

• • • • • • • • • • • • • • • • • • • • • • • • • • •

**GPS TRAILHEAD COORDINATES** N39° 14.398'   W76° 51.048'

**DIRECTIONS**  Take I-95 S 3 miles to Exit 49B (I-695 W). Take I-695 W 5 miles to Exit 16 and merge onto I-70 W. Take US 29 south to MD 108 west toward Clarksville. Go 1 mile and turn right onto Centennial Park Lane, into the main south entrance of the park. Then take your first right, following signs for the boat ramp. Make another right, passing the E, F, and G pavilions and park in the lot at the end of the road. The trail begins at the asphalt path heading down to the lake.

Centennial Lake sparkles in the winter sun.

This stream connects Wilde Lake—just to the northwest—with Lake Kittamaqundi.

**TAKE AN EASY STROLL** around Lake Kittamaqundi.

## DESCRIPTION

Sandwiched between Little Patuxent Parkway and US 29, the 27-acre man-made Lake Kittamaqundi bears the name of the first recorded American Indian settlement in Howard County. Kittamaqundi means "meeting place," which is appropriate for the lake's position adjacent to Columbia Town Center.

From the back of the Sushi Sono restaurant, head left onto the asphalt path down the hill, and then make your first hard right toward the lakefront plaza and onto a wooden boardwalk. The Soundry, a music venue, and Clyde's Restaurant, a local institution, sit on the hill above the lake. The boathouse here has a ramp for launching boats and canoes. The adjacent wooden pier offers nice views of the lake, which provides good habitat for hundreds of ducks and geese.

At 0.1 mile you'll see a ramp with metal railings directly in front of you. Take that uphill to the next landing. Once there, you'll see a bronze statue, entitled *Dealings*, of Jim Rouse, the founder of Columbia, and his brother Willard, who served as executive vice president, on your left. Turn left, passing a fountain inspired by the one in Tivoli Gardens in Rome, Italy, on your right. When you see the red sculpture in front of you, look left and take the asphalt path to continue your hike around the lake.

**DISTANCE & CONFIGURATION:** 2.25-mile loop with spur

**DIFFICULTY:** Easy

**SCENERY:** Lake Kittamaqundi, Patuxent River, mixed hardwoods

**EXPOSURE:** Half and half

**TRAFFIC:** Moderate–heavy

**TRAIL SURFACE:** Asphalt, dirt, brick

**HIKING TIME:** 1 hour

**DRIVING DISTANCE:** 19 miles

**ELEVATION GAIN:** 300' at trailhead, with no elevation change

**ACCESS:** Open 24-7; no fees or permits required. MTA runs buses to downtown Columbia, including Columbia Mall across from Lake

Kittamaqundi; for a complete MTA schedule, call 866-RIDE-MTA or visit mta.maryland.gov.

**WHEELCHAIR ACCESS:** Yes, full trail is asphalt.

**MAPS:** USGS *Savage*

**FACILITIES:** Food, drinks, restrooms in restaurants along west side of lake

**CONTACT:** 410-715-3000, columbiaassociation. org/about-us/ca-open-spaceparks-recreation /lake-management

**LOCATION:** 10215 Wincopin Cir., Columbia

**COMMENTS:** The mileage markers included in the Description start at the entrance to the trail loop behind the Sushi Sono restaurant, but the abundance of parking in a variety of areas surrounding the lake make it possible for you to start your hike elsewhere.

Cattails and willow trees make this section of the lake more scenic. Stay straight, passing a path on your right that leads to Whole Foods, and stay straight again when another trail to the right leads to a residential area. At just under 0.4 mile, the trail splits. A path leads right to the Downtown Columbia Trail. Instead, head left. You'll see some benches on your left and then another junction at 0.4 mile; go left (east) over the wooden footbridge. You'll now be on the opposite end of the lake from where you started. A decent-size wooded buffer separates you from US 29, which is not far to the right. The Patuxent River runs in between. You won't be able to see the river here, but you will a little farther down the trail.

Pass through Kennedy Gardens, which include Yoshino cherry trees grown from saplings of the original cherry trees donated to Washington, D.C., by Japan. In this area, many of the plants and trees are labeled, and it's a great place to take a break—sit on one of the many benches and soak in the peaceful beauty. The trail splits into a loop at 0.7 mile; you can head either way. Note the contrast between this section of the hike and the beginning. Here, white-tailed deer run in the woods; fish, turtles, frogs, and snakes make their homes in the river; and you'll probably have the trail all to yourself. In the grassy area between the two paths, metal sculptures depict the various neighborhoods that make up Columbia.

At 0.85 mile you'll gain a better view of the Patuxent on your right as the trail saddles up next to it, following it upstream. At just over 1 mile, you'll cross over a wooden boardwalk and see town houses on the right. Continue straight on the wide asphalt path as it meanders through mature trees, and at 1.25 miles you'll reach a trail junction. A left takes you back to the Lakefront Plaza, where you parked. Instead, take a right to head north toward Wilde Lake. The woods here are thick and mature, full of sassafras, maple, beech, sycamore, oak, gum, tulip poplar, and sumac; these

223

## Lake Kittamaqundi

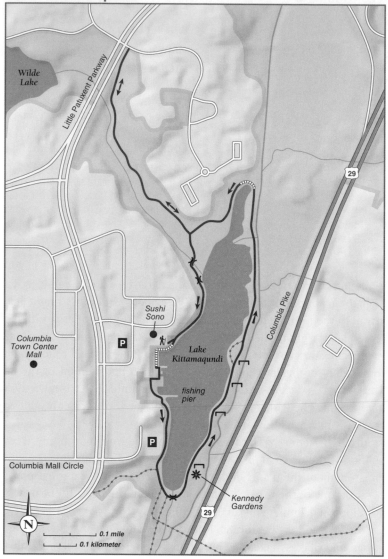

fantastic foliage trees turn the path into a rainbow of color in the fall. This portion of trail includes a parcourse fitness circuit, so you'll pass stations along the way.

Unfortunately, you can hear the traffic from Little Patuxent Parkway. This section of the trail has a nice mix of fairly short, immature trees alongside centuries-old walnuts that soar hundreds of feet above. At 1.6 miles you'll reach the Little Patuxent Parkway. Here, you can choose to cross Little Patuxent Parkway and do the Wilde Lake Loop on the other side. However, to continue on the Lake Kittamaqundi Loop, turn around and head back. When you reach the main trail intersection again at 2 miles, turn right. You'll have a good view of Nomanisan Island, reachable only by boat, on your left; during summer you can rent a canoe, rowboat, or paddleboat at the pier. Cross two wooden footbridges in quick succession; the little creek below connects Lake Kittamaqundi with Wilde Lake. A small buffer of trees stands between you and the lake, with some apple trees on the right. At 2.2 miles you'll reach the trail junction with the boardwalk on your left. Veer right, uphill, to reach Sushi Sono restaurant and the end of your hike.

## NEARBY/RELATED ACTIVITIES

Check out what's happening at **The Soundry** (thesoundry.com) or nearby **Merriweather Post Pavilion** (410-715-5550, merriweathermusic.com), the "Mid-Atlantic Fillmore East," which has hosted virtually every big name in rock and pop music. Designed by famed architect Frank Gehry, it has been rocking for more than 50 years. You'll find it just southwest of Lake Kittamaqundi across Little Patuxent Parkway.

• • • • • • • • • • • • • • • • • • • • • • • •

**GPS TRAILHEAD COORDINATES** N39° 12.962'   W76° 51.315'

**DIRECTIONS** Take I-95 S 3 miles to Exit 49B (I-695 W). Take I-695 W 5 miles to Exit 16 and merge onto I-70 W. Continue to US 29 south (toward Columbia and Washington, D.C.). Take Exit 20B (MD 175) toward Columbia Town Center. Go 1 mile and turn left onto Wincopin Circle; park anywhere in the nearby lots or garages and walk east toward the lake. The trail described in this hike starts roughly behind the Sheraton Hotel, in front of the Sushi Sono restaurant.

You'll follow the Middle Branch of the Patuxent River for much of this hike.

**SEARCH FOR A** variety of wildlife in a swath of buffer woods around the Middle Branch of the Patuxent River.

## DESCRIPTION

The varied topography and ecosystems of the 1,021-acre Middle Patuxent Environmental Area (MPEA) host an impressive diversity of wildlife, including roughly 150 bird species, more than 40 mammal species, and many amphibians, reptiles, and fishes.

Pick up an informative trail brochure at the bulletin board before you head out. At 0.2 mile you'll come to a clearing and see marker #1 for the Woodcock Habitat Management Area. The wooden post marks the beginning of the interpretive Wildlife Loop Trail, which was not entirely easy to follow during my visit, but it's worth a shot for wildlife aficionados. In just another 0.1 mile, you'll come to marker #2; head right and pass a bench on your left.

You're now leaving the Wildlife Loop Trail, using a connector path to the Southwind Trail. Walk through a field of midlevel growth (blueberry, sweet cicely, azalea, and mountain laurel) with a few pines beyond as you head toward the Middle Branch of the Patuxent River.

This very lovely spot in thick woods shows no sign at all of humanity. At 0.5 mile the scenery takes on an Appalachian feel, with ferns, big hunks of rock, moss, and

**DISTANCE & CONFIGURATION:** 3.5-mile combination

**DIFFICULTY:** Easy–moderate

**SCENERY:** Varied flora and fauna, the Middle Branch of the Patuxent River

**EXPOSURE:** Slightly more shade than sun

**TRAFFIC:** Light–moderate

**TRAIL SURFACE:** Initially crushed rock and then mostly packed dirt

**HIKING TIME:** 1.5 hours

**DRIVING DISTANCE:** 21 miles

**ELEVATION GAIN:** 380' at trailhead, 280' at low point

**ACCESS:** Sunrise–sunset; no fees or permits required; see Comments for additional information

**WHEELCHAIR ACCESS:** No

**MAPS:** USGS *Clarksville;* trail maps and informational brochures available at the trailhead bulletin board and online at howardcountymd.gov/MPEA

**FACILITIES:** Restroom at Trotter Rd. trailhead

**CONTACT:** 410-313-4726, howardcountymd.gov/MPEA

**LOCATION:** 5795 Trotter Rd., Clarksville

**COMMENTS:** The Trotter Rd. entrance was under construction at press time, with a scheduled reopening in summer 2019. Enhancements will include additional parking, a trailhead kiosk, a bathroom, and a park office. During closure, trails are accessible via South Wind Cir.

the river winding its way through the big trees. You'll cross a feeder stream of the Middle Branch at 0.6 mile, and then turn left, paralleling it on your right.

At 0.75 mile turn right onto the wide trail with a hiker icon. You'll be walking alongside the Middle Patuxent River and soon cross over a wooden bridge. Here the trail can become a bit muddy, but it eventually turns grassy.

At just over 1 mile, you'll see a trail post pointing to the right; head right, uphill and into an open field. Known as edge habitat, this area provides important hunting and nesting grounds for a variety of animals. Many of the trees in the approaching field are persimmons. A grassland-restoration project is under way in this open area, called Clegg's Meadow, with plantings of bluestem, Indian, switch, and Eastern gamma grasses. Also look for purple martin housing here. Head left, following the treeline around the pasture. Watch for deer, red foxes, and hawks, all of which frequent this area.

When the trail splits at 1.25 miles, go left to extend the hike. A few private homes will shatter the isolation for a while, but as you continue on the trail you'll soon regain a feeling of seclusion. Be on the lookout for a trail on your left. If you miss it and continue straight, you'll reach the South Wind Circle entrance to the area.

When you see the trail split on your left, you'll have two options, both heading south. Take the one on the right, and then almost immediately the trail splits again. Again, stay right. Here, you're on a wide, grassy trail with some sunshine and brush on either side. Spicebush is dominant here, providing food for numerous songbirds, including wood thrushes and veeries.

At 1.7 miles you'll come to a stream and veer left, following the little hiker icon. As you parallel Carroll's Branch on the right, the path becomes wide, grassy, and muddy, and you'll begin to see numbered wooden posts again. If you still have the

## Middle Patuxent Environmental Area

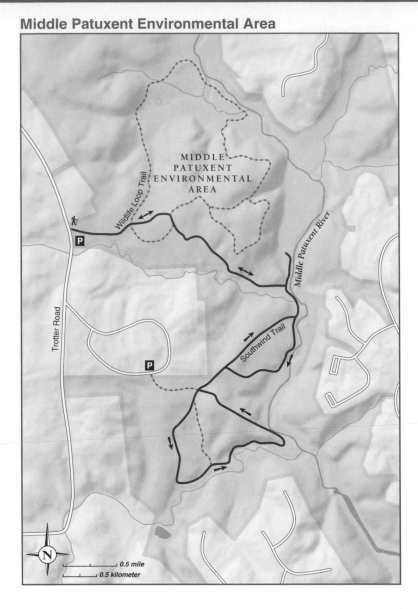

Wildlife Loop Trail brochure you picked up at the hike's beginning, you may find the numbers a bit misleading because they don't correspond to the map; that's because you left the Wildlife Loop Trail. Instead, this is the Southwind Trail. This, too, is an interpretive trail, and you can retrieve the corresponding information online at issuu.com/hocorec/docs/mpeavirtualtour.

Jump over a small feeder stream at just under 1.9 miles and then head right. Going left is a quicker way back to the loops' starting point. You'll soon come to a big stream on your right—a nice spot for a picnic.

Continuing on, at 2.1 miles, the trail opens up into a little pasture with multiple trail options. Veer left (north), hiking back into the woods and winding through mature upland forest, with beautiful views of the Middle Patuxent on the right.

At 2.4 miles you'll be back on the trail you hiked coming in earlier. Turn right (northeast) and head uphill toward the pasture, but this time, instead of making a right to return on the same trail, go straight, walking along the treeline with the pasture on your right. You'll reach the other side of the pasture in around 2.8 miles and head left (north) to return on the same route you took before.

At just under 3 miles, turn left onto the connector trail you took earlier. The option to the right (north) toward the wooden footpath will lead you to a dead end but does give you a chance to check out marker #13 from the nature trail. At just under 3.5 miles, head left when the trail splits to catch another portion of the Wildlife Loop. After walking through a pasture, you'll return to your car. Here, you can spend more time exploring the other wildlife markers in this part of the MPEA.

## NEARBY/RELATED ACTIVITIES

You might enjoy seeing **Centennial Park** (page 218), just 4 miles to the east on MD 108. Take time to walk through the park's Centennial Arboretum, an immaculately maintained treasure trove of diverse tree species. For good restaurants and shopping, head to **Columbia Town Center** and **Lake Kittamaqundi** (page 222); go east on MD 108 to US 29 south and follow the signs to Town Center.

• • • • • • • • • • • • • • • • • • • • • • • • • •

**GPS TRAILHEAD COORDINATES** N39° 12.750'   W76° 55.096'

**DIRECTIONS** Take I-95 S 3 miles to Exit 49B (I-695 W). Take I-695 W 5 miles to Exit 16 and merge onto I-70 W. Take US 29 south and then MD 108 west toward Clarksville. Go 5 miles and turn left onto Trotter Road. Drive 0.5 mile to the gravel parking area on the left. The trail starts behind the wooden posts at the edge of the parking area next to the informational bulletin board.

A sycamore towers over the Glen Artney Area.

**TAKE IN THE** best of the Glen Artney Area on this hike: two branches of the Patapsco River, mature forest, and Lost Lake.

## DESCRIPTION

The trailhead leads onto the purple-blazed Soapstone Trail. A long, flat ridge drops off both sides of the trail, with Soapstone Branch to the right and very big beech trees all around. Just before 0.2 mile, the trail heads into a deep gully; follow it down to level ground.

Before you reach 0.5 mile, you'll have already crossed two small streams. You'll traverse quite a few more while following the Soapstone Trail. Midlevel growth includes mountain laurel and sumac, with oak and beech trees towering above.

At 0.5 mile a trail leads up to your left. You'll take this alternate path on your return. For now, continue straight. As you move on, huge rocks dominate the trail. You'll make several easy crossings over Soapstone Branch in this section. At 0.8 mile, after two more stream crossings, you'll see the orange-blazed Bull Run Trail uphill to the right; this trail will be part of your return route. For now, stay on Soapstone Trail.

Immediately after the Bull Run Trail, you'll come to the longest crossing over Soapstone Branch; the large rocks here make this manageable. On the other side is a little parking area with a pavilion, restrooms, and a playground.

**DISTANCE & CONFIGURATION:** 4.7-mile out-and-back with 2 loops

**DIFFICULTY:** Moderate

**SCENERY:** Soapstone and Santee Branches, Patapsco River, forest

**EXPOSURE:** More shade than sun

**TRAFFIC:** Moderate

**TRAIL SURFACE:** Packed dirt

**HIKING TIME:** 1.5–2 hours

**DRIVING DISTANCE:** 7 miles

**ELEVATION GAIN:** 300' at trailhead, 40' at low point

**ACCESS:** 9 a.m.–sunset; no fees or permits required at Rolling Rd. entrance. The official parking area for Glen Artney (5120 South St.) is $3/person on holidays and weekends April–October; otherwise, it's $2/vehicle.

**WHEELCHAIR ACCESS:** On Grist Mill Trail

**MAPS:** USGS *Relay;* trail map available online at dnr.maryland.gov/publiclands/documents /Patapsco_Avalonmap.pdf or purchase one at shopdnr.com/PVSP-Avalon_GlenArtney _OrangeGrove_Hilton.aspx.

**FACILITIES:** Restrooms, water, pavilions, and playground at the paved area at 0.8 mile of this hike

**CONTACT:** 877-620-8367, dnr.maryland.gov /publiclands/pages/central/patapsco.aspx

**LOCATION:** South Rolling Rd., Catonsville (by Park and Ride)

**COMMENTS:** Due to flooding in 2018, portions of the Grist Mill Trail are being repaired. This may continue into 2019. Check the website before your trip; an alternative route is described below.

From the parking area, head diagonally uphill to the right (with the restrooms on your left) to stay on the Soapstone Trail. At 1 mile you'll see the Santee Branch Trail to your right. Continue straight on the same purple-blazed Soapstone Trail. In 0.1 mile you'll come to a park road and see trails heading off in several directions. Take a hard left to continue on the Soapstone Trail.

*Note:* If you're visiting while the Grist Mill Trail is inaccessible (see Comments), instead, turn right here on the park road and take the second trail on your right, about a quarter mile up the road. When that trail splits, head left, and you'll reach the Vineyard Spring Trail. Turn right to continue on the trail (and jump below to the description of the Vineyard Spring Trail).

Almost immediately, you'll come to another trail intersection. Stay straight, going downhill. At 1.5 miles you'll reach a park road. Turn right and walk toward the stone tunnel, with the CSX railroad tracks overhead. Walk through the tunnel, under the tracks, and you'll come to Glen Artney Road, with official parking to your left.

Head toward Lost Lake. On your left, you'll come to a wooden notice board, informing you of the happenings in the park. Walk to your left, over a little wooden footbridge to reach Lost Lake, which was once a feeder pond for the mill race that powered the iron works downstream. Facing the lake, turn left, walking clockwise around the water. Here, the path might not be quite as visible, but continue around the lake, which has little benches where you can sit and enjoy the scenery.

After completing the loop around Lost Lake, you'll come to the trailhead for the Grist Mill Trail on your left, at 1.7 miles. This wide, paved trail is a great option for those with wheelchairs or strollers.

## Patapsco Valley State Park: Glen Artney Area

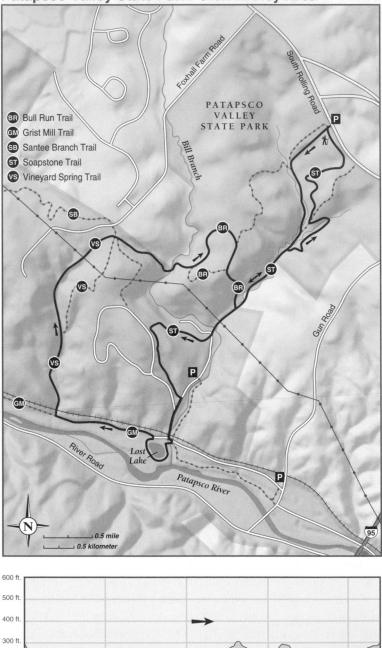

Continue along the Grist Mill Trail, passing a fishing area on your left, and at 2 miles turn right onto Vineyard Springs Trail. You'll walk through another stone tunnel that brings you under the CSX train tracks. This red-blazed trail is steep and rocky, and you'll be surrounded by large oaks as you walk alongside a large gully to your right.

At 2.6 miles you'll reach a power line cut and cross it. Here the topography changes drastically. Before, it was soaring old-growth trees; here, it's short, nubbly trees and lots of underbrush. Obviously, people used this area as an open field sometime in the last 20–30 years, but vegetation is now filling it in nicely.

When you reach a trail intersection at 2.7 miles, cross over the wide Santee Branch Trail and head straight, taking the white-blazed trail. Almost immediately after, head left on the orange-blazed Bull Run Trail, which will lead you back to Soapstone Branch. The descent is quite steep, and at 3 miles you'll reach a stream. Use the large stones to cross, and then continue left, with the stream on your left. Follow the trail back up a fairly steep incline, away from the water, and at 3.1 miles you'll intersect with the main orange-blazed Bull Run Trail loop. Turn left here, and soon after, at the next intersection (with orange blazes going in both directions), make another left.

Continue following the orange-blazed Bull Run Trail all the way back down into the gully, reaching Soapstone Branch at 3.6 miles. Though you can cut down at this point and cross the branch to rejoin the Soapstone Trail on the other side, the easier route in high water would be to continue straight on Bull Run until it officially joins back to the Soapstone Trail and then turn left. However you get there, once you reach the Soapstone Trail, begin retracing your steps north. At just over 4 miles, you'll see a trail to your right; take this alternate path to enjoy a higher elevation route back up to the trailhead. Once you see Rolling Road, you can turn left to walk back to the main parking area through the woods, rather than walking on the side of the road.

## NEARBY/RELATED ACTIVITIES

You might enjoy hiking through the nearby **Orange Grove and Hilton Areas of Patapsco Valley State Park;** for hike descriptions and directions, see pages 234–243. I-195 runs from the Park and Ride at the Glen Artney trailhead to BWI Airport at the other end. If you can't fly off to paradise, check out the **BWI Trail** (page 254).

• • • • • • • • • • • • • • • • • • • • • • • • •

**GPS TRAILHEAD COORDINATES** N39° 14.675'    W76° 43.152'

**DIRECTIONS** Take I-95 S 5.5 miles to I-195. Take I-195 W toward Catonsville/Park and Ride; continue toward the Park and Ride to where I-195 ends at Rolling Road. Turn left and continue on Rolling Road; immediately look for the gravel parking area on the right shoulder across from the Park and Ride lot. You'll see several trails leading from this area; begin at the one with the sign for the Soapstone Trail.

Pigs Run Stream in autumn

**THIS HIKE PROVIDES** enough elevation changes for a great workout and some kid-friendly pit stops to keep everyone happy.

## DESCRIPTION

Begin your descent on the blue-blazed Forest Glen Trail. At 0.3 mile Pigs Run Trail comes in on your right, but continue down the Forest Glen Trail. When you reach Pigs Run Stream, turn left to continue on the Forest Glen Trail, paralleling the water on your right. Pigs Run Stream becomes a bit wider as you reach an old stone bridge, which supports the CSX train tracks above. Walk through the tunnel and climb onto the paved Grist Mill Trail at 0.5 mile.

*Note:* If the Grist Mill Trail is inaccessible (see Comments), instead, turn right onto the Buzzards Rock Trail before the tunnel and cross the stream. Head up Buzzards Rock Trail, and when you reach a junction, turn right onto Sawmill Branch Trail, which will take you back down on a nice loop to Pigs Run Stream. Return on the Pigs Run Trail (described below).

The Grist Mill Trail parallels the Patapsco River. To the right, the trail leads to Ilchester Road. When I visited, this portion of the trail was closed for the removal of Bloede's Dam, which was built in 1907 and removed in 2018 due to safety and environmental concerns. The project is expected to be complete in 2019, restoring

**DISTANCE & CONFIGURATION:** 4.4 miles, 2 loops

**DIFFICULTY:** Moderate–strenuous

**SCENERY:** Patapsco River, historical structures, Cascade Falls

**EXPOSURE:** Mostly shade

**TRAFFIC:** Light–moderate

**TRAIL SURFACE:** Packed dirt, rock, and asphalt

**HIKING TIME:** 3 hours

**DRIVING DISTANCE:** 9 miles

**ELEVATION GAIN:** 285' at trailhead, 45' at low point

**ACCESS:** 9 a.m.–sunset; $2/vehicle day-use fee or $3/person on weekends and holidays April–October (usually collected by honor system—place the money in an envelope at the tollgate)

**WHEELCHAIR ACCESS:** On paved Grist Mill Trail and in Hilton-area structures; the All Sensory Trail provides an experience for those who are visually impaired, have autism, or use wheelchairs.

**MAPS:** USGS *Relay, Savage, Ellicott City, Baltimore West;* you can order a trail map online at shopdnr.com/trailguides.aspx.

**FACILITIES:** Phone, restrooms, campsites, pavilions, and playgrounds

**CONTACT:** 877-620-8367, dnr.maryland.gov /publiclands/pages/central/patapsco.aspx

**LOCATION:** 1101 Hilton Ave., Catonsville

**COMMENTS:** Due to flooding in 2018, portions of the Grist Mill Trail are being repaired. This may continue beyond 2019. Check the website before your trip; an alternative route is described below.

access to Ilchester Road and surrounding areas. If you'd like to explore more in the area, many trails lead off Grist Mill Trail to your right. However, turn left onto the Grist Mill Trail, walking with the Patapsco River on your right, for this hike.

At 0.8 mile you'll come to the Patapsco Swinging Bridge and old remains of the Orange Grove flour mill on your left. The flour mill operated from 1856 to 1905 as one of the largest on the East Coast.

The swinging bridge to your right once allowed mill workers who lived in a company-owned community across the river to walk to work. The current Grist Mill Trail Bridge was built in 2006 by the Maryland Department of Natural Resources.

Reaching the other side of the bridge, you'll find the Avalon parking area. This area once supported the Orange Grove Milltown, with 41 mill workers, and was also the site of Maryland's first recreational campground. Here, you'll now find the welcome respite of restrooms and a water fountain across the street to your left, as well as the Cascade Falls trailhead just in front of you to the right.

Take the blue-blazed Cascade Falls Trail that winds uphill, navigating a little switchback, before quickly coming to Cascade Falls. Ferns, mossy rocks, and oaks surround a narrow ridge where the falls spill over; the trail becomes a series of rocks that leads across the falls and give you a fantastic view. On the other side of the falls, you'll find yourself at the bottom of a big stone staircase. Climb up, and at the top, the Ridge Trail goes left and the blue-blazed Cascade Falls Trail goes right. Turn right, walking with Cascade Falls on your right and following it upstream. At 1.7 miles cross the stream and continue to the left upstream. You will pass trails on your right and left, but continue along the main path paralleling the water, still following the blue blazes.

At just under 2 miles, cross the wooden footbridge on your right over the stream. At 2 miles you'll come upon a trail junction. Following the trail straight will

## Patapsco Valley State Park: Hilton Area

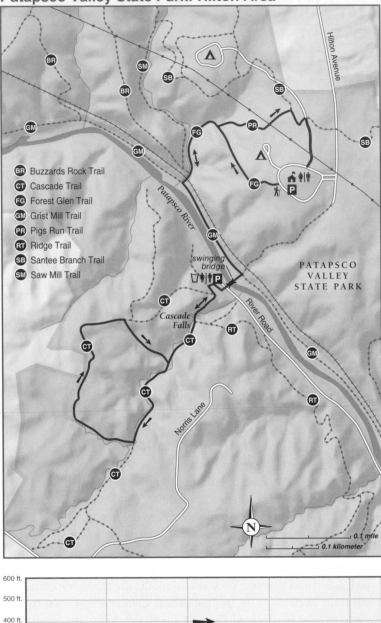

**BR** Buzzards Rock Trail
**CT** Cascade Trail
**FG** Forest Glen Trail
**GM** Grist Mill Trail
**PR** Pigs Run Trail
**RT** Ridge Trail
**SB** Santee Branch Trail
**SM** Saw Mill Trail

Patapsco River

swinging
bridge

Cascade
Falls

Norris Lane

River Road

Hilton Avenue

PATAPSCO
VALLEY
STATE PARK

N

0.1 mile
0.1 kilometer

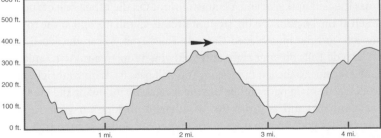

bring you to an alternative entrance for this hike at Landing Road. However, to continue on this hike, turn right. At the four-way junction at 2.1 miles, continue straight uphill, following the blue-blazed trail.

Immediately after, a small trail on the left leads to a residential area, but you should continue straight on the main trail. At the junction at 2.4 miles, turn left. When the trail splits again, follow the blue-blazed trail down to the right. At 2.8 miles you'll reach the main trail that parallels the river. Turn left to continue back, following the blue markers across the stream. At 3 miles you'll reach the waterfall again. At the base of the waterfall, cross the stream and follow the blue-blazed trail back down to the Avalon parking area, with the water on your right. Walk back over the swinging bridge, pausing to enjoy the beautiful view of the Patapsco River.

Turn left onto the paved Grist Mill Trail (this should look familiar); the river will be on your left. At 3.3 miles turn right to go back through the stone tunnel. Take the blue-blazed Forest Glen Trail. At 3.6 miles, after ascending the trail, if you look carefully you'll see a trail junction you passed at the beginning of your hike. Turn left on the purple-blazed Pigs Run Trail. (Going right here to continue on the Forest Glen Trail will take you directly back to the Hilton Area park entrance). A thick upland forest surrounds you on the Pigs Run Trail, and wildflowers are abundant. You'll cross a wooden footbridge and then pass through a power line cut before reaching the white-blazed Santee Branch Trail at 4 miles. Turn right onto the Santee Branch Trail and soon reach a road; turn right and follow the road to the main Hilton entrance and parking lot. If you parked closer to the Forest Glen trailhead, walk along the road to the right or straight through the playground to reach the trailhead.

## NEARBY/RELATED ACTIVITIES

The Hilton Area also offers a 2-acre tire playground, as well as a nature center that hosts many activities throughout the year. You might also want to hike through the nearby **Glen Artney and Orange Grove Areas of Patapsco Valley State Park** (see pages 230 and 238). Also nearby is historic **Ellicott City** (ellicottcity.net), a former mill town founded in 1772, where you will find shops and restaurants on the main street.

• • • • • • • • • • • • • • • • • • • • • • • • • •

**GPS TRAILHEAD COORDINATES** N39° 14.701'   W76° 44.817'

**DIRECTIONS** Take I-95 S 3 miles to Exit 49B (I-695 W). Take I-695 W to Exit 13. Follow Frederick Road west 2 miles, and then turn left onto South Rolling Road. Make your first right onto Hilton Avenue. Continue 1.5 miles until you reach the park; turn right and follow the park road around to a parking area, about 0.2 mile. A sign on the right marks the Forest Glen Trail.

# 50 PATAPSCO VALLEY STATE PARK:
## Orange Grove and Avalon Areas

Cascade Falls is a highlight on this hike.

**SEE WATERFALLS, RIVERS,** streams, upland forest, historical structures, and a pasture in one of the more diverse hikes in Patapsco Valley State Park. This hike begins in the Orange Grove Area and takes in the Avalon Area before returning to Orange Grove.

## DESCRIPTION

The 300-foot suspension swinging bridge provides one of the few places for easy access across the Patapsco River. You can cross it to go to the paved Grist Mill Trail and the Hilton Area of the state park, but to hike in the Orange Grove Area, turn around and head uphill on the stone steps to the blue-blazed Cascade Trail. It winds uphill, taking in a little switchback, before quickly coming to Cascade Falls at 0.2 mile. Ferns, mossy rocks, and oaks surround a narrow ridge where the falls spill over; the trail becomes a series of rocks that leads across the falls and gives you an unobstructed and fantastic view. It's a superb way to start your hike.

On the other side of the falls, you'll see the orange-blazed Ridge Trail on the left; you'll take that trail on the way back, so head right instead to continue on the Cascade Trail. The trail becomes very rocky as it winds through mature beech, oak, dogwood, maple, redbud, and sassafras trees; you'll see and hear the stream that

**DISTANCE & CONFIGURATION:** 6.4-mile loop

**DIFFICULTY:** Moderate

**SCENERY:** Cascade Falls, historical ruins, abundant wildlife, mature forest

**EXPOSURE:** Shady

**TRAFFIC:** Light

**TRAIL SURFACE:** Packed dirt

**HIKING TIME:** 3 hours

**DRIVING DISTANCE:** 11 miles

**ELEVATION GAIN:** 55' at trailhead, 380' at high point

**ACCESS:** 9 a.m.–sunset; $2/vehicle day-use fee or $3/person on weekends and holidays April–October (usually collected by honor system—place the money in an envelope at the tollgate)

**WHEELCHAIR ACCESS:** No

**MAPS:** USGS *Relay*; trail map available online at dnr.maryland.gov/publiclands/documents /Patapsco_Avalonmap.pdf or purchase one at shopdnr.com/PVSP-Avalon_GlenArtney _OrangeGrove_Hilton.aspx.

**FACILITIES:** Restrooms and water at trailhead

**CONTACT:** 877-620-8367, dnr.maryland.gov /publiclands/pages/central/patapsco.aspx

**LOCATION:** River Rd., Elkridge

feeds the falls to the right. At just over 0.3 mile, cross the water again. Once on the other side of the river, head left, paralleling the water upstream. At 0.4 mile cross the water again, continuing to parallel the stream and following the blue-blazed trail upstream. You'll come to a creekbed and small wooden footbridge at just over 0.6 mile, followed by a little gully full of moss and ferns. A few eastern hemlocks are visible here; also look for plant species more commonly found in the mountains, such as erect trillium, false hellebore, and wild sarsaparilla. At 0.7 mile cross the water again, this time on a wooden footbridge, and then again on another wooden footbridge soon after.

At 0.8 mile the trail levels out and quiets down a bit. You're now away from the water, walking among beech and oak trees in a mature forest. At a little under 0.9 mile, the trail splits; head left up the hill. Soon after making a left, you'll reach another trail junction at 0.9 mile with a sign pointing left to the yellow-blazed Morning Choice Trail. Go left, following the Morning Choice Trail. (If you go straight, you'll wind up leaving the park boundary in another 0.3 mile.) At 1 mile check for cars and cross Norris Lane, a paved park road, and continue straight. You'll immediately come to a T-intersection and turn left.

At 1.2 miles make another left at the trail junction. In another 0.1 mile, you'll reach a sign for the Old Track Loop. For a short section, the red- and yellow-blazed trails run together. Stay on the yellow-blazed Morning Choice Trail. When the trail splits again, you can either go right on the yellow-blazed trail or left on the red-blazed trail. Turn left, following the short portion of the red-blazed Old Track Loop, and at 1.5 miles cross over a wooden footbridge. Soon after, you'll reach another junction and make a left. Immediately on your right up the hill, you'll see an old iron fence enclosing a cemetery that sits at the edge of Belmont Manor and Historic Park. In just another 0.1 mile, where the other portion of the Old Track Loop links up, you'll

# Patapsco Valley State Park:
# Orange Grove and Avalon Areas

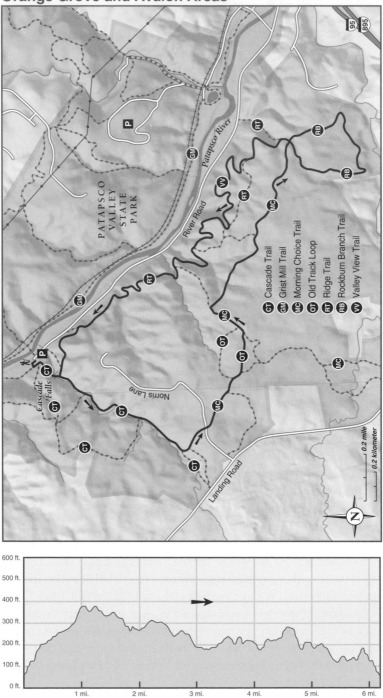

CT Cascade Trail
GM Grist Mill Trail
MC Morning Choice Trail
OT Old Track Loop
RT Ridge Trail
RB Rockburn Branch Trail
VV Valley View Trail

once again be back on the yellow-blazed Morning Choice Trail. Soon you'll reach the green-blazed Old Connector Trail, which would shave off a good portion of your hike if you decided to continue straight. Instead, turn right downhill to continue on the yellow-blazed trail.

Cross over a little stream at about 2 miles; soon after, the path becomes a cut groove along the treeline of the field before winding back through the woods. You'll soon pass the ruins of two old houses on the left. Once past the house ruins, at 2.1 miles, you'll reach a second junction for a connector trail on the left. Instead, make a right and you'll come back to the field again, where you'll follow the treeline. Look across the field for deer. As a bonus, you'll see loads of jays, cardinals, blackbirds, and cedar waxwings flitting about the mountain laurel and holly on the edge of the field.

At 2.6 miles you'll come to the purple-blazed Rockburn Branch Trail. You'll eventually return to this intersection to go north. For now, turn right to hike the nice 1-mile Rockburn Branch Trail loop. The route winds through mature forest, and while you'll see several trail junctions, sticking to the purple-blazed trail will keep you on the right track. At 3.6 miles, back at the intersection, go right for 100 yards on the purple-blazed trail and then turn left onto the thin orange-blazed Ridge Trail. Soon after, at just over 4.3 miles, you'll see a sign for the white-blazed Valley View Trail. Take a right onto it and enjoy a more meandering path above River Road with fewer mountain bikers.

Valley View Trail provides a good sense of the topography—hills rising and falling all around, with the piedmont river valley below. You should be able to catch glimpses of the Patapsco River and River Road below you.

At 5 miles turn right at the T-intersection to get back on the orange-blazed Ridge Trail, which winds along a series of drainage cuts. You've lost your valley views, but you'll gain a level area in mature upland forest, with abundant groves of mountain laurel. Head downhill and soon pass the connector on the left to the yellow-blazed Morning Choice Trail that you hiked earlier. You'll still see lots of mountain laurel and now also an abundance of beech trees. In 0.2 mile another stretch of the Valley View Trail links up with the Ridge Trail; turn left to stay on the Ridge Trail, which will take you all the way back to Cascade Falls. When the Ridge Trail splits, turn left. And then at 5.4 miles, you'll see the second connector trail you saw earlier that leads to the Morning Choice Trail. Continue on the orange-blazed Ridge Trail.

The ruins of a series of stone houses, some with collapsed wooden roofs, mark the trail here. You'll soon cross a little stream running over beautiful pink-hued, striated rocks and see a wooden shelter ahead with a bench if you'd like a rest. While you've seen River Road and the Patapsco River at a distance along this portion of the hike, it now comes into view as you parallel it on your right. At 6 miles a path leads down to River Road; turn the other direction and head to the left. You'll soon hear Cascade Falls and, at 6.2 miles, reach the path to the right that leads to the falls. When you reach the falls, cross the water and head back to your car.

## NEARBY/RELATED ACTIVITIES

Satisfy your thirst for history by driving (or walking) on River Road through the developed section of the **Avalon Area of Patapsco Valley State Park.** All that remains of Avalon, a thriving mill town until it was wiped out by a massive flood in 1868, is one stone building that now houses the visitor center, which features exhibits on about 300 years of history in the Patapsco Valley. The 704-foot-long Thomas Viaduct is about 1.5 miles south of the swinging bridge; completed in 1835, the viaduct is the world's largest multiple-arched stone railroad bridge.

• • • • • • • • • • • • • • • • • • • • • • • • • • •

**GPS TRAILHEAD COORDINATES** N39° 14.456'  W76° 44.999'

**DIRECTIONS**  Take I-95 S 5.5 miles to Exit 47 (BWI Airport) and travel east on I-195 to Exit 3 heading toward Elkridge. Turn right (south) onto US 1, and then take the next right onto South Street. You will see the park entrance immediately on the left. Follow the park road past the WELCOME TO ORANGE GROVE SCENIC AREA signs, turn left onto Gun Road, and then make an immediate right onto River Road. Continue to the parking area on the left across from the Swinging Bridge over the Patapsco River. The trail starts at the CASCADE FALLS TRAIL sign, up the hill from the parking area.

The ruins of several stone houses are visible along the trail.

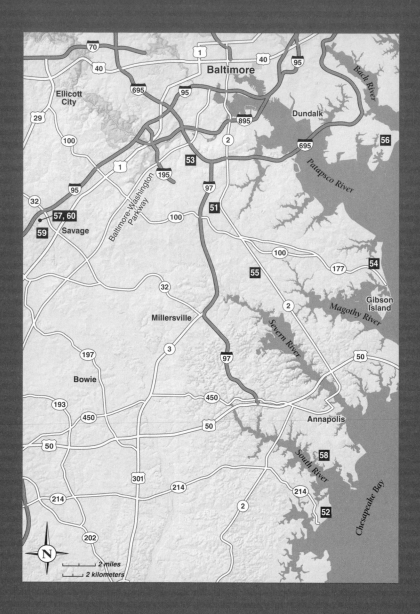

244

# SOUTHERN SUBURBS

Keep an eye out for ducks, turtles, and other wildlife as you pass this nice stretch of marsh.

**THE B&A TRAIL** is Anne Arundel's linear island in the most congested part of the county. This park is a haven for bikers, strollers, and hikers.

## DESCRIPTION

The B&A Trail, part of the East Coast Greenway, is a rails-to-trails park that follows the old Baltimore & Annapolis Railroad (1880–1968) from Glen Burnie in the north (not quite Baltimore) to Annapolis in the south. The park itself is 115 acres, running as a 10-foot-wide paved path that follows a more or less straight line along Ritchie Highway and the twistier Baltimore Annapolis Boulevard to US 50 heading into Annapolis. Along the trail, look for historical markers, labeled A–Z and pointing out interesting historical events and people, that were created as part of an Eagle Scout project.

Beginning in the north at Glen Burnie, the trail is fairly urban, with businesses, residences, roads, and parking lots never too far away. From this vantage, it's easy to believe an oft-quoted statistic about the trail: one third of Anne Arundel County's more than 400,000 residents live within a mile of it. The hike begins behind the parking garage at a swing set and benches.

At 1 mile the Planet Walk begins and you'll see an interesting solar sculpture with some explanatory signs on the sun. Signs for each of the planets are spaced out proportionally along the trail from here until the Earleigh Heights Ranger Station

**DISTANCE & CONFIGURATION:** 12.7-mile point-to-point (13.3 miles for complete trail)

**DIFFICULTY:** Moderate–strenuous

**SCENERY:** Mixed hardwoods, railroading structures, pocket wetlands

**EXPOSURE:** Mostly sunny

**TRAFFIC:** Heavy

**TRAIL SURFACE:** Asphalt

**HIKING TIME:** 4–4.5 hours

**DRIVING DISTANCE:** 11 miles

**ELEVATION GAIN:** 60' at trailhead, 125' at high point

**ACCESS:** Sunrise–sunset; no fees or permits required

**WHEELCHAIR ACCESS:** Yes

**MAPS:** USGS *Relay, Curtis Bay, Round Bay, Gibson Island;* trail map online at aacounty.org /departments/recreation-parks/parks/trails /forms-and-publications

**FACILITIES:** All along the trail in nearby businesses

**CONTACT:** 410-222-6244, aacounty.org /locations-and-directions/ba-trail-ranger-station

**LOCATION:** 7480 Baltimore Annapolis Blvd., Glen Burnie

**COMMENTS:** The hike as described here begins at the Glen Burnie Parking Area and moves south, totaling 12.7 miles. An additional 0.6 mile of trail heads north, terminating at Baltimore Annapolis Blvd., and a bike lane alongside Governor Ritchie Hwy. adds another 2 miles to Jonas Green Park in the south. Several parking areas along the way make shortening the hike easy.

to follow the pattern from the sun of actual distance in outer space. Beyond the solar sculpture, a wooded buffer turns a bit marshy, with some cattails, a reminder of the area's dominant ecozone: nearby, the Severn and Magothy Rivers make their eventual ways to Chesapeake Bay.

After 1.4 miles a nice wooded stream valley full of honeysuckle appears to the left. The first of several old railroad bridges follows soon after, this one crossing Marley Creek in a forest full of maple, hickory, and oak trees. Marley Station Mall soon appears on the left, with abundant parking, which makes it a popular access point for the B&A. Wildflowers line the edge of the trail.

Cross over MD 100 on a bridge at 2.2 miles. Once beyond, the trail becomes more pleasant and wooded, arriving at another parking area at 3 miles on Jumpers Hole Road. A gazebo with benches stands just beyond Jumpers Hole, beginning a nice stretch with flower plantings on both sides of the trail that leads to a marsh full of ducks and sunning turtles, clearly the nicest spot so far.

Cross East West Boulevard at 4.2 miles on a railroad bridge and enter a wooded residential neighborhood. A third parking area can be found soon after, at 5 miles, at Earleigh Heights. This is a good area to rest up, with several places to eat nearby off the trail. A ranger station (closed for renovations March–December of 2019), restrooms, water fountains, and a pond are also just on the other side of Earleigh Heights. A trail map there allows you to check your position.

The area feels a bit more aquatic suddenly, and in summer, you'll see dragonflies shuttling back and forth over the trail. Every now and again, you'll cross a tiny one-lane road, but this stretch for the next few miles is nicely wooded and semi-isolated. Pass another series of wildflower plantings—lilies, daffodils, petunias, peonies,

# Baltimore & Annapolis (B&A) Trail

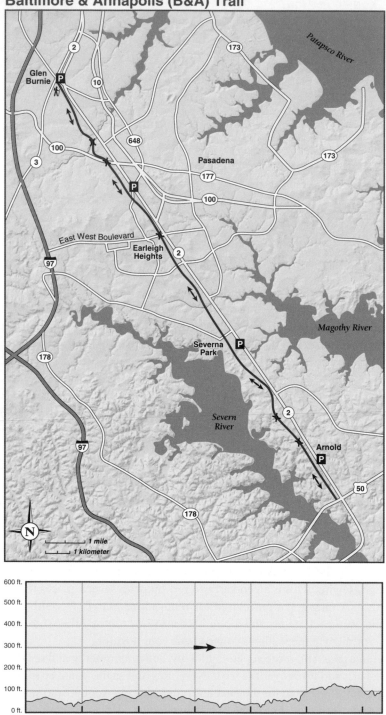

coneflowers—at 7 miles. You'll also see the old Severna Park Railroad Station, one of the few intact structures left over from the railroad. You have probably noticed several switch boxes and a power house along the trail as well, but the Severna Park Station (aside from the ranger station at Earleigh Heights) is the starkest reminder of this corridor's earlier incarnation. Most "stations" along the route were nothing more than small platforms. These are indicated along the trail by rectangular outlines in stone, along with a little sign telling which station it was.

Cross another wooden railroad bridge at 7.6 miles. A trails maintenance shop follows at 8.4 miles. Just beyond is the only spot along the trail where you can still see railroad tracks—only about 20 feet worth, to the left. By 9 miles, you can hear Baltimore Annapolis Boulevard to the left, but a big wooded gulley sits between. To the right is a thickly wooded forest of oak, poplar, and maple trees. The trail is soon lined with dense stands of bamboo.

At 9.5 miles, as you cross the steel railroad bridge, look left for a series of wire-contained rocks, a drainage system. A nice rural scene of rolling hills with horses soon comes into view on the right, providing a quick glance of what the area looked like when the trains still came through. The Arnold Parking Area is at 10.9 miles, followed by a very pleasant couple of miles with nice buffers between the road to the left and neighborhoods to the right. Sometimes these buffers extend to a couple hundred feet. The hike ends at Boulters Way. There, a sign points to US 50 to the left, where you can find the Annapolis parking area and the bike path extension. (If you've done the trail in reverse, beginning at Annapolis, head up Boulters Way east from the parking area, and you'll quickly reach the trail.)

## NEARBY/RELATED ACTIVITIES

Because of the B&A's location and configuration, you can choose from a historic capital (Annapolis—just across the bridge on US 50 W), a big city (Baltimore's Inner Harbor is just a few miles north of the trail's beginning in Glen Burnie), town centers (Glen Burnie, Severna Park, Pasadena, Arnold), or more hiking (BWI Trail is connected by the John Overstreet Connector Trail [page 254] and Kinder Farm Park [page 263]).

• • • • • • • • • • • • • • • • • • • • • • • •

**GPS TRAILHEAD COORDINATES** N39° 09.775'   W76° 37.452'

**DIRECTIONS** Take I-95 S 3.3 miles to Exit 49A (I-695 E). Take I-695 E to I-97 S to Exit 16 and follow MD 648/Baltimore Annapolis Boulevard toward Ferndale/Glen Burnie. Keep left at the fork and merge onto MD 648 South. Cross Crain Highway and turn right onto Barbara Moeller Lane, just after the Glen Burnie District Court building, following signs for parking. Turn right and park in the garage. The trail is just behind the parking garage, across Post 40 Road.

The beginning of this hike features spectacular views of Chesapeake Bay.

**TAKE IN SWEEPING** views of the Chesapeake Bay, followed by a hike around Deep Pond for a peaceful respite from the beachgoers.

## DESCRIPTION

Beverly–Triton Beach Park is a popular destination in Anne Arundel County for fishing, boating, windsurfing, and beach-going. While no swimming is permitted, you can wade into the water and walk along the sandy beaches. The 340-acre park was once the location of the most popular private resort along the Chesapeake Bay, with a lively, cabana-filled beachfront, big bands, and slots. It still retains some of that private aura compared to the neighboring Chesapeake Bay–front parks. It has approximately 5 miles of trails, and this hike treats you to 3 of the most beautiful miles—first along the beach, and then around Deep Pond.

Begin by walking down the gravel beach access road. You'll pass portable toilets and a stationary park map on your right. Continuing, you'll quickly pass the Heritage Trail, also on your right. You'll return on this trail, but for now, veer left on the main road, and the Chesapeake Bay will come into view in front of you.

When you reach the beach, at just under 0.2 mile, take in the beautiful vista. If it's a nice day, you'll likely be sharing the space with windsurfers and other boaters putting in for the day. When you've had your fill, head right (southwest) and look

**DISTANCE & CONFIGURATION:** 2.9 miles, 2 loops

**DIFFICULTY:** Moderate

**SCENERY:** Chesapeake Bay, Deep Pond

**EXPOSURE:** Half and half

**TRAFFIC:** Heavy by main Chesapeake beach area; light on surrounding trails

**TRAIL SURFACE:** dirt, crushed rock, sand

**HIKING TIME:** 1 hour

**DRIVING DISTANCE:** 36 miles

**ELEVATION GAIN:** 23' at trailhead, with no significant rise

**ACCESS:** 7 a.m.–sunset; no fees or permits required. On summer afternoons, the park can reach capacity. Check aacounty.org/services-and -programs/recreation-and-parks-alerts or Twitter (@AACountyGovt) for updates.

**WHEELCHAIR ACCESS:** No

**MAPS:** Stationary trail map at trailhead

**FACILITIES:** Wading beach, portable toilets (at trailhead and near beach)

**CONTACT:** 410-222-7317, aacounty.org /locations-and-directions/beverly-triton -beach-park

**LOCATION:** 1202 Triton Beach Rd., Edgewater

for the trailhead for the Beach and Triton Trails. Head southwest on this blue-and-yellow-blazed trail, paralleling the Chesapeake on your left.

The trail is equal parts grass and sand. On your left, listen for the lapping Chesapeake, and on your right, gaze into a thick forest. At just over a quarter mile, you'll come to a yellow marker pointing you straight ahead and a bench on your left. Several benches along the trail offer beautiful vantage points of the Chesapeake. Here, the trail turns to packed dirt and briefly heads a little farther away from the bay before returning shortly to another bench overlooking the Chesapeake. This portion of the beach is currently closed as it undergoes a shoreline restoration project—volunteers and park staff planted native trees, grasses, and flowers to help with erosion.

Here, you'll also come to a junction, with the blue Beach Trail leading straight ahead and the yellow Triton Trail going right. Continue straight on the blue-blazed Beach Trail into a pine forest. At 0.4 mile the path narrows and briefly turns to crushed gravel before returning to dirt. At 0.5 mile the Beach Trail intersects the red-blazed Heritage Trail and orange-blazed Pond Trail. These two trails run together briefly. Turn left (southwest) to take these trails. You'll quickly see an entrance to the orange-blazed Pond Trail on your right. You'll return on this trail, but for now, keep straight on the wide trail.

Another junction comes up quickly. Both options meet up shortly, but heading left gives you a nice view of a jetty out into the Chesapeake. The trail turns to sand and enters an open area at just under 0.6 mile. On your left you have the Chesapeake, and on your right are long grasses with Deep Pond just beyond that. Making your way down the beach, you'll see a sign for the Heritage Trail. On some maps, the trail continues along the beach at this point, but due to the shoreline restoration project, instead head right, with Beverly Lake to the left and Deep Pond to the right. Both offer fishing and require a Maryland Chesapeake Bay & Coastal Sport Fishing license. Deep Pond is not stocked on a regular basis, but it's tidal, so fish can swim in and out

## Beverly–Triton Beach Park

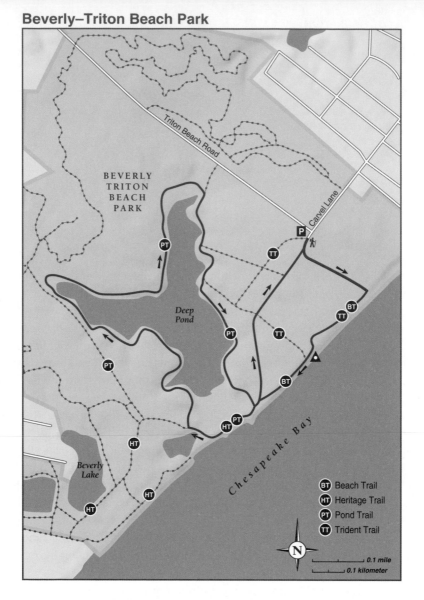

BEVERLY
TRITON
BEACH
PARK

Triton Beach Road

Canvel Lane

P

Deep
Pond

Chesapeake Bay

Beverly
Lake

**BT** Beach Trail
**HT** Heritage Trail
**PT** Pond Trail
**TT** Trident Trail

N

0.1 mile
0.1 kilometer

through a connecting pipe. It's fairly brackish, with commonly sought-after carp and white perch in the spring. Here, the trail heads away from the bay. At 0.7 mile take the orange-blazed Pond Trail to your right. (Continuing straight leads to two other trails within the park, which are also enjoyable to explore if you want to extend your hike.)

The narrow dirt Pond Trail brings you to a lovely view of the pond at 0.8 mile. Here, you'll have sweeping views of the grasslands, with Chesapeake Bay on your right and the pond on your left. Head left and follow the shady trail as it meanders around the lobed outline of the pond. Be on the lookout for some of the wildlife often seen around the park—bald eagles, osprey, otters, white-tailed deer, red foxes, gulls, monarch butterflies, zebra and eastern tiger swallowtail butterflies, king snakes, black rat snakes, green rough snakes, box turtles, and mud turtles all make common appearances. I once startled an adolescent white-tailed deer during a trip around the pond.

At the intersection at 1.3 miles, turn right to stay on the orange-blazed Pond Trail. The trail to your left cuts back down to the Heritage Trail. Very soon after, a path continues straight, but you'll see an orange arrow pointing to your right. Veer right (north) to stay on the orange-blazed trail. Going straight brings you to some local access points to the park.

You'll continue to closely follow the pond on your right. Well-placed boards help keep your shoes dry at spots along this portion of the path, and you'll be surrounded by towering oak and maple trees. At the intersection at just over 2 miles, turn right, passing a bench and area marked for fishing. The trail here is wide and sandy, and you'll soon come to another trail intersecting with the Pond Trail. Head straight to continue following the contours of the pond.

At 2.3 miles a well-placed board helps you walk over a swampy area without getting wet—you'll be glad if you have on bug spray at this point. You'll quickly come to another junction and head right. The Pond Trail soon concludes at the Heritage Trail at 2.5 miles, with the bay in front of you. Here, you can choose to retrace your steps along the Beach Trail back to your car or turn left on the Heritage Trail for a change of scenery. If you opted for the Heritage Trail, when you reach your next trail intersection, head straight (north). To your right, you'll see another pathway down to the bay. At 2.75 miles you'll pass another trail on your left, but continue straight and you'll soon see the parking area come into view in front of you.

## NEARBY/RELATED ACTIVITIES

Just north of Beverly–Triton Beach Park is **Annapolis,** with plenty of dining and shopping options. If you'd like to enjoy another hike with water views, visit nearby **Quiet Waters Park** (page 275).

• • • • • • • • • • • • • • • • • • • • • • • • • •

**GPS TRAILHEAD COORDINATES** N38° 53.087'    W76° 29.725'

**DIRECTIONS** Take I-95 S 3.3 miles to Exit 49A (I-695 E). Take I-695 E to I-97 S. Follow I-97 S 18 miles to Exit 22 (MD 665 E/Riva Road), and then take the MD 2/Solomons Island Road ramp toward Parole/Edgewater. Follow MD 2 for 4.8 miles to MD 214 East/Central Avenue. Turn left onto MD 214 East/Central Avenue and continue onto Shoreham Beach Road, then onto Triton Beach Road. Parking for Beverly–Triton Beach Park will be on your right (overflow parking is on your left). The trail begins along the beach access road.

One of the many spots along the BWI Trail where you can wait to catch a plane landing.

**HIKING AT AN** airport? It's a lot more pleasant than it sounds. Marvel at the woods and wetlands that still coexist with the airport and be awed by jets flying just above your head.

## DESCRIPTION

One caveat: the BWI Trail is an absolute must for aviation aficionados, but it's not for those who crave the solitude of a walk in the woods. However, even if you count yourself in that latter group, the BWI Trail is worth a go; it's not hard to find something to like along its well-used route.

Starting across from the Linthicum Light Rail station, take the asphalt path adjacent to the tracks as it parallels a small buffer of woods to the right with a residential neighborhood beyond. You'll quickly come to two small streets: Shipley Road at 900 feet and Music Lane at 0.3 mile. Beyond that, the trail is simply the sidewalk that runs along Hammonds Ferry Road. Cross Andover Road, turn left at the school, and continue to Camp Meade Road. Ignore the signs pointing right to the airport and follow the BIKE ROUTE signs straight ahead over Camp Meade. At just under 0.7 mile, cross the light rail tracks and swing around into a little wooded section. There's a parking area for the airport beyond a small pond fed by Cabin Branch with cattails

**DISTANCE & CONFIGURATION:** 11.6-mile loop

**DIFFICULTY:** Moderate

**SCENERY:** BWI airport, pines, wetlands

**EXPOSURE:** Mostly sunny

**TRAFFIC:** Moderate–heavy

**TRAIL SURFACE:** Asphalt, boardwalk

**HIKING TIME:** 3.5–4 hours

**DRIVING DISTANCE:** 6.5 miles

**ELEVATION GAIN:** 150' at trailhead, with no significant rise

**ACCESS:** Sunrise–sunset; no fees or permits required

**WHEELCHAIR ACCESS:** Yes, full trail is paved.

**MAPS:** USGS *Relay;* trail map available online at aacounty.org/locations-and-directions/bwi-trail

**FACILITIES:** None on the trail, but food is available at BWI Plaza, and restrooms and water are at various airport and transportation buildings.

**CONTACT:** 410-222-7317, aacounty.org /locations-and-directions/bwi-trail

**LOCATION:** End of Oakdale Rd., Linthicum Heights (across from the Linthicum Southbound Light Rail station)

**COMMENTS:** The lot sometimes fills up, but you can alter the hike distance and configuration by parking at the Tom Dixon Observation Area at 1911 Dorsey Rd. in Glen Burnie.

and (usually) Canada geese. It's a fairly nice stretch of woods here, and it makes up for the initial suburban feel.

At about 1 mile, cross Aviation Boulevard and continue to the Benson-Hammond House, owned by the Ann Arrundell County Historical Society. Built in the late 1820s and the only structure left from the farming period of a postcolonial settlement, the house now serves as a farm museum and shop.

At 1.25 miles stands a grove of pines, the dominant trees around the airport. You'll also see cattails, a reminder that this is a marshy Chesapeake watershed area. At 1.3 miles cross a little driveway that parallels Aviation Boulevard and heads into the BWI General Aviation Facility, and continue to the Maryland Aviation Administration at 1.8 miles. The area becomes very boggy, with more cattails and marshland. You'll come to Dorsey Road at 2.9 miles and Newport Road at just under 3.2 miles. Going straight here takes you to the John Overstreet Connector Trail to the B&A Trail (page 246); to stay on the BWI trail, turn right and follow the sign for the BWI Bike Trail. You'll soon enter arguably the nicest stretch of the trail.

Immediately to the left is busy I-97, but you'll quickly turn away from the road and head into the woods, where you'll see red oaks, tulip poplars, and, of course, the dominant pines. Even though you're deep within the woods, planes roar overhead, maybe only a couple of hundred feet or so above the ground. It's an amazing dichotomy: serene woods shattered by screaming jet engines, retreating to serenity again, and on and on. In all, this wooded stretch lasts 0.7 mile. On the other end of it, at 4.2 miles, fields that are a part of Friendship Park open up to the right; this is a great spot to sit and watch the planes. They come roaring over the treeline in descent and zoom past, barely a hundred feet in the air. In addition to this perfect natural place to watch the planes, you may want to stop at the Thomas A. Dixon

# BWI Trail

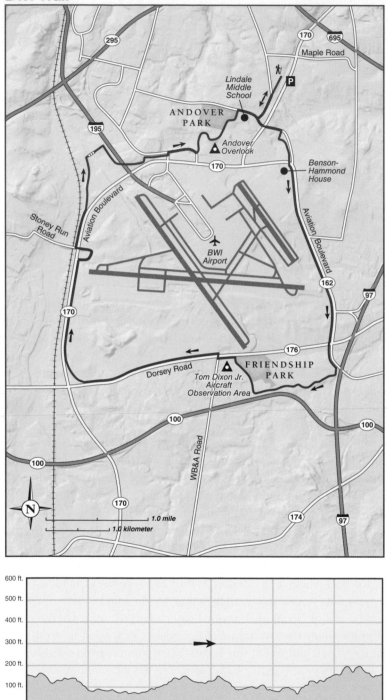

Jr. Aircraft Observation Area just ahead at 4.3 miles; the trail runs to the left of the parking area, which includes benches, portable toilets, and a playground.

At 4.4 miles you'll reach Dorsey Road. Head left, and when you reach WB&A Road at 4.7 miles, cross Dorsey Road and turn left. You'll pass a VFW hall on the left at 5.25 miles. Just beyond is the BWI Plaza if you need a quick pit stop for food or drink.

Continuing on, the trail turns into one of many boardwalks; these wooden walkways denote environmentally sensitive wetland sections. At just over 6 miles, you'll come to another nice wooded area away from the roads where again you'll have a good view of planes taking off, but they're fairly high at this point. Pass through a large pine grove, and then cross a 900-foot boardwalk at 6.7 miles.

At 7.2 miles you'll come to the metal CAR RENTAL RETURN sign; if you hang out for a moment, a plane will come roaring over the hill to your right—you'll be directly under it and can see its belly from a pretty close distance. At the top of the hill at 7.6 miles, head left on Stoney Run Road. As you go over MD 170 on the bridge, look for the green bicycle icon to the right; when you see it, head down the ramp, passing thick woods to the left.

At 8.2 miles you'll see the light rail tracks to the left, in a nice section full of sycamore and tulip poplar trees with water on both sides of the tracks. A big marsh, often filled with herons, geese, and ducks, appears on the left. The trail begins paralleling Amtrak Way, heading toward the BWI Amtrak Station. At 8.7 miles go right across the street to follow the path along a long wooden boardwalk. Stop for a moment on the boardwalk—this is one of the nicest spots on the trail. Herons often wade here, the vegetation is abundant and aquatic, and the marsh itself is ringed with pines.

When you climb the big ramp over I-195 at 9 miles, you'll have a decent view of the entire airport to the right; but the view is not all mechanical—a wildflower meadow sits to the right at 9.2 miles. The trail splits at 9.4 miles; head left in the direction of the sign pointing toward Andover Park.

At 9.7 miles cross Elkridge Landing Road and turn right. At 10 miles you'll come to an open area that runs up a hill and into a field, where you'll see some old farm equipment, a reminder of what the area looked like before the airport was built. From the late 18th century until 1947, when construction began on today's Thurgood Marshall BWI (formerly Friendship International Airport), farmers cultivated the land for tobacco and grains, as well as fruits and vegetables. At Andover Park, you'll find a pasture observation area and an equestrian park, as well as the continuation of the loop that will take you back to the Linthicum Light Rail station.

At the Andover Overlook at the top of the hill, you can see the layout of the entire airport—runways, arriving and departing planes, and control towers. Just beyond, you'll come to the Andover equestrian area—not surprisingly, you'll see horses in the field in front of the farmhouse.

Follow the asphalt path until it turns into a sidewalk in front of Lindale Middle School at 10.8 miles. At 11 miles you'll reach Hammonds Ferry Road and turn left; you've now made a complete loop back to the sidewalk where you entered the trail.

## NEARBY/RELATED ACTIVITIES

The late 1820s **Benson-Hammond House** on the first part of the BWI Trail is owned by the Ann Arrundell County Historical Society and serves as a shop and farm museum. It is open seasonally; confirm hours at aachs.org. For more hiking, take the John Overstreet Connector to the **B&A Trail** (page 246).

• • • • • • • • • • • • • • • • • • • • • • • • • •

**GPS TRAILHEAD COORDINATES** N39° 12.141'   W76° 39.334'

**DIRECTIONS** Take I-95 S 3.3 miles to Exit 49A (I-695 E). Take I-695 E to Exit 6 (MD 170/ S. Camp Meade Road); take the second right onto Maple Road and follow it to the first light. Turn left onto Hammonds Ferry Road, and then turn left onto Oakdale Road. The trail begins at the end of Oakdale Road across from the Linthicum Southbound Light Rail station.

Don't forget to check out the beach after your hike.

**ENJOY A NICE** combination of mature forest, boggy marshland, self-guided nature trails, golden-sand beach, and stunning water views.

## DESCRIPTION

This land, owned by the Anne Arundel County Department of Parks and Recreation, comes well stocked not only in natural beauty but also in human history. Downs Park stands on Bodkin Neck, a peninsula at the confluence of the Patapsco River and Chesapeake Bay. Deeds to its earliest settlement date to 1670 and include Charles Carroll, a signer of the Declaration of Independence, among its initial landowners.

After entering the park, immediately turn right into the first parking area. You'll find two trailheads, one closest to where you've pulled in and the other on the far end of the parking area; take the one closest to the entrance. The trail begins in the woods under the overhanging sign that reads ECO TRAIL—SELF GUIDED NATURE TRAIL, with a wooden platform helping you over some swampy area. Immediately, a trail heads right, but you should continue straight on the Eco Trail.

This stand of hardwoods contains oak, poplar, beech, birch, sycamore, holly, gum, and sassafras trees. At 180 feet, you'll see a bench and little sign suggesting that hikers stop and listen to the sounds of the forest. Interpretive signs such as this one are all along the Eco Trail; they describe the bark, trees, moss, leaves, insects, and animals you'll see as you hike.

**DISTANCE & CONFIGURATION:** 4.4-mile loop

**DIFFICULTY:** Easy

**SCENERY:** Chesapeake Bay, beach, pond, mature trees

**EXPOSURE:** More shade than sun

**TRAFFIC:** Light on trails, moderate–heavy at overlooks and pavilions

**TRAIL SURFACE:** Mostly asphalt

**HIKING TIME:** 2 hours, including time to linger on the beach

**DRIVING DISTANCE:** 22 miles

**ELEVATION GAIN:** 20' at trailhead, with no significant rise

**ACCESS:** Park open daily, 7 a.m.–sunset; visitor center open Monday–Friday 9 a.m.– 4 p.m. and weekends 10 a.m.–3 p.m.; $6/vehicle entrance fee.

**WHEELCHAIR ACCESS:** Perimeter trail is paved.

**MAPS:** USGS *Gibson Island;* trail maps available at gatehouse and information center and online at aacounty.org/departments/recreation-parks /parks/downs

**FACILITIES:** Restrooms, water, playground, picnic, fishing pier, basketball courts, ball fields

**CONTACT:** 410-222-6230; aacounty.org /departments/recreation-parks/parks/downs

**LOCATION:** 8311 John Downs Loop, Pasadena

**COMMENTS:** No swimming is allowed.

At 0.1 mile you'll come to a map that, like all others in the park, has a YOU ARE HERE marker to help you keep your bearings. The trail splits here, and you go to the right, still on the Eco Trail. Accordingly you'll see more signs; the next one gives a rundown of Maryland's official state tree (white oak), flower (black-eyed Susan), dog (Chesapeake Bay retriever), bird (Baltimore oriole), insect (Baltimore checker spot butterfly), and fish (rockfish).

Soon, follow an unpaved sand trail to the left (southeast) to reach the asphalt Perimeter Trail. You're now off the Eco Trail but will finish the portion you've skipped toward the end of the hike. On the Perimeter Trail, which is close to Mountain Road, you'll hear some car traffic, but soon you'll leave the road behind and follow the trail deeper into the thick woods. Look closely through the dense tree cover to see a chain-link fence that delineates the park boundary. The woods beyond the fence give the trail a remote feel. At 0.4 mile you'll pass a trail to your left and a wooden Eagle Scout Project trail to your right, but continue straight. In 0.5 mile the Perimeter Trail links with the Senior Trail, which is paved and leads to the left; keep going straight, and you'll soon pass a basketball court on the left.

At just under a mile, you'll pass through another stand of trees before the view opens up again and the South Overlook appears. Walk up the wooden boardwalk toward a gazebo that once belonged to H. R. Mayo Thom, a wealthy Baltimorean; his family's estate included this area from 1913 through 1937. The gazebo provides a quintessential Maryland view of the Chesapeake Bay.

When you've had your fill of the vista, head down from the overlook and continue along the path, enjoying views of the Chesapeake to your right. You'll pass a little beach area on your right and a playground to your left.

At the junction at 1.15 miles, go right (north) toward the sign pointing to the dog beach. A trail soon heads left to a parking area, but you should stay straight. At

## Downs Park

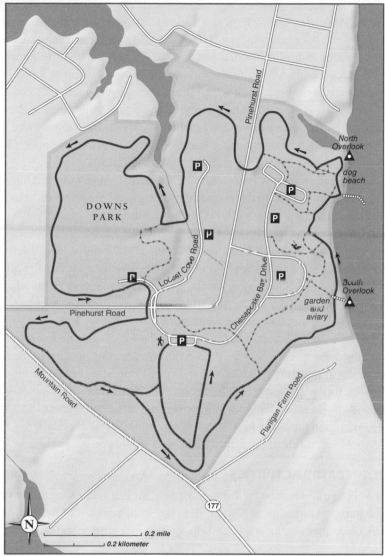

1.2 miles the trail opens up with a kayak and canoe launch to your right and a paved trail leading to a fishing pier. Turn right to take a look at the Downs Park Fishing Pier, built in 2006. When you're done at the pier, head back toward the asphalt trail and continue on, passing a volleyball net on your left at 1.3 miles.

Go right at the next trail junction to reach the dog beach, where dogs can roam off leash. Heading back to the paved path from the dog beach, you'll see a wooden boardwalk trail immediately to the right; it heads through the woods and takes you to a big stagnant pond, where you'll likely see a few frogs and snakes. Next, head back up

261

to the paved Perimeter Trail, where you'll see picnic benches to the left. Stay to the right, and, at just under 1.5 miles, you'll come to bathroom facilities and a water fountain with pavilions and volleyball nets just beyond. Turn right after the bathrooms.

At 1.6 miles you'll see your first option to cross over Pinehurst Road, but continue on a bit farther, where you'll go uphill and cross over Pinehurst Road. Pick up the trail on the other side. Side trails to the left will take you to tennis, basketball, and handball courts, but keep straight, cutting back into the woods away from all the facilities. You'll come to one more stand of picnic benches and open play areas before you hit a valley of marshy aquatic plants to the right.

When the trail splits at 2.3 miles, turn right (north). At just under 3 miles, you'll pass wetlands to your right. In this increasingly boggy and marshy area, you're barely above sea level. Invariably, both sides of the trail will be muddy, and you'll appreciate the fact that the trail is a bit raised in this section.

Pass a camping area and fields on your left at 3.25 miles, and then the trail crosses Pinehurst Road again. Your car is just ahead, but to continue the hike, head right at the gatehouse. The Perimeter Trail parallels first Pinehurst Road and then Mountain Road.

At a bench with a trail behind it, turn right down that trail, and when you reach a V, take the right path, allowing you to link up to the Eco Trail where you first began. Even though you've already been on this section, you're now heading in the opposite direction and will soon link up with the section you skipped earlier. At 4.2 miles where the trail splits, turn left to finish hiking the Eco Trail. About midway down this section, you'll be walking on an old farm road once traversed by horses and carriages and later used by farmers and lumberjacks. When you come to Chesapeake Bay Drive, turn left to return to the other side of the parking area from where you began the hike.

## NEARBY/RELATED ACTIVITIES

Plenty of opportunities exist for fishing or picnicking at one of the many pavilions inside the park. If you haven't had your fill of bay-view parks, visit nearby **Fort Smallwood Park** (aacounty.org/locations-and-directions/fort-smallwood-park).

• • • • • • • • • • • • • • • • • • • • • • • • •

**GPS TRAILHEAD COORDINATES** N39° 06.521'   W76° 26.394'

**DIRECTIONS** Take I-95 S 3.3 miles to Exit 49A (I-695 E). Take I-695 E 3.4 miles to I-97 S. Follow I-97 S 3.5 miles to Exit 14 and take MD 100 E to Mountain Road E. When Mountain Road veers to the right, stay straight on Pinehurst Road, and then turn right into the park entrance at Chesapeake Bay Drive. The gatehouse is straight ahead.

These goats are just some of the animals greeting visitors to Kinder Farm Park.

**STROLL AROUND THE** Perimeter Trail and take in the natural habitat before enjoying the many amenities of this 288-acre park.

## DESCRIPTION

As you begin your hike just opposite the parking lots, you'll see why Kinder Farm Park is so popular. Managed by Anne Arundel County, the park offers a disc golf course, community gardens, and a large playground. Just beyond the playground are farm animals to greet eager young visitors. Year-round you'll find cows, goats, sheep, pigs, and chickens, and, if you visit in March and April, you're likely to see lots of baby animals.

The Perimeter Trail begins northeast as you pass the community garden on your right and the disc golf course on your left. Heading southwest at just under 0.4 mile, you'll come to a four-way intersection and see a sign for the East West Boulevard Trail to your right (ending at the boulevard) and a road to your left; continue straight. This portion of the trail meanders through mature forest and can be surprisingly empty for such a busy park. If you keep a close watch, you're likely to stumble upon deer in this area. Also be on the lookout for eastern bluebirds—Kinder Farm Park has 65 bluebird boxes scattered throughout the park.

**DISTANCE & CONFIGURATION:** 2.5-mile loop

**DIFFICULTY:** Easy

**SCENERY:** Woods, fields

**EXPOSURE:** Mostly shade

**TRAFFIC:** Moderate; heavy at trailhead

**TRAIL SURFACE:** Asphalt

**HIKING TIME:** 45 minutes

**DRIVING DISTANCE:** 15 miles

**ELEVATION GAIN:** 117' at trailhead, with no significant rise

**ACCESS:** 7 a.m.–sunset; $6/vehicle entrance fee

**WHEELCHAIR ACCESS:** Perimeter trail is paved.

**MAPS:** aacounty.org/departments /recreation-parks/parks/forms-and-publications /KinderFarmParkMap.pdf

**FACILITIES:** Restrooms, picnic tables, grills, playground and tot lot, disc-golf course, visitor center (open Monday–Friday 9 a.m.– 4 p.m. and weekends 10 a.m.–3 p.m.)

**CONTACT:** 410-222-6115, aacounty.org /departments/recreation-parks/parks /kinder-farm

**LOCATION:** 1001 Kinder Farm Park Rd., Millersville

**COMMENTS:** Playgrounds and farm animals make this a great area for those with children. If you're interested in birding, stop in at the visitor center for a list of birds commonly seen in the area, or visit the Kinder Farm Park site of the Maryland Ornithological Society at mdbirdingguide.com/Kinder_Farm.

In another 0.3 mile, you'll pass the Blackberry Trail heading to your left. This is one of several miles of unpaved trails interlinked throughout the park that provides some nice scenery and meanders through Kinder Farm Park's grass meadows. If you're interested, taking one of these trails gives you a chance to spot some of the other birds popular in the area, including hawks, woodpeckers, wrens, and chickadees.

However, to continue on the main Perimeter Trail, stay straight. A sign here identifies that this area of the trail is being encouraged to return to its natural condition through re-growth in order to help provide a habitat for wildlife. At 1.2 miles you'll pass the Wildflower Trail on your left. Continue straight and reach the sports fields at 1.5 miles. Continue on the paved path, walking with the fields on your left.

At just under 1.75 miles, you'll continue straight through a four-way intersection, passing a tot lot on your left and additional free parking on your right (though this lot fills up with those using the fields). At 2.1 miles head over a wood-and-metal bridge and you'll soon reach the main gatehouse. Cross at the crosswalk and turn left, passing a beautiful rock tribute to the victims of September 11th, and then the community gardens. Your car is just up the road on the left. If you haven't already, take some time to visit the animals or try your luck at the catch-and-release pond, located just beyond the barns. Several museum buildings in this area offer a snapshot of farm life in the early 1900s: there's a Farmhouse Museum, Ice House and Outhouse, and Tobacco Barn Museum.

• • • • • • • • • • • • • • • • • • • • • • • • • • •

**GPS TRAILHEAD COORDINATES** N39° 06.047'    W76° 34.904'

## Kinder Farm Park

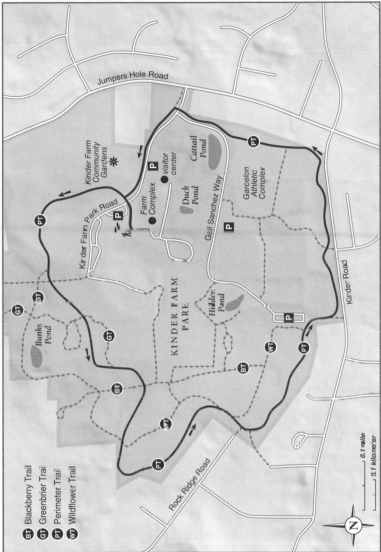

Jumpers Hole Road

Kinder Farm Community Gardens

visitor center

Cattail Pond

Farm Complex

Duck Pond

Gail Sanchez Way

Garcelon Athletic Complex

Kinder Farm Park Road

Kinder Road

KINDER FARM PARK

Hidden Pond

Bunks Pond

Rock Ridge Road

0.1 mile
0.1 kilometer

**BT** Blackberry Trail
**GT** Greenbrier Trail
**PT** Perimeter Trail
**WT** Wildflower Trail

**DIRECTIONS** Take I-95 S 3.3 miles to Exit 49A (I-695 E) toward Glen Burnie/Annapolis. In 3.4 miles, take I-97 S 3.5 miles to Exit 14 (MD 100 E). In 3 miles, take Exit 16A to merge onto MD 2/South Ritchie Highway. In just under 1 mile, turn right onto Jumpers Hole Road. Kinder Farm Park will be on your right. Continue past the gatehouse and pass the visitor center on your left. You'll see the paved Perimeter Trail on your right, just before you reach the second parking area and playground on your left. Park in either lot and make your way to the trailhead.

265

Remains of the Bay Shore Amusement Park pier

**SEE HOW THINGS** have changed in an area of undeveloped bayfront property, including evidence of the old Bay Shore Amusement Park from the early 1900s.

## DESCRIPTION

Begin your hike on the white-blazed Black Marsh Trail. You'll quickly come to a T-intersection and see the gatehouse on your left. Turn right to stay on the trail, which is initially shaded by tall, thick trees. At 500 feet a trail begins to parallel you on the left, but stay on the narrow dirt path, and then, at just over a quarter mile, you'll come to the Black Marsh Wildlands. Turn right onto the wider gravel path and walk through the Black Marsh area. At 0.3 mile, on the left, you'll come to the Observation Trail. Unfortunately, beaver activity in this area has blocked the path to an observation deck that allows you to take in a nice view of the marsh. This short 0.6-mile out-and-back may be passable for you, depending on the whims of the beavers.

Continue along the wide white-blazed path. The marsh is protected as a Maryland Wildland and Natural Heritage Area and provides a haven for birds, including bald eagles, American bitterns, northern harriers, great horned owls, red-tailed hawks, and black rails. The marsh is also home to wading birds such as herons and egrets. For an exhaustive list of the hundreds of birds found in North Point State

**DISTANCE & CONFIGURATION:** 3.4-mile loop with short spurs

**DIFFICULTY:** Easy–moderate

**SCENERY:** Chesapeake Bay, Black Marsh Wildlands, historical structures

**EXPOSURE:** Slightly more shade than sun

**TRAFFIC:** Light–moderate

**TRAIL SURFACE:** Dirt, asphalt

**HIKING TIME:** 1.5 hours

**DRIVING DISTANCE:** 20 miles

**ELEVATION GAIN:** 16' at trailhead, with no elevation gain

**ACCESS:** 8 a.m.–sunset. Entrance fee is $4/vehicle on weekends in season and $3/vehicle on weekdays and in the off-season. The park is known to fill to capacity during warm weather; arrive before noon for the best chance of entry.

**MAPS:** USGS *Sparrows Point;* trail map available at gatehouse and online at dnr.maryland.gov /publiclands/Documents/NorthPoint_Map.pdf

**FACILITIES:** Portable bathroom at parking area; restrooms, water, and concessions at the Takos Visitor Center (open Memorial Day–Labor Day, Wednesday–Sunday, 11 a.m.–4 p.m.); swimming area and pavilions

**CONTACT:** 410-592-2897, dnr.maryland.gov /publiclands/pages/central/northpoint.aspx and northpointstatepark.homestead.com

**LOCATION:** 8400 North Point Rd., Edgemere

**COMMENTS:** Bring bug spray.

Park, visit northpointstatepark.homestead.com/birds.html. Many frogs, snakes, skinks, salamanders, and turtles (including the state reptile, the Diamondback Terrapin) make homes in and around the water.

At just under 0.6 mile, turn left at the yellow-blazed Muskrat Trail and make your way down to the edge of the marsh. Here, the remains of a small boat, almost completely overtaken by vegetation, sit by the water's edge. In addition to muskrats, you'll also have a decent chance of spotting beavers, foxes, and otters.

Returning on the Muskrat Trail, you'll see the purple-blazed Holly Trail about 200 feet to the left. Take the Holly Trail, and at just over 0.8 mile, you'll see a cavernous abandoned structure through the woods to your right; you'll get a closer look at this remnant of Bay Shore Amusement Park a little later on. Continue on, and you'll arrive at the Power House Trail at a T-intersection and turn left (north). This trail is muddy, tight, and overgrown, but some well-placed boards help you stay dry. Very soon, you'll see a beautiful little rocky beach, complete with small, lapping waves. This is one of the quieter spots to enjoy views of the Chesapeake.

When you're ready, head back to the T-intersection where you went left earlier, but now continue straight. Take a left onto the green-blazed spur trail to enjoy another view of the water, this time from a nice sandy beach. Return to the Power House Trail and continue on.

On your right, the abandoned building you saw earlier will come into closer view, posted with NO TRESPASSING. PRIVATE PROPERTY signs. This used to house a reverse transformer that powered the Bay Shore Amusement Park, which operated at North Point from 1906 to 1947. Bay Shore boasted a dance hall, a bowling alley, a restaurant (where the visitor center now stands), and a pier. Pass the building and turn left to continue on the orange-blazed Power House Trail as it widens considerably.

## North Point State Park

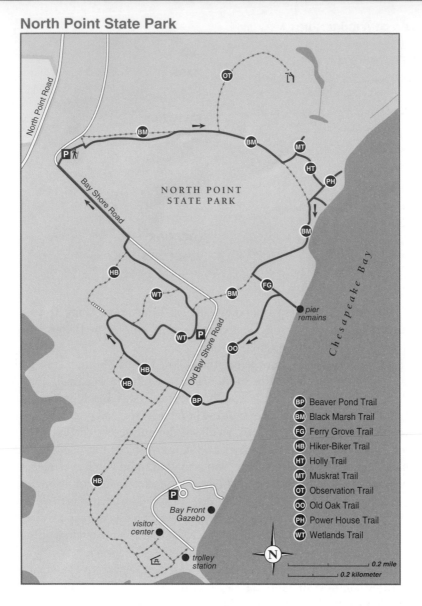

North Point Road

Bay Shore Road

NORTH POINT
STATE PARK

Old Bay Shore Road

Chesapeake Bay

pier
remains

Bay Front
Gazebo

visitor
center

trolley
station

BP Beaver Pond Trail
BM Black Marsh Trail
FG Ferry Grove Trail
HB Hiker-Biker Trail
HT Holly Trail
MT Muskrat Trail
OT Observation Trail
OO Old Oak Trail
PH Power House Trail
WT Wetlands Trail

N

0.2 mile

0.2 kilometer

As you continue on, you'll pass trails to your left offering nice vantage points of the Chesapeake and begin to see white blazes marking your trail. At 1.4 miles head left (east) on the blue-blazed Ferry Grove Trail. You'll come to the green-blazed Old Oak Trail at 1.5 miles on the right, but for now, pass it and head toward the water for a nice view of a sunken jetty and the bay. Turn around, and then turn left onto the Old Oak Trail, which is surrounded by oaks and thick underbrush. At just under 2 miles, you'll come to a post marking the Old Oak Trail and see double red blazes on trees both to your right and left. Turn right (west) onto the Beaver Pond Trail. This wide, exposed trail follows cut grass through an area that provides good habitat for raccoons, gray squirrels, cardinals, great horned owls, red foxes, red-tailed hawks, spotted salamanders, American kestrels, killdeers, plovers, and robins.

At just over 2.1 miles, cross a park road on the crosswalk and head into the woods. If you want to check out the busy swimming beach area and enjoy the many interesting exhibits at the visitor center, turn left to parallel the road on the Hiker-Biker Trail. To continue on the hike described here, however, head right (north). You can always drive to the swimming area after you complete your hike.

You'll pass some marshes to your right and then come to an open field at 2.3 miles. Head straight (north), walking along the left side of the field. Just on the other side, you'll see a sign for the Wetlands Loop. Take this loop through the pines, and be on the lookout for deer and red foxes. At the junction at just over 2.5 miles, continue straight, and then at 2.6 miles, you'll reach a little boardwalk, offering you some protection from the wetland area.

At 2.7 miles, you'll come to another field and head left (north). You'll see a parking area on your right and a stationary park sign on your left, indicating that you're on the Wetlands Loop. Head straight. Soon after, you'll come to a junction and an observation platform. Going right here takes you to the Black Marsh Trail, so go straight (northwest) and pass the platform on your right.

At just under 2.9 miles, the Wetlands Trail veers left, but continue straight (northwest) and begin paralleling the road on your right. Soon after, you'll come to a cornfield in front of you; turn right to head toward the road, and then take a left, walking northwest alongside the road to return to your car, which you'll see on the right.

Heading back to the parking area along the road isn't nearly as unpleasant as it sounds. You'll parallel the cornfield on the left, and a big buffer separates the cornfield from the road. In summer, the sounds of the grasshoppers and crickets will drown out the noise of the cars going by at low speed. You can follow the paved road around to the parking area where you began.

One of the nice things about this park is that the vast majority of visitors come here for the beach, which means the trails are fairly free of traffic. When you're finished hiking, though, you can head down to the beach area for a pleasant diversion. The visitor center mimics the original Bay Shore Park Restaurant. The swimming beach (unguarded) is also nearby, and in between sits Trolley Station Pavilion, a holdover from the days when passengers paid 30 cents to ride the #26 trolley car that ran between Baltimore and the amusement park.

## NEARBY/RELATED ACTIVITIES

The route for British troops to Baltimore during the War of 1812 passed through North Point. Linking nearby **Fort Howard** and **Todd's Inheritance** with this trip provides additional hiking, as well as excellent history lessons. Fort Howard is another 2.2 miles south down North Point Road. You'll find Todd's Inheritance a half mile north of Fort Howard on North Point Road. Thomas Todd settled on this spot in 1664. Retreating British soldiers, defeated at the Battle of Fort McHenry, burned the original Todd home; the house standing here now was built on the original homesite in 1816 and was remodeled in 1867. You can find details on these trails at the **Takos Visitor Center.**

• • • • • • • • • • • • • • • • • • • • • • • • •

**GPS TRAILHEAD COORDINATES** N39° 13.236'   W76° 25.811'

**DIRECTIONS** Take I-95 N 5.5 miles to Exit 59. Follow Eastern Avenue for just under a mile, and then take the ramp on the right to turn onto MD 151 S/North Point Boulevard. In 5.2 miles, turn left onto Bethlehem Boulevard, which then veers right and turns into North Point Road. Go 1.8 miles to the park entrance on the left at Bay Shore Road; pass the gatehouse and make your first left into the Lot A parking area on the left. The trail starts at the edge of the parking area.

A mature forest borders this section of the Patuxent River.

**HIKE A SCENIC** forested river valley along the Patuxent River through a portion of an old B&O railbed from Savage north to Lake Elkhorn in Columbia.

## DESCRIPTION

At the trailhead you'll find a stationary map of the trails, as well as signs indicating the distance to various points of interest. Inaugurated by a ribbon-cutting ceremony on November 2, 2002, Patuxent Branch Trail connects many sections of Columbia's extensive pathway network. Patuxent River runs on the right as you walk upstream; mature walnut, sumac, sassafras, oak, and tulip poplar trees flank this section of the trail, which runs along the railbed of the main line of the B&O Railroad. This particular spur of the B&O's Washington Branch served the textile mills and quarries between Savage and Guilford until 1928.

This hike gives you the chance to marvel at the existence of a long stretch of thick woods running through a heavily populated suburban center. In addition, the scenery is often very lovely. On the downside, you'll hear cars every now and again, even though you will rarely see them; the traffic noise grows especially loud at just over 0.5 mile, when you walk under the two I-95 bridges soaring several hundred feet above your head. On the trail under the interstate, which is in a wetland protection area, you can see the river, the mature trees, and the occasional deer, all up

**DISTANCE & CONFIGURATION:** 10.4-mile out-and-back with lake loop

**DIFFICULTY:** Moderate due to length

**SCENERY:** Patuxent River, Lake Elkhorn, historical bridge

**EXPOSURE:** More shade than sun

**TRAFFIC:** Heavy

**TRAIL SURFACE:** Asphalt, packed dirt, crushed rock

**HIKING TIME:** 3–3.5 hours

**DRIVING DISTANCE:** 16 miles

**ELEVATION GAIN:** 280' at trailhead, with no significant rise

**ACCESS:** Sunrise–sunset on the trail; Lake Elkhorn open daily 6 a.m.–10 p.m.; no fees or permits required

**WHEELCHAIR ACCESS:** Yes

**MAPS:** USGS *Savage*

**FACILITIES:** Restrooms and water at Lake Elkhorn

**CONTACT:** 410-313-4700, howardcountymd.gov /PatuxentBranchTrail

**LOCATION:** Vollmerhausen Rd., Jessup

**COMMENTS:** You can shorten your hike by parking at any of the parking areas on the route, and you can make the hike a point-to-point by setting up shuttles at the parking area and Lake Elkhorn.

close. Walk over a wooden boardwalk protecting the wetlands under I-95 S. You'll cross over quite a few boardwalks along this trail.

The woods grow especially thick along the trail after passing the I-95 bridges. Many paths lead to the river; head down to see for yourself why it was named Patuxent, the Algonquian word for "rapids." The big rocks in the river create eddies and pools that make enough babbling noise to drown out the traffic above.

At just over 1 mile, a paved trail intersects from the left. You'll see a couple of these offshoot trails along the way; they offer access from adjoining neighborhoods.

At 1.25 miles the trail leads uphill and comes out to an open area, providing a good opportunity on the right to see birds; from the high angle here you can look into the tops of the trees and see finches, cardinals, blue jays, red-winged blackbirds, and bluebirds flitting around the branches.

Just before 1.5 miles, the trail splits at a mileage marker indicating 2 miles to Lake Elkhorn; follow the trail right (north), and you'll soon come to and cross over the Pratt Through-Truss Railroad Bridge, built in 1901. Nearby are the remains of a granite quarry that operated until 1928. The second parking area option for this hike is just beyond this bridge on the right. (To begin your hike here, from MD 32 East, turn south onto Broken Land Parkway, take a left at Guilford Road and a right onto Old Guilford Road, and then turn left into the parking lot. This is the best trailhead for those with mobility issues or strollers.)

Turn left to follow Old Guilford Road west, which is now closed to westward traffic, for a while before it reverts to a narrower asphalt path. This section of the trail is less shaded and will also remind you that you're walking through suburban Columbia; every so often a building or house will pop into view, but just as often, thick stands of woods will crowd both sides of the trail. The result is a strange battle between the sounds of moving cars and birdcalls.

## Patuxent Branch Trail

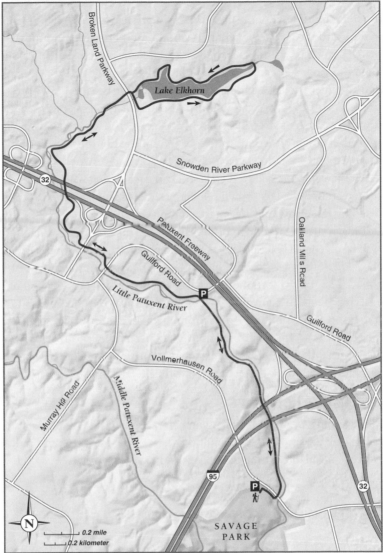

Cross a power line cut and then walk under Guilford Road Bridge. At 2.7 miles pass under Broken Land Parkway as the trail winds through an area with a little creek. A 3,000-foot wooden boardwalk takes you across the boggy, marshy, thickly wooded land. At 2.5 miles a sign indicates 1.2 MILES TO LAKE ELKHORN, and another says 0.2 MILE TO BLUE SEA DRIVE on the left. Stay straight (north).

Two more wooden boardwalks start at 2.7 miles and take you across a marshy area and under MD 32. This area is full of cattails and aquatic life, and wildflowers here attract a multitude of butterflies. When the trail splits less than 0.1 mile later, head right toward the lake through thick woods and underbrush. Another wooden bridge carries you past a little creekbed at 3.3 miles. Come to a steel bridge at just under 3.5 miles, and, soon after crossing the bridge, you'll come to a junction. Stay straight to go under Broken Land Parkway, heading northeast.

The man-made 37-acre Lake Elkhorn, created in 1974, averages only 8 feet in depth, but its watershed stretches some 2,500 acres. Since the lake trail is a loop, you can head in either direction; to follow the mileage in the hike described here, go right. At just under 4 miles, a pavilion with water and restrooms sits on the right. A fishing pier juts into the lake, which is stocked each spring with trout and bass. As you continue around the lake, you'll see many side paths; stay left each time. These paths head into the residential areas surrounding the lake.

You'll reach the farthest edge of the lake at 4.6 miles. Cross a small footbridge here at the lake's edge. Generally speaking, the majority of the waterfowl live at this end of the lake. Houses get closer to the trail here, but so does the lake itself; in a few places the trail has only 5 feet of open space on either side. This portion of the trail has identifying labels on many of the trees along the path. At 5.25 miles turn left as the trail turns to a wooden waterfront promenade; a platform with benches, tables (with checkerboards), and chairs makes this a convenient place to sit. On your right is a large playground. At 5.5 miles veer left and come to Lake Elkhorn Dam and, soon after, your entry point back to the Patuxent Branch Trail. Backtrack to your car.

## NEARBY/RELATED ACTIVITIES

Nearby **Savage Park** (page 279), which you can reach by trail from the parking area, includes historic **Savage Mill** (savagemill.com), a 19th-century textile mill that has been restored and adapted for use as an arts and crafts retail center.

• • • • • • • • • • • • • • • • • • • • • • • •

**GPS TRAILHEAD COORDINATES** N39° 08.954'   W76° 49.963'

**DIRECTIONS** Follow I-95 S 16.2 miles toward Washington, D.C. Take MD 32 east toward Fort Meade (Exit 38) and a quick exit onto MD 1 south toward Savage. Stay in the right lane and take an immediate right onto Howard Street, which soon turns into Baltimore Street. Go three blocks and turn right onto Savage Guilford Road. Go 0.7 mile and turn left onto Vollmerhausen Road. Continue on Vollmerhausen for 0.5 mile to a parking area on the left. You'll see a sign there that reads SAVAGE PARK WINCOPIN TRAIL ACCESS. To reach the trailhead, turn right, walking along the sidewalk on Vollmerhausen Road and look for the second path on the left in 0.15 mile. Cross Vollmerhausen at the crosswalk and begin the trail on the wide gravel path.

Take a break here to admire the beautiful South River.

**ENJOY A BEAUTIFUL** hike around this waterfront park, taking in views of Harness Creek and the South River.

## DESCRIPTION

Quiet Waters Park has something for everyone, and you won't regret making a visit. The 340-acre park served as a farm before it was eventually sold to Anne Arundel County in 1987. Now, visitors to the park enjoy a myriad of recreational, environmental, and cultural activities.

Begin your trek at the edge of the visitor center parking area and head north on the paved trail. This mile-long portion leads you up toward the entrance and includes a fitness course, with various exercise stations along the route. The trail is initially shaded, with trees flanking you on both sides. In 0.5 mile you'll begin to see houses on your right, and you lose some of your shade as the trees thin out. At just over 1 mile, you'll cross Quiet Waters Park Road at a crosswalk, heading straight (going right takes you to the park entrance).

On the other side, take the path into the woods, where the trail becomes quite peaceful and shaded. Several benches along the route offer a place to rest. At just over 1.5 miles, you'll pass a picnic pavilion area—one of many in the park—and soon after cross a wooden bridge. This is one of three bridges you'll cross in close

275

**DISTANCE & CONFIGURATION:** 5-mile loop

**DIFFICULTY:** Easy

**SCENERY:** Chesapeake Bay

**EXPOSURE:** Half and half

**TRAFFIC:** Moderate

**TRAIL SURFACE:** Paved

**HIKING TIME:** 1.5 hours

**DRIVING DISTANCE:** 33 miles

**ELEVATION GAIN:** 53' at trailhead, with no significant rise

**ACCESS:** 7 a.m.–sunset; $6/day parking fee (credit and debit cards are not accepted); visitor center open Monday and Wednesday–Friday

9 a.m.–4 p.m. and Saturday and Sunday 10 a.m.–4 p.m.

**WHEELCHAIR ACCESS:** Yes

**MAPS:** park map available at aacounty.org /departments/recreation-parks/parks/quiet-waters

**FACILITIES:** Restrooms, vending machines, and grill at visitor center; portable toilets, boat rental, playground, dog park, and rentable pavilions

**CONTACT:** 410-222-1777, aacounty.org /departments/recreation-parks/parks/quiet-waters

**LOCATION:** 600 Quiet Waters Park Rd., Annapolis

**COMMENTS:** In winter, the fountain in front of the visitor center is converted into an ice-skating rink.

succession over the next 0.5 mile. At just over 2.2 miles, a playground and pavilion appear on your left, and then as the trail begins heading west, you'll see the Blue Heron Center on your left. This venue, which includes a private garden, is available for rent for special events and weddings.

At just over 2.4 miles, you'll reach the trailhead for the Wildwood Trail. If you'd like to extend your hike, continue straight for an out-and-back that adds a total of 0.4 mile. The Wildwood Trail takes you through the woods to a composting demonstration area, with self-instructional signs and brochures guiding you through a dozen different composting methods.

However, to continue on our hike, head left. After passing the Dogwood Pavilion on your left, you'll reach the trailhead for the Harness Creek Trail at 2.5 miles. Take this trail, and at just over 2.75 miles, you'll reach the boat dock at Harness Creek. In season, you can rent canoes and kayaks, and portable toilets are available. Though not as obvious as the recreational activities, you're also looking at an oyster nursery! There are 22 oyster baskets hanging off the Harness Creek docks, which help filter the water and maintain a healthy coastal ecosystem.

Be on the lookout here for osprey, red-tailed hawks, and great blue herons. For birding aficionados, a full list of the birds often seen at Quiet Waters is available at the visitor center and online at aabirdclub.org. When you're ready, turn around and reach the main trail at just over 3 miles. Turn right and pass the visitor center on your left. If you didn't get the chance to do so before your hike, I'd recommend popping into the visitor center to check out the art gallery, which features rotating exhibits of local and regional artists. And, if you need a break or a snack at this point, there are also restrooms, indoor and outdoor seating areas, a café, and vending machines.

## Quiet Waters Park

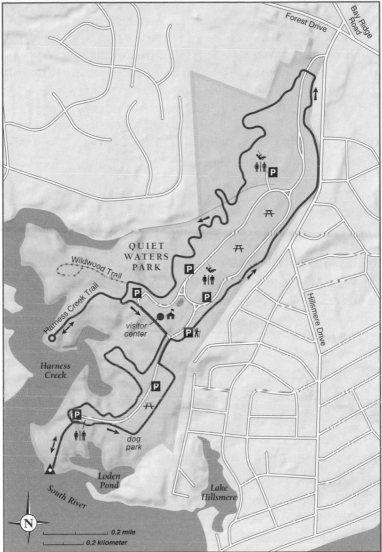

Continuing on, just before you reach the main park road, turn right to head south along the paved path (you'll see the parking lot where you parked in front of you). At 3.25 miles you'll have the option to cross the road heading left, but stay straight. At just under 3.5 miles, take a right into the woods, just before another pavilion. You'll soon come upon a beautiful area with benches and another great view of Harness Creek.

At 3.8 miles turn right just before you reach another parking lot, and soon you'll come to a roundabout. Skirt around it to the right and turn right on the trail labeled SOUTH POINT OVERLOOK. When the trail splits, stay straight to reach the overlook, which provides a beautiful vantage point to take in the South River. You can use the binoculars to look over to Selby, or head down the stairway to get a closer look at the water (there's also a dog beach available down and to the left).

Once you've finished taking in the views, retrace your steps and reach the main path at just under 4.5 miles. Head right and back into the woods. You'll very quickly reach a dog park and then a concert pavilion, where they host Saturday night concerts in summer, on your left.

At just under 5 miles, you'll reach a stop sign. Head right, going uphill toward the parking area, which you'll see shortly on your right. Reach the parking area and your car at 5 miles.

## NEARBY/RELATED ACTIVITIES

Just south across the South River is **Beverly–Triton Beach Park** (page 250). Though it would be quicker to boat there, you can reach it by car by heading back to MD 655 and then going south on MD 2. Just north is **Annapolis,** which provides ample shopping and dining options.

• • • • • • • • • • • • • • • • • • • • • • • • •

**GPS TRAILHEAD COORDINATES** N38° 56.227'   W76° 30.040'

**DIRECTIONS** Take I-95 S 3.5 miles to Exit 49A (I-695 E) toward Glen Burnie/Annapolis. In 3.4 miles, take I-97 S 18 miles to Exit 22 for MD 665 E/Riva Road. Follow MD 665 E, which turns into Forest Drive, for 5.7 miles. Turn right onto Hillsmere Drive, and then take an immediate right onto Quiet Waters Park Road. Follow signs for the visitor center parking. As you enter the lot, you'll see a paved path on your left; this is the start of the trail.

The end of this hike follows a beautiful rapids-filled portion of the Little Patuxent River.

**TAKE A LEISURELY STROLL** along the Little Patuxent River and enjoy the shops and stores at historic Savage Mill.

## DESCRIPTION

From the asphalt trailhead, you will go immediately into a stand of mature trees—mostly oaks and tulip poplars. Look for white-tailed deer, which congregate in this area. At 250 feet the trail splits; turn right (north) on the Patuxent Branch Trail, following the sign that gives the mileage to Vollmerhausen Road, the Pratt Railroad Bridge, and Lake Elkhorn.

You'll pass some houses on your right, a reminder that you're not too far from civilization. At 0.3 mile cross a wooden bridge and look for the Panther Branch of the Patuxent on the left and lots of beautiful beech trees in this section. At 0.5 mile a dirt path leads to the left, but stay straight. Very shortly after, look for a second dirt path on the left and take it down to link up with a riverside path. If the trail opens up and you see Patuxent Middle School and Bollman Bridge Elementary, you've gone too far. (However, staying straight on this paved path is how you link up with the Patuxent Branch and Wincopin Trails, if you wish to hike them.)

Admire the many beautiful beech trees in this section. When you reach the Little Patuxent River, head left on the narrow, dirt River Trail, paralleling the river on

**DISTANCE & CONFIGURATION:** 4.4-mile out-and-back with loop

**DIFFICULTY:** Easy–moderate

**SCENERY:** Little Patuxent River, Savage Mill historical sites

**EXPOSURE:** Mostly shade

**TRAFFIC:** Moderate

**TRAIL SURFACE:** Packed dirt, some asphalt and sidewalk

**HIKING TIME:** 2 hours

**DRIVING DISTANCE:** 17 miles

**ELEVATION GAIN:** 265' at trailhead, 145' at low point

**ACCESS:** 7 a.m.–sunset; no fees or permits required

**WHEELCHAIR ACCESS:** Portions around Savage Mill and Patuxent Branch Trail

**MAPS:** USGS *Savage;* park map available at howardcountymd.gov/SavagePark

**FACILITIES:** Restrooms, water, ball fields, pavilions, concessions near Savage Mill

**CONTACT:** 410-313-4700, howardcountymd.gov /SavagePark

**LOCATION:** 8400 Fair St., Savage

**COMMENTS:** If you'd like to explore trails on the opposite side of the Little Patuxent River, check out the adjoining Wincopin Trails (page 283).

your right. This trail is at water level and simply follows the contours of the river, providing many places to stop and take in the beautiful and wild scene. At 1.1 miles a gravel trail splits off to your left, which is how you'll return, but for now continue past it on the River Trail. Check out the beautiful rock formations all around—on the hills and in the water, creating more sections of rapids.

At 1.3 miles go over a wooden footbridge, and soon after the trail becomes a bit shadier and the river's rapids add an enjoyable soundtrack to your hike. At 1.6 miles another gravel path leads up to your left, while another path heads down to your right. Take the gravel path to the left.

As you hike this trail uphill, you'll see a dirt trail leading left (northeast), but stay on the wider gravel trail. To your left is Savage Park and a baseball diamond. You'll emerge onto a gravel parking lot at the top of the hill.

Head through the parking lot; at 1.8 miles a little path cuts through to the Savage Mill parking lot. Take that path, and you'll see Savage Mill cattycorner on the other side of the parking lot. Cross the lot, passing Terrapin Adventures on your right, and reach Savage Mill at just under 2 miles. Constructed in 1822 as a cotton mill, Savage Mill now houses antiques stores, historical displays, restaurants, and specialty shops. It also has restrooms and water on the bottom floor if you need a quick break.

Assuming you haven't stopped to shop, go through and around the main stone mill building, skirting the parking area on the opposite side, and take the red metal stairs down toward Gorman Road. Follow the sidewalk to the Bollman Truss Bridge at just over 2 miles. A national Civil Engineering landmark completed in 1869, it is the sole surviving example of the bridging system invented in 1850 by Wendell Bollman, a Baltimore engineer.

Cross over the Little Patuxent River on the wooden walkway that parallels the Bollman Bridge and then turn right onto the Savage Mill Trail. There's trailhead

# Savage Park

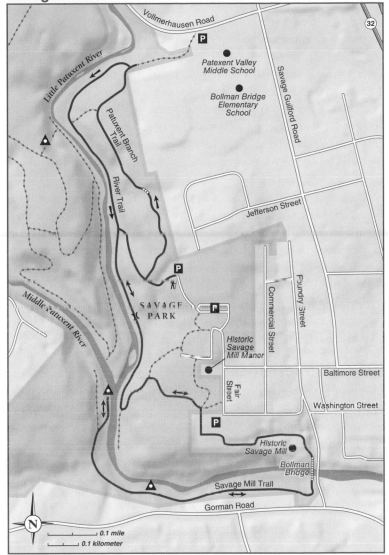

32

Little Patuxent River

Vollmerhausen Road

Patexent Valley Middle School

Bollman Bridge Elementary School

Savage Guilford Road

Patuxent Branch Trail

River Trail

Jefferson Street

Middle Patuxent River

SAVAGE PARK

Commercial Street

Foundry Street

Historic Savage Mill Manor

Baltimore Street

Fair Street

Washington Street

Historic Savage Mill

Bollman Bridge

Savage Mill Trail

Gorman Road

N

0.1 mile

0.1 kilometer

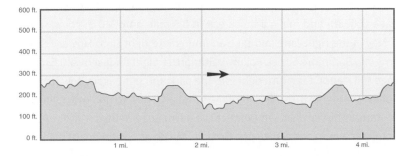

parking available, should you prefer to begin your hike here (9040 Gorman Road), as well as portable bathrooms and a picnic table. The gravel path is relatively flat the entire way; however, you'll have several opportunities to hike on a less-manicured trail, closer to the Patuxent River on your right. The first of these opportunities comes at 2.2 miles. You can take this down, make a left, and parallel the gravel path on your left. Just when it looks like it disappears, you'll see a wooden staircase on your left, bringing you back up to the main Savage Mill Trail.

At 2.5 miles, when you see a stone staircase on your right, take a moment to walk down and sit on the rocks overlooking the many rapids in the Patuxent River. It's a beautiful, serene spot.

At 2.7 miles another trail leads down to your right. Take it down to reach a sandy beach. If you walk upstream a bit, you'll see where the Little and Middle Patuxent Rivers join.

Retrace your steps back up to the main trail and turn left on the Savage Mill Trail to begin your return. At 3.4 miles you'll make it back to the trailhead and retrace your steps, walking through Savage Mill, across the parking lots, and reach the Patuxent River Trail at 3.8 miles. Turn right, this time walking upstream. When you reach the gravel path at 4.3 miles, turn right and you'll soon rejoin the asphalt path and see the trailhead parking at 4.4 miles.

## NEARBY/RELATED ACTIVITIES

Save some time to explore **Savage Mill** (410-792-2820, savagemill.com). Nine buildings remain that date back to 1820. The mill was placed on the National Register of Historic Places in 1974. It is open Monday–Thursday, 10 a.m.–6 p.m.; Friday and Saturday, 10 a.m.–9 p.m.; Sunday, 11 a.m.–6 p.m.

For more hiking, the **Patuxent Branch Trail** (page 271) runs from Savage Park all the way to Lake Elkhorn.

• • • • • • • • • • • • • • • • • • • • • • • •

**GPS TRAILHEAD COORDINATES** N39° 08.432'    W76° 49.807'

**DIRECTIONS** Take I-95 south 14 miles toward Washington, D.C. Take MD 32 east toward Fort Meade (Exit 38) and make a quick exit in 0.5 mile onto MD 1, going south toward Savage. Stay in the right lane and take an immediate right onto Howard Street, which soon turns into Baltimore Street. Follow Baltimore straight for just over 0.5 mile until you see Savage Mill Manor, then turn right into the park and right again, toward the baseball fields. Follow the lot north, to the left of the baseball fields, to find the trailhead parking. The trail starts at the farthest left point at the north edge of the lot next to the baseball fields; you'll see a map of the Patuxent Branch Trail on a bulletin board there.

A sandbar on the Middle Patuxent River

**TAKE A LEISURELY** stroll through beech, oak, and pine trees, and take in views of the Patuxent River.

## DESCRIPTION

The Wincopin hike begins on the Red Trail, an asphalt path that quickly turns to packed dirt. Consequently, the trail becomes narrower and tighter, but it's well maintained and easy to follow. Thick woods of beech, oak, and poplar trees crowd the trail.

At just under 0.4 mile, the trail splits. To the left is the Green Trail; you'll return on this trail. For now, stay straight on the Red Trail, following the post indicating that the Blue, Yellow, White, and Red Trails are ahead of you.

Very soon after, the Blue Trail splits off to the left and leads to the most thickly wooded section of the park, running along the Middle Patuxent. For now, continue on the Red Trail. At the next trail junction, head right (northwest) to stay on the Red Trail (rather than the Green Trail, which heads southwest).

At just under 0.5 mile, you'll come to another junction where the Red Trail continues in both directions. This is a loop, and we'll return to this spot eventually. For now, go straight (northwest). Very soon after, the Yellow Trail branches off to your right. This is another short loop you can take to extend your hike, but to continue on, remain on the Red Trail, heading southwest.

**DISTANCE & CONFIGURATION:** 4.2-mile combination

**DIFFICULTY:** Easy

**SCENERY:** Middle Patuxent and Little Patuxent Rivers

**EXPOSURE:** Mostly shade

**TRAFFIC:** Moderate

**TRAIL SURFACE:** Packed dirt, some asphalt and sidewalk

**HIKING TIME:** 2 hours

**DRIVING DISTANCE:** 16 miles

**ELEVATION GAIN:** 280' at trailhead, with no significant rise

**ACCESS:** Sunrise–sunset; no fees or permits required

**WHEELCHAIR ACCESS:** Extremely limited (initial asphalt path quickly turns to packed dirt)

**MAPS:** USGS *Savage;* trail map available at howardcountymd.gov/trail-directory

**FACILITIES:** Portable bathroom at trailhead parking lot

**CONTACT:** 410-313-4700, howardcountymd.gov /trail-directory

**LOCATION:** Vollmerhausen Rd., Jessup

**COMMENTS:** You can easily extend this hike by continuing to Savage Park.

As you descend the rocky trail toward a horseshoe in the river, the Middle Patuxent River comes into view on both the right and left. Though you'll hear I-95 in the background, the views more than make up for the noise. At just under 0.8 mile, a red trail marker guides you to the left, but continue straight for a short distance to a peaceful, sandy overlook of this bend of the Middle Patuxent River.

When you've had your fill of the view, backtrack and make a right to finish your loop of the Red Trail. The easternmost portion of the loop runs alongside the river and then heads back up to rejoin the original main Red Trail. In addition to the beech, oak, and poplar trees you've already seen, pines begin to make an appearance. The trail heads uphill a bit as it winds through the aforementioned trees. At just under 1.4 miles, the trail splits, with one path heading uphill to your left and another path going northeast to your right. Continue right, on the Red Trail. The rocky path leads uphill, passing another trail, this one currently closed for resource recovery. Continue on, rejoining the main trail at just under 1.5 miles. Turn right (east) on the Red Trail. Soon you'll pass the Green Trail on your right and then make your second right onto the Blue Trail at just under 1.6 miles.

Walking along the Blue Trail, you'll soon see the Green Trail join you from the right. Continue straight, following the trees blazed with blue and green. At the junction at just under 2 miles, with green blazes to your right (south) and blue straight ahead, veer right to take the Green Trail. The Blue Trail cuts off a significant portion of the hike. At 2.1 miles you'll reach the river again and see an overgrown trail to your right, which has been closed for restoration. Turn left (east), paralleling the Patuxent on your right.

At 2.4 miles you'll see the Blue Trail again to your left, but continue on the Green Trail, heading south. You'll immediately reach a T-intersection, with a green arrow pointing left. You'll return that way, but for now head right (southwest) to see the remains of the historic Gabbro Bridge. This bridge was used by the B&O Railroad

# Wincopin Trails

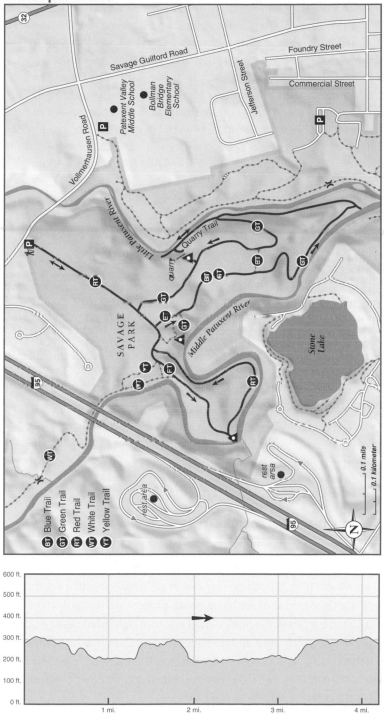

to carry stone from the Guilford Quarry to the main track. It was removed in 1925 when the quarry flooded. Here, at the bridge, you'll be standing high above the confluence of the Middle Patuxent (to your right) and the Little Patuxent (to your left).

Head back to where you took a right and continue straight on the Green Trail. This portion of the trail will largely follow the Little Patuxent River upstream, though for a few moments it will seem as if you're walking away from it. This section is flat and wide with lovely views of the Patuxent. You'll pass an old stone finishing plant, where up until 1925 stone finishers would cut raw granite into usable stones.

At just over 2.8 miles, you'll reach a junction where the Green Trail heads up to your left. You'll return that way, but if you'd like to take a look at the abandoned quarry (and extend your hike by 0.5 mile), continue straight along the Quarry Trail. Walk past the remnants of the Stone Crib Dam, which was used to provide water power to the Savage Grist Mill. At 3 miles you'll see a path to your left. If you continue straight, the trail ends at private property, so turn left here to have a look at the abandoned quarry, and then turn around and return to the Green Trail junction you passed moments ago and head right uphill.

At 3.5 miles at a T-intersection, turn right (northwest) to follow the sign guiding you back to parking and the Red and Blue Trails. Soon after, a trail intersects on your left, but continue straight. Just 0.2 mile later, a marker points you to a trail to your right. This is a short path that leads you to an overlook of the quarry you were standing in just moments ago. At just over 4 miles, you'll reach the main Red Trail and turn right (north) to follow it back to the parking lot.

## NEARBY/RELATED ACTIVITIES

To hike the rest of Savage Park's trails, go right roughly 500 feet along Vollmerhausen Road from the original trailhead and look for the asphalt trail to the right. For a description of this hike, see pages 279–282.

• • • • • • • • • • • • • • • • • • • • • • • • • • •

**GPS TRAILHEAD COORDINATES**  N39° 08.987'   W76° 50.065'

**DIRECTIONS** Take I-95 S 14 miles toward Washington, D.C. Then take MD 32 east toward Fort Meade (Exit 38) and quickly exit in 0.5 mile onto MD 1 south toward Savage. Stay in the right lane and take an immediate right onto Howard Street, which soon turns into Baltimore Street. Go three blocks and turn right onto Savage Guilford Road. Go 0.7 mile and turn left onto Vollmerhausen Road. Continue on Vollmerhausen for another half mile to a parking area on the left. You'll see a sign there that reads SAVAGE PARK WINCOPIN TRAIL ACCESS. There's parking and a portable toilet there, and the trailhead is just at the end of the parking area.

This hike is mostly shaded as you stroll along the Middle Patuxent River.

# APPENDIX A: Outdoors Stores

**BASS PRO SHOPS**
basspro.com
7000 Arundel Mills Circle
Hanover, MD 21076
410-689-2500

**H&H OUTDOORS**
hhsurplus.net
5406 Harford Road
Baltimore, MD 21214
410-752-2580

**REI**
rei.com
63 W. Aylesbury Road
Timonium, MD 21093
410-252-5920

6100 Dobbin Road B
Columbia, MD 21045
410-872-1742

# APPENDIX B: Map Stores

**GIS INTEGRATED SOLUTIONS**
gisintegratedsolutions.com
3235 Elliott Street
Baltimore, MD 21224
443-524-1550

**KAPPA MAP GROUP**
kappamapgroup.com
800-829-6277

**REI**
rei.com
63 W. Aylesbury Road
Timonium, MD 21093
410-252-5920

6100 Dobbin Road B
Columbia, MD 21045
410-872-1742

**UNITED STATES GEOLOGICAL SURVEY**
usgs.gov
888-275–8747

### HIKE IT BABY
Baltimore and Annapolis Chapters
hikeitbaby.com/find-your-city, info@hikeitbaby.com

### MARYLAND OUTDOOR CLUB
mdoutdoorclub.com

### MOUNTAIN CLUB OF MARYLAND
mcomd.org, contact@mcomd.org

### OUTDOOR AND ADVENTURE MEETUPS
meetup.com
Various meetup groups for a variety of interests (Hiking Around Baltimore, 20s and 30s Hiking Around Maryland, Maryland Hiking and Adventuring, etc.)

### SIERRA CLUB–GREATER BALTIMORE CHAPTER
sierraclub.org/maryland/greater-baltimore-group
301-277-7111

### SIERRA CLUB–MARYLAND CHAPTER
sierraclub.org/maryland

This wooden dock on Lake Elkhorn is a great spot for fishing.
(see Hike 57, Patuxent Branch Trail, page 271)

# INDEX

# ABOUT THE AUTHOR

Photo: Catherine Aldrich

**Allison Sturm** is a writer living in Baltimore County, Maryland. Her love for travel and the outdoors has taken her on hikes all over the world, including Italy, Spain, Ireland, and Saba, where she spent her honeymoon hiking up a volcano with her husband, Steven. She loves exploring all of the wonderful recreational options in and around Baltimore, and looks forward to instilling a spirit of adventure in their baby boy, who joined the family in fall (a month after finishing this third edition!).

**DEAR CUSTOMERS AND FRIENDS,**

**SUPPORTING YOUR INTEREST IN OUTDOOR ADVENTURE** travel, and an active lifestyle is central to our operations, fror the authors we choose to the locations we detail to the way w design our books. Menasha Ridge Press was incorporated in 198 by a group of veteran outdoorsmen and professional outfitters. Fc many years now, we've specialized in creating books that benefit th outdoors enthusiast.

Almost immediately, Menasha Ridge Press earned a reputatior for revolutionizing outdoors- and travel-guidebook publishing For such activities as canoeing, kayaking, hiking, backpacking and mountain biking, we established new standards of quality that transformed the whole genre, resulting in outdoor-recreatior guides of great sophistication and solid content. Menasha Ridge Press continues to be outdoor publishing's greatest innovator.

The folks at Menasha Ridge Press are as at home on a whitewater river or mountain trail as they are editing a manuscript. The books we build for you are the best they can be, because we're responding to your needs. Plus, we use and depend on them ourselves.

We look forward to seeing you on the river or the trail. If you'd like to contact us directly, visit us at menasharidge.com. We thank you for your interest in our books and the natural world around us all.

**SAFE TRAVELS,**

*Bob Sehlinger*

**BOB SEHLINGER**
**PUBLISHER**